Purifica
of the Mind
(Jila Al-Khatir)

Discourses by

Shaikh 'Abd Al-Qadir Al-Jilani

Translated by

Shetha Al-Dargazelli   Louay Fatoohi

Based on an Arabic edition by

Shaikh Muhammad Al-Kasnazani Al-Hussieni

Luna Plena Publishing   Birmingham

First published: March 2008

Production Reference: 1010308

Published by:
Luna Plena Publishing
Birmingham, UK.
www.lunaplenapub.com

ISBN 978-1-906342-02-9

Cover design by:
Mawlid Design
www.mawliddesign.com

Front cover image:
The school and shrine of Shaikh 'Abd Al-Qadir Al-Jilani in Baghdad, Iraq.

About the Translators

Shetha Al-Dargazelli was born in Baghdad, Iraq, in 1946. She graduated from the Physics Department, the College of Sciences, University of Baghdad, in 1966. She completed an MSc in 1970, and obtained a PhD in Physics from the Physics Department, Durham University, in 1979.

Dr Al-Dargazelli taught at Universities in Iraq where she became "Professor" in 1991. She moved with her husband Louay to the United Kingdom in 1992, where she worked at Durham University and Aston University. She has published several books, including four university text books on Physics one book on Sufism, and another on the position of woman in Islam.

Louay Fatoohi was born in Baghdad, Iraq, in 1961 to a Christian family. He converted to Islam when he was twenty years old. He obtained a BSc in Physics from the College of Sciences, University of Baghdad, in 1984. He obtained his PhD in Astronomy from the Physics Department, Durham University, in 1998.

The author of several books and over forty scientific and general articles in Arabic and English, Dr Fatoohi is particularly interested in Qur'anic exegesis (*Tafsir*), history in the Qur'an, and comparative religion. His most recent books are *The Mystery of the Historical Jesus: The Messiah in the Qur'an, the Bible, and Historical Sources* and *The Prophet Joseph in the Qur'an, the Bible, and History: A new detailed commentary on the Qur'anic Chapter of Joseph.*

Contents

Introduction to the Second Edition

The first edition of this translation came out in 1998. Ten years later, we are proud to present this revised and much improved translation. One aspect of the improvement is that the first translation was too literal. The problem with that approach is that the original Arabic text is so metaphorical, poetic, and full of imagery. The revised translation also corrects a number of mistakes in the first attempt. Furthermore, we have removed any Arabic text, and only a small number of transliterations were left. As a result, the revised translation reads much better and is more faithful and accurate than the translation of the first edition. One other change we have made is to make the translated title, *Purification of the Mind*, the main title and the original Arabic title, *Jila' Al-Khatir*, the subtitle, which is the opposite to what we did in the first edition. We think this is more appropriate given that the book is for English readers.

The book consists of 45 discourses that were given by Shaikh 'Abd Al-Qadir Al-Jilani in his school in Baghdad. These discourses, like the ones found in some of his other books, would have been transcribed by some of his listener. There are a number of surviving manuscripts of the book.

Our translation is based on an edition of the Arabic book by Shaikh Muhammad Al-Kasnazani Al-Husseini and published in 1989 in Baghdad, Iraq. At the time, one of us took a small part in proofreading the edited text and finalizing it for printing. That edition relied on three copies of the manuscript in Iraq: one at the department of manuscripts of the Iraqi Museum, one at the Library of the Ministry of *waqf* and religious affairs, and the third at the Library of the Mosque of Shaikh 'Abd Al-Qadir al-Jilani. Before embarking on this revised translation, we checked the Iraqi Arabic source with a separate edition done by Khalid Az-Zar'i and 'Abd An-Nāṣir Sirrī and published in 1994 by Dār Ibn Qayyim, Syria. This allowed us to improve the source text of our translation significantly by correcting mistakes and adding missing passages that were probably lost during the editorial work on the Iraqi edition. This improvement to the Arabic source has contributed to improving the translation.

Shaikh Al-Kasnazani Al-Husseini did not publish the manuscript in its original form but chose to classify the contents of the discourses into forty sections each of which deals with a specific subject, such as "patience," "mercy," "love"....etc. However, as each discourse covers a number of different topics, often in short statements, it was inevitable that such classification would be only very approximate. In fact, there are many instances where a paragraph that has been placed under a particular section could have been as appropriately, or may be even more accurately, put under a different one. These issues made us consider the possibility of canceling the classification and publishing the discourses in their original form in the second edition, but at the end we decided to leave the text as is for two reasons. First, although the classification is far from being accurate, it is still useful in clustering related sayings of the Shaikh. Second, the discourses have been published in their original form in both English and Arabic, so interested readers can consult those publications.

We also considered for the second edition removing some topics and adding their contents to other sections, as the contents had very little relation to the topics under which they were originally classified. However, it looks like the goal of introducing these topics, such as "pardoning," is to emphasize their importance, so we decided not to change them.

In order to differentiate between consecutive paragraphs that belong to different discourses, we have left space between them. Additionally, we have started any paragraph that belongs to a different discourse from the one before it with the special symbol ⊛.

As mentioned earlier, the language of Shaikh 'Abd Al-Qadir's discourses is often permeated by symbolic references, metaphorical images, and poetic expressions. This is an example passage of this immensely beautiful use of the language which the Shaikh ends with a reference to the fact that Allah used in the Qur'an parables and symbolic language:

> When the lover arrives to his Beloved (mighty and glorified is He), could there still be any tiredness? Tiredness turns into comfort, remoteness into nearness, absence into presence, and the hearing of news into direct seeing. He will come to view His secrets. He will take His servant on a tour in His house and He will open for him His treasures and show him His garden. Can you not comprehend this? "And Allah strikes parables for people" (from 14.25). It is the people of signs who understand the signs.

This style, which is characteristic of Shaikh 'Abd Al-Qadir's discourses, reflects a number of facts. First, the Shaikh often speaks about spiritual matters that are completely unfamiliar to the layperson and which the language is incapable of describing with accuracy. These, in the Shaikh's words, are states, stations, visions, and experiences that "no eye has ever seen, no ear has ever heard, and has never occurred to any human being." Second, the Shaikh's words spring as much from his heart as from his mind, describing feelings as well as thoughts. He is forced to use common words to describe feelings that are known only to those who have had those spiritual experiences. No language is equipped enough to describe these feelings, in the same way that no words can assist in describing color to one born blind because it requires visual experience. Third, the Shaikh often speaks about secret and intimate spiritual issues that he does not want to or cannot fully disclose, thus wrapping his words in metaphors. This is how the master ends one of those descriptions:

This is something beyond the comprehension of the creatures. All that appears of it is merely an atom from its mountain, a drop from its sea, and a lamp from its sun. O Allah, I apologize to you for speaking about these secrets, but You know that I am overwhelmed. A certain righteous person once said: "Beware of what merits an apology." But when I get up to sit on this chair [to preach], I become unaware of you [O people!] to the extent that no one is left in front of my heart to apologize to and restrict myself because of.

The words of Shaikh 'Abd Al-Qadir do not describe one spiritual state and are not targeted at one person. They paint a fascinating picture of a myriad of spiritual states and stations and apply to people of very different beginnings, paths, and ends. The destination is the same, but the routes are different. Also different wayfarers end their journeys at different points. What is good for someone might not good for another, and what is required of two different people might be completely different, even though both have the same goal. This is why understanding the Shaikh's words and their applications is a science in its own right. As Sufis say: "The ways to Allah are as many as the creatures."

The words of Shaikh 'Abd Al-Qadir remain as relevant to the seeker of the truth and nearness to God as they were when he uttered them almost one thousand years ago. For sure, the world has changed a lot, but man's nature has not, and the diseases of his heart remain the same. The Shaikh's words address these diseases and show man the way to salvation. His words lived a thousand years and will live to the day when this transient world is no more and is replaced by the permanent one.

Like all beacons of truth, Shaikh 'Abd Al-Qadir has been the target of attacks of the ignorant, the narrow-minded, and the misguided. As happened to others who understood Islam to be about works of the heart not acts of the body, this pious servant, whose life was fully dedicated to serving his Lord, has often been accused of distorting the message of Prophet Muhammad by those who wanted to hijack Islam and turn it into a spiritless, legalistic system to serve their worldly ambitions. But, as history has been confirming everyday, the voice of truth can never be silenced and the words of wisdom will remain inerasable.

It is ignorance of this fact, as well as mistaking falsehood for truth, that must have made some misguided individuals to use terrorism against the Shaikh as they bombed his shrine in Baghdad on 28th May 2007, damaging parts of it. These and similar criminals do not realize that what made great masters such as Shaikh 'Abd Al-Qadir Al-Jilani live forever is not buildings that commemorate them or books written about them, but the teachings and examples they set that live in people's minds and love for God that they helped them develop in their hearts. This is why almost one thousand years after his departure from this world people still feel immensely honored to serve the Shaikh and his sacred cause, including making his words more accessible to people.

19/2/2008
Birmingham, UK

A Biography of Shaikh 'Abd Al-Qadir Al-Jilani

Shaikh 'Abd Al-Qadir Al-Jilani was born in Gilan,[1] west of Iran, in 1077 CE to two well-known saints. He is a descendant of Prophet Muhammad (Allah's prayer and peace be upon him) from both of his parents sides. His father, sayyid[2] 'Abdullah az-Zāhid, is son of sayyid Yaḥya, son of sayyid Muhammad, son of sayyid Dāwūd, son of sayyid Mūsā, son of sayyid 'Abdullah, son of sayyid Mūsā Aj-Jūn, son of sayyid 'Abdullah Al-Maḥdh, son of sayyid Al-Ḥasan Al-Muthanna, son of Imām[3] Al-Ḥasan, son of Imām 'Alī bin Abī Tālib, cousin of Prophet Muhammad, and sayyida Faṭima Az-Zahrā', daughter of Prophet Muhammad.

Shaikh 'Abd Al-Qadir Al-Jilani's mother is Um Al-Khayer Faṭima, daughter of sayyid 'Abdullah Aṣ-Ṣawma'ī Az-Zāhid, son of sayyid Jamāl Ad-Dīn Muhammad, son of sayyid Maḥmūd, son of sayyid Abī Al-'Atā' 'Abdullah, son of sayyid Kamāl Ad-Dīn 'Īsa, son of Imām Abi 'Alā' Ad-Dīn Muhammad Aj-Jawād, son of Imām 'Alī Ar-Ridhā, son of Imām Mūsā Al-Kādhim, son of Imām Ja'far Aṣ-Ṣādiq, son of Imām Muhammad Al-Bāqir, son of Imām 'Alī Zayn Al-'Ābidīn, son of Imām Al-Ḥussein, son of Imām 'Alī bin Abī Tālib and sayyida Faṭima Az-Zahrā'.

Both of Shaikh 'Abd Al-Qadir's parents lived a pious life, in total detachment from this world, and in complete obedience to Allah. This is how they are described in the words of their saintly son: "My father renounced this world despite his ability to earn a lot in it, and my mother agreed with him on that and was pleased with his action. They were among the people of righteousness, religion, and compassion for the creatures."

Sayyid 'Abdullah Az-Zāhid was renowned for having his prayers answered by Allah and for his accurate predictions of future events. Sayyid 'Abdullah Aṣ-Ṣawma'ī was also known for performing numerous miracles, so people used to ask for his spiritual intervention when they found themselves in distress. It is reported that one day a caravan of merchants from Gaylan was heading toward Samarkand when a group of bandits stopped it. The merchants could not do anything other than invoke the help of sayyid 'Abdullah Aṣ-Ṣawma'ī whom they suddenly saw among them reciting a prayer. The bandits then fled the place, and sayyid

---

[1] He is also called "Al-Gīlānī" or "Al-Gaylānī" in various countries, but "Al-Jīlānī" is more widely used in English speaking countries.

[2] The word *sayyid* means literally "master." It is usually used as a title for the descendants of Prophet Muhammad because he described his two grandsons Imām Al-Ḥasan and Imām Al-Ḥussein, from whom all his lineage descended, as follows: "Al-Ḥasan and Al-Ḥussein are the masters (*sayyida*) of the youth of Paradise."

[3] The word "Imām" means literally "the leader or guide."

'Abdullah Aṣ-Ṣawma'ī disappeared as suddenly as he appeared. When they returned to their home city and related the story to the people of Gaylan, they were told that sayyid 'Abdullah Aṣ-Ṣawma'ī never left Gaylan throughout their journey.

Shaikh 'Abd Al-Qadir Al-Jilani started to show miraculous wonders soon after his birth. When he was an infant he would not suckle his mother during the day in the fasting month of Ramadhan. When the overcast sky prevented people from watching the crescent for the first day of Ramadhan, they asked his mother about him and she told them that he did not take milk on that morning. It turned out later that this was indeed the first day of Ramadhan.

After the departure of his father from this world, Shaikh 'Abd Al-Qadir Al-Jilani stayed with his mother until the age of eighteen when, after having a vision, he asked for her permission to move to Baghdad, the capital of Sufism and knowledge. In Baghdad, he accompanied Shaikh Ḥammād Ad-Dabbās, a well-known Sufi saint of the time, who predicted that Shaikh 'Abd Al-Qadir would attain such a high spiritual station to declare: "My foot is on the neck of every saint."

For almost twenty five years, Shaikh 'Abd Al-Qadir traveled the deserts and ruins of Iraq, and for several years he did not eat more than what was essential to keep him alive. For about forty years he never slept at night in order to worship Allah, and as a result he performed the prayer of dawn with the ablution of the evening prayer.

One of the major miraculous wonders that sheds light on the exceptional spiritual status of Shaikh 'Abd Al-Qadir and the role that Allah had assigned to him in promoting Islam took place on a Friday in 1117 CE. While on his way to Baghdad, Shaikh 'Abd Al-Qadir came across a frail and sick man who saluted him saying: "Peace be on you." As Shaikh 'Abd Al-Qadir returned the greeting, the man asked him for help to sit up. When Shaikh 'Abd Al-Qadir gave the requested help, the sick man started to grow big in stature. The person then asked Shaikh 'Abd Al-Qadir if he knew him, but Shaikh 'Abd Al-Qadir answered in the negative. So the man explained to: "I am the religion of your grandfather. I have become sick and miserable but Allah has revived me with your help." After this strange encounter Shaikh 'Abd Al-Qadir continued on his way to the mosque to perform the Friday prayer. At the mosque, a man approached him and gave him a pair of shoes and addressed him with the title of *Muḥyī ad-Dīn* which means "the reviver of religion," which became his title. Shaikh 'Abd Al-Qadir did indeed spread Islam everywhere in the world and his influence and guiding efforts were so great that many of today's Sufi schools trace their origin to him.

Shaikh 'Abd Al-Qadir then accompanied the Sufi Shaikh Abu Sa'īd Al-Makhzūmī who, in 1127 CE, put Shaikh 'Abd Al-Qadir in charge of his well-known school in Baghdad. Shaikh 'Abd Al-Qadir first did not preach. In that same year, one day before the prayer of midday, Shaikh 'Abd

Al-Qadir saw in a visionary dream his grandfather Prophet Muhammad who asked him why he was not preaching to the people. The grandson replied that he could not speak in the presence of the orators of Baghdad as his mother tongue was not Arabic. The Prophet then ejected his saliva seven times in his grandson's mouth and asked him to start preaching to people by both words and works. After the prayer, Shaikh 'Abd Al-Qadir sat to preach and people gathered around him, but he felt nervous. At this point, he saw his other great grandfather Imām 'Ali bin Abi Talib before him who ejected his saliva six times into the mouth of his grandson. When Shaikh 'Abd Al-Qadir asked him why he did that six rather than seven times, Imām 'Ali replied that it was out of respect to the Prophet. This is one of the miraculous events which underlines Shaikh 'Abd Al-Qadir's following reply to the question about the source of his divine knowledge: "In the past, it was my Master Hammad Ad-Dabbas, but now I drink from two seas: the sea of Prophethood and the sea of chivalry (*futuwwa*)".[4] The large number of books that Shaikh 'Abd Al-Qadir wrote on both the Law and Sufism attest to the depth of his divine knowledge.

This miracle provided Shaikh 'Abd Al-Qadir with a great deal of spiritual knowledge and the ability to preach to the people with eloquence and perfect command of the language. Thus, the school of Shaikh 'Abd Al-Qadir, where he used to lecture three days a week, became the destination of the seekers of truth and divine knowledge. He lectured at his school for about forty years since it was handed over to him in 1127 CE until his departure from this world in 1166 CE. The present book consists of 45 discourses that Shaikh 'Abd Al-Qadir gave at his school. He also taught and acted as a jurisprudent for thirty three years from 1133 CE.

Shaikh 'Abd Al-Qadir attained spiritual states and stations that no other Sufi Master after him reached. He was raised to such a status in the world of sainthood that in 1165 CE Allah ordered him to make his unique, well-known declaration: "My foot is on the neck of every saint", as had already been predicted of him by Shaikh Ḥammād Ad-Dabbās and a few other saints. All saints of the time heard his words and all of them bent their necks in compliance with this divine order. This is how he came to be known as *Sultān Al-Awliyā'* (the sultan of saints).

---

[4] The term *futuwwa* is derived from *fata* which literally means "noble knight" and which is one of the titles of Imām 'Alī bin Abī Tālib.

Good Behavior in the Company of Shaikhs

❀ O young man! When you come into my presence, give up your appreciation for your deeds and self-admiration. Come in with nothing, as one who is bankrupt. If you have high regard for your deeds and yourself you will be astonished at what I am talking about and you will hate me because I speak the truth and disagree with you. No one hates me other than the enemy of Allah and no one is ignorant of me except one who is ignorant of Allah (mighty and glorified is He), given to much talk and little action. No one loves me but one who is knowledgeable of Allah (mighty and glorified is He), given to much action and little talk. The sincere person loves me, whereas the hypocrite hates me. One who follows the *Sunna*[5] loves me, whereas one who follows heretical innovations hates me. If you love me, you are the one who will receive the benefits of that; and if you hate me, you are the one who will suffer the harm. I pay no attention to the praise and dispraise of the creatures.

❀ The person who wishes for success must become a piece of ground under the feet of shaikhs. What are the attributes of these shaikhs? They are those who have abandoned this world and the creatures and have bidden farewell to everything from beneath the Throne down to beneath the surface of the earth — that is the heavens and what is therein and the earths and what is therein. They are those who have given up all things and bidden them the farewell of one who will never return to them again. They have said farewell to all creatures including their own selves, for they are in the presence of their Lord (mighty and glorified is He) in all of their states. Anyone who seeks a company that guides him to the True One (mighty and glorified is He) yet keeps his lower self is in illusion and fantasy.

The person whose renunciation and belief in the oneness of God are sound does not see the existence of the creatures, does not see a giver other than the True One (mighty and glorified is He), and does not see a benefactor other than Him. How great your need is, O all of you people of this world, to listen to these words! How great your need is, O ignorant ascetics, to listen to these words! Most ascetic worshippers are servants of the creatures, associating them with God.

---

[5] The Arabic word *sunna* generally means "way" or "method." Usually written in English with a capital S, the term *Sunna* refers specifically to the way of life of Prophet Muhammad (prayer and peace be upon him), including his sayings and doings.

❀ O hermits and recluses, come and get a taste of my words, if only a single letter! Accompany me for a day or a week so that you may learn something that benefits you. Woe to you! The majority of you are in illusion, worshipping the creatures in your cells. This business does not come about by sitting in retreats while being ignorant. Woe to you! Walk in search of Knowledge and knowledgeable scholars until no further walking is possible. Walk until nothing obeys you [in your wish to walk]. When you become unable to walk, sit down. Walk with your outward, then with your inward,[6] then with your heart, and then with your essence. When you have become totally exhausted outwardly and inwardly and have to sit, nearness to Allah (mighty and glorified is He) and attainment to Him will come to you.

❀ If you come to me but do not put my teachings into practice you would only be a nuisance to the audience. As long as you are in your shop, you continue to think of your failing business, and when you come to me it is only to comfort yourself. No matter how many times you come to listen, it is as if you heard nothing. O property owner! Forget about your property and come and sit among the poor and be humble to Allah and to them.

❀ Be sensible, abandon your prestigious position and come and sit here like one of the group so that my words get planted in the land of your heart. If you have sense you will accompany me, be content with a morsel from me every day, and endure with patience the harshness of my words. Anyone who has faith will stand firm and grow, whereas the person who lacks faith will run away from me. Woe to you, O you who claim to know the spiritual states of others! How can we believe you when you have not managed to know your own state? This is nothing but telling of lies, so repent from the telling of lies. O Allah, grant us truthfulness under all conditions and "give us good in this world and good in the hereafter and protect us from the torment of the Fire" (from 2.201).

❀ Woe to you, O you who associate creatures with God! How often you knock on doors behind which there is none to answer you, and how often you hammer cold iron without heating it with fire! You have no sense, you have no proper reasoning, and you do not know the proper behavior. Woe to you! Come close to me and have a morsel from my food. If you taste my food you will renounce the food of others. If you get a taste of the food of the Creator, your heart and innermost being will renounce the food of the creatures. This takes place in the heart — behind the clothes, the flesh, and the skin. This heart will never be sound as long

---

[6] The *dhāhir* (outward) refers to the body, appearance, and visible actions. The *bāṭin* (inward) denotes inner feelings, thoughts ...etc.

as it is inhabited by any creature. Certainty [of faith] will remain incomplete as long as there is an atom of love of this world in the heart. When faith has become certitude, certitude has become knowingness, and knowingness has become Knowledge, you will become an expert in distinguishing between the good and the bad in the service of Allah (mighty and glorified is He). You will take from the hand of the rich and give back to the poor. You will become the owner of the kitchen, dishing out sustenance with the hand of your heart and innermost being.

O hypocrite, you are unworthy of respect until you come to be like this! Woe to you! You have not acquired good manners at the hand of an ascetic shaikh who practices pious restraint and is learned in the Law of Allah (mighty and glorified is He) and His Knowledge. Woe to you! You want something in return for nothing, so you will get nothing. Worldly things cannot be earned without diligence, so what of that which is in the presence of Allah (mighty and glorified is He)?

⊛ When the seeker's company of the shaikh has become sound, the shaikh will feed and nourish him from his heart with the food and drink of knowingness. O seekers, empty your hearts of the creatures and then you will see wonders! Tomorrow it will be said to the people of Paradise: "Enter Paradise," and today, when the True One (mighty and glorified is He) examines the hearts of the elite of His servants and finds them empty of this world, Paradise, and anything other than Him, He will say to them: "Enter the Paradise of My nearness now and later on."

⊛ Adhering to what I say is a sign of faith and running away from it is a sign of hypocrisy. O Allah, forgive us, do not expose us in this world and the hereafter, and "give us good in this world and good in the hereafter and protect us from the torment of the Fire!"

⊛ Refined behavior is as much an obligatory duty on the knower as is repentance on the disobedient person. How can he fail to be well-mannered when he is the nearest of all creatures to the Creator? If someone builds social relationships with kings but behaves ignorantly, his ignorance will bring him near to being put to death. Everyone who lacks polite behavior is detested by the creatures and the Creator. Any time in which good manners are lacking is loathed. Refined behavior in the company of Allah (mighty and glorified is He) is essential.

O young man, if you know me you will not leave me and you will follow me wherever I go. You will be incapable of leaving whether I assign you work to do or leave you without work, take from you or give you, impoverish you or enrich you, tire you or rest you. The requirements for becoming like this are to think well [of me] and cultivate good intention, both of which you lack. How could you, then, be fit for my company and benefit from my words? Victory lies in cultivating good behavior in the company of the Creator (mighty and glorified is He) and the creatures. O Allah, do not let their hearing of these words be evidence against them but render it evidence in their favor! "O our Lord, give us good in this world and good in the hereafter and protect us from the torment of the Fire!"

⊛ My enemy and one who loves me are both equal in my sight. I have no friend or foe left on the face of the earth. This happens only after one loves Allah, cultivates sound belief in His oneness, and sees the creatures as powerless. One who is pious to Allah (mighty and glorified is He) is my friend, whereas one who disobeys Him is my enemy. The former is the friend of my faith and the latter is its enemy. O Allah, let this be always true of me, establish it firmly, and make me totally committed to it! Make it a genuine attribute of mine, not merely something that I pretend. You know that I twine the fibers of the ropes of Your religion and of the ropes of Your will, and that I am the servant of Your servants — those who have renounced everything other than You in seeking Your satisfaction.

⊛ O ignorant one, O you who embrace the gold coin and the silver one, O you who rejoice in the praise and commendation of the creatures! You are the servant of praise, applause, and rewards. If you have sense you will weep over yourself. "We belong to Allah, and to Him we return" (from 2.156). There is no might or strength but by Allah, the High, the Great. O Allah, grant us fulfilling the servitude to You and being truthfulness in seeking You and "give us good in this world and good in the hereafter and protect us from the torment of the Fire!"

O young man, the truthful person has no backward movements. He is always moving forward. He has a front but no back. He keeps to his truthfulness until his atom becomes a mountain, his drop a sea, his little bit so much, his lamp a sun, and his shell a kernel. If you are ever fortunate to come across a truthful person, stay always close to him. If you are ever fortunate to meet one who has your remedy, keep always close to him. If you ever have the good fortune to come across one who guides you to what you have lost, remain always close to him. You may never get to know such people for they are a few, rare individuals. The shell is abundant but the kernel is rare. The shells are in the garbage dumps, whereas the kernel is in the treasuries of the kings.

⊛ The people of Allah are ill and their Physician is with them. They are ill in the presence of their Physician, on the lap of His generosity and His subtle kindness. He handles them with His favor, grace, and mercy. One who does not see a successful person will never succeed. Sit in the presence of the people of Allah, listen to their utterances, and accompany them for the sake of Allah (mighty and glorified is He) not for the sake of this world, and then you will benefit from them.

⊛ You are unworthy of respect! I speak the truth to you so it is up to you whether you wish to come or not, whether you wish to praise or dispraise me. The Invincible One has said: "And say [O Muhammad!] '[this is] the truth from your Lord,' so let him who will, believe; and let him who will, disbelieve" (from 18.29). No one runs away from the sharpness of my words other than one who is a hypocrite, impostor, swindler, follower of his passion, obedient to his lower self; violates the Book of Allah (mighty and glorified is He) and the Sunna of the Messenger of Allah (Allah's prayer and peace be on him); hates the truth; loves falsehood; takes no steps with his heart to draw near to his Master (mighty and glorified is He).

O young man, hear and look with your heart without doubts and you will see wonders! Relinquish your doubts about the people of Allah. Believe them and believe in them without asking "why" and "how," so they will accept you in their company, admit you to their service, and give you a share of what has been sent down to them. Favors and graces come down from the heaven on the hearts of the truthful, and the rewards of the innermost beings come down on their innermost beings, by night and day. If you wish them to accept you for their service you must purify your outward and inward. Be at the ready before them. Purify your heart of any heretical innovation, for the doctrine of the people of Allah is the doctrine of the prophets, the messengers, and the truthful (Allah's prayer and peace be on all of them). They follow in the footsteps of the righteous predecessors. Their creed is the creed of the elderly. They do not lay claim to anything unless they have evidence on it.

⊛ Woe to you! You claim that your heart has attained to Allah when it is in fact fettered and burdened. It is imprisoned behind doors and locked gates. Go and pass off your counterfeit coins on someone else. If you come here to pass off your counterfeit coins on me, do not come, for you will only tire yourself, as I will not accept your counterfeit coins. But if you come so that I cast your gold and separate out from it the impurities, silver, and any covering layer, then come. Have you not known that the people of Allah are money changers, assay the gold coins of religion and distinguish between the good and the bad — between what belongs to Allah (mighty and glorified is He) and what belongs to the creatures? The people of Allah are ambassadors, guides, physicians, experts, diligent workers, agents, and callers on people to their Lord (mighty and glorified is He).

O people, love your Lord (mighty and glorified is He) and make His creatures recognize that He is worthy of all love! Love Him and guide the creatures to Him so that they join you in loving Him. Remind those who are forgetful of Him. Remind them of His favor to them so that they come to love Him. Allah (mighty and glorified is He) revealed to David (prayer and peace be on our Prophet and on him) the following: "O David, make

My creatures love Me!" He has foreknowledge of whom will love Him. He ordered David (prayer and peace be on our Prophet and on him) to make His creatures love Him in order for that foreknowledge to become manifest. If you were inside a dark house, with a fire iron and a flint, and you rub the two together, would not that generate fire? The fire that was in the fire iron is old but the act of rubbing made it appear. Similarly, the duties imposed by the Creator reveal and unveil the foreknowledge about the creatures. The commandments and prohibitions differentiate between the obedient servant and the disobedient one. They distinguish between the good debtor who pays his dues and the bad debtor who defaults.

The people of the innermost being were few in ancient times, and today they are the fewest of the few. The believer loves Allah (mighty and glorified is He) even if He tests him with afflictions; reduces his share of food, drink, clothing, social prestige, and well-being; and drives creatures away from him. He does not run away from His door but rather sleeps at it, taking its doorstep as a pillow; and he does not feel alienated from Him. He does not object to Him should He give favors to others and deprive him. If He grants him favors, he offers thanks to Him, and if He withholds things from him, he endures that with patience. His aim is not to receive favors, but his goal is to see Him, come near to Him, and enter into His presence.

⊛ O you who waste your time in your houses and cells in the company of the lower self, natural inclination (*tab'*), passion, and little knowledge! You have to accompany practicing knowledgeable shaikhs. Obey them and follow in their footsteps. Show humility to them and be patient with their humiliation of your lower selves until your passions have disappeared, your lower selves have been subjugated, and the fire of your natural inclination has been put out. Only then will you come to know this world and so you will avoid it. It will become your maidservant and it will give you what it has been ordered to give you, which are your allotted worldly shares. It will then bring your shares to you while you are at the door of your nearness to your Lord (mighty and glorified is He). It and the hereafter are both maidservants for the person who serves the True One (mighty and glorified is He).

⊛ This business cannot be done by merely sitting in retreats in the company of ignorance. Woe to you! Walk in search of Knowledge and practicing knowledgeable scholars until no further walking can be done. Keep walking until your legs no longer obey you. So, when you become unable to walk, sit down with your outward, then with your inward, then with your heart, and then with your essence. When you become totally exhausted outwardly and inwardly and have to sit, nearness to Allah (mighty and glorified is He) and attainment to Him will come to you. If the footsteps of your heart come to a halt and you lose all your energy in your way to Him, that will be a sign of your nearness to Him. At that point, surrender and throw yourself prostrate. Then, He will either build a cell for you in the wilderness and lodge you in the ruins, or return you to society and order this world, the hereafter, jinn, people, angels, and spirits to be at your service.

⊕ It is being said to you: "Only if you listen and put into practice what you hear!" How often you attend these sessions with passion, disobedience, and objection! Your attendance is a falsehood with no truth, punishment with no reward, evil with no good. Repent and stop attending in this manner. Attend with the intention of deriving benefits and then you will benefit. I hope and pray that Allah (mighty and glorified is He) will benefit you through me and amend your hearts, intentions, and aims. I do not lose hope of you, in compliance with His words: "Allah may bring after that something new to pass" (from 65.1). You will wake up: "And you will know its tidings after a while" (38.88).

O Allah! Grant us the wakefulness of the vigilant. Treat us like You treated them. Let us enter their spiritual states with forgiveness, good health, and permanent well-being in religion in this world and the hereafter. O Allah, grant us Your nearness with forgiveness and well-being. Grant us the goodness of today and the goodness of every day! Grant us the goodness of those who are present and the goodness of those who are absent. Drive away from us the evil of the present and the absentees. Grant us the goodness of the sultans whom you put in charge of Your land and guard us against their evil. Guard us against the evil of the wicked, the scheming of the disbelievers, the evil of all of your servants and lands, and the evil of every crawling creature You grasp "by the forelock. Certainly, My Lord is on a straight Path" (from 11.56). Give the disobedient persons to the obedient ones, the ignorant persons to the knowers, the absentees from Your presence to those who are in Your presence, the idle ones to those who have put their knowledge into practice, and those who have gone astray to the guided ones. Amen.

⊕ O young man, what is yours will not go past you or be consumed by others. What is others' will not come to you by wishing for it and being keen on obtaining it. There is only yesterday that has already past, today that you are in, and tomorrow that is yet to come. Yesterday of yours is a lesson for you, today of yours is your current state, and tomorrow that is yet to come you may or may not witness. You do not know what your name will be tomorrow.

You will remember what I am saying and regret. Woe to you! You trade being in my presence for earning a grain or two! What cuts you off from me is your ignorance of what I am involved in and what I teach. You are ignorant of its root and branch. You are ignorant of its stream, mountain, and source. If you have known and understood what I do and say you would not have left me. You will remember after a while the advice that I am giving you. You will see after death the aftermath that I am talking about: "So you shall remember what I say to you, and I entrust my affair to Allah" (from 40.44). Say: "There is no might or strength but by Allah, the High, the Great (*lā ḥawla wa lā quwwata illā billāhi al-'Aliy al-'Adhīm*)".

⊛ Learn from me, O ignorant ones! Follow me for I guide you to the way of righteousness. Woe to you! You claim that you seek obedience to me, yet you hide your wealth from me! You have lied in your claim. The seeker has no shirt, turban, gold, or wealth in addition to his shaikh. He eats from his shaikh's plate what he orders him to eat, while he is in a state of extinction, waiting for the commandments and prohibitions of his shaikh. He knows that this has benefits from Allah (mighty and glorified is He) for him and is a tightening of His ropes. If you harbor doubts about your shaikh, you better leave his company, for in this case accompanying him and obeying him would bring no benefit to you. If the patient develops doubts about his physician, he cannot be cured by his medicine.

⊛ Accompany the people of Allah, for one of their attributes is that if they look at a person and direct to him their spiritual influence they love him, even if the person they looked at was a Jew, Christian, or fire-worshipper. And if he was a Muslim, his faith, certitude, and steadfastness will increase. If he was in a different state, Allah will expand his breast to Islam.

O you who are forgetful of the True One (mighty and glorified is He), it is piety and righteous works that draw you near to Him! The disbelievers used to draw close to the sultans and kings by means of their wealth and sons, and they used to say: "If on the Day of Resurrection Allah (mighty and glorified is He) wishes us to draw near to Him by means of our property and sons we will do," so Allah (mighty and glorified is He) revealed: "It is not your wealth or your children that bring you near to Us, but [our nearness is for] those who believe and do righteous deeds — these will have a double reward for what they did, and they shall be safe in the chambers" (34.37). If you draw near to Allah (mighty and glorified is He) by means of your property while you are still in this world, this will be beneficial to you. If you teach your children how to write, how to read the Qur'an, and how to worship with the intention of drawing near to Allah (mighty and glorified is He), you will benefit from this. You will get the rewards for this after your death. I am telling you that all that you are involved in will bring you no benefit. It is faith, righteous deeds, truthfulness, and belief that are beneficial.

The believer who has become a knower (may Allah be satisfied with him) keeps on pleasing the Messenger (Allah's prayer and peace be on him) by working with him until his heart asks for the permission to enter into the presence of his Lord (mighty and glorified is He). He will be like a servant before him, and after he has served him for a long time, he will say to him: "O Master, show me the King's door. Make me do business with Him. Put me in a position where I can see Him. Let me hold with my hand the ring of the door of His nearness." He will then take him along with him and bring him near to the door. Then it will be said to him: "O Muhammad (Allah's prayer and peace be on him), who is the person with you, O ambassador, O guide, O teacher?" To this he will reply: "You already know, a young bird that I have brought up and accepted for Your service." Then he will say to his (the servant's) heart: "Here you are with your Lord," as Gabriel (peace be on him) said to him when he flew him to heaven and he drew near his Lord (mighty and glorified is He): "Here you are with your Lord."

Repentance

✸ Piety is the key to repentance, and adhering to it is the key to the nearness to Allah (mighty and glorified is He). Repentance is the root and branch of every goodness, which is why the righteous people never abandon it under any circumstances. Repent, O backsliders, O disobedient ones! Seek reconciliation with your Lord by means of repentance. This heart remains undeserving of the True One (mighty and glorified is He) as long as it contains an atom of this world and longing for any creature. Therefore, when you seek His company, evict both of these attachments from your hearts. This will not cause you any harm. For once you have established a connection with Him, this world and the creatures will both come to you while you are with Him, at His door. This is an experienced thing; it has been experienced by the ascetics who renounced everything.

✸ Repent and acknowledge your shortcomings and weaknesses. Repentance is the water of the True One (mighty and glorified is He). He revives the earth after its death with rain and quickens the hearts after their death with repentance and wakefulness. O disobedient ones, repent, never despair of the mercy of Allah (mighty and glorified is He), and never lose hope of His mercifulness!

✸ You must repent and ask for forgiveness frequently, for these are two great means to achieving success in the affairs of this world and the hereafter. Noah (prayer and peace be on our Prophet and on him) ordered his people to pray for forgiveness, and he promised them that He will respond by granting them forgiveness and putting this world at their command and at their service. So he said, quoting Him (high is He): "And ask forgiveness of your Lord, He is Forgiving. He will send the rain on you in torrents, help you with wealth and sons, appoint for you gardens, and appoint for you rivers" (from 71.10-12). Repent from your sins and turn away from your current attribution of partners to God so that He will grant you all that you wish for of things of this world and the hereafter.

You have sinned as your father Adam (prayer and peace be on our Prophet and on him) sinned, so repent as he did. When he and his wife Eve (prayer and peace be on our Prophet and on them) ate from the tree that their Lord forbade them to eat, He punished them with remoteness and stripped them of the rewards of His generosity. He left them naked, so they picked up leaves from Paradise [to cover their bodies]. But the leaves dried up and fell, so they remained naked. They were then sent down to earth. All that occurred as a result of the evil of disobedience and noncompliance. The poison of disobedience flowed in their bodies so He expelled them. Then Allah (mighty and glorified is He) taught them how to repent and ask for forgiveness. They repented and asked for forgiveness, so He pardoned and forgave them.

✣ When will you repent, O backsliders, O disobedient ones? Be reconciled with your Lord (mighty and glorified is He) by means of repentance. Was it not for my sense of shame in the presence of Allah (mighty and glorified is He) and in relation to His patience, I would get up and grab each one of you by the hand and say to him: "You have committed such and such. Repent to Allah (mighty and glorified is He)". You must not speak and you will not be spoken to until your faith, certitude, and knowingness of your Master (mighty and glorified is He) have strengthened. Then, you will clinch to the firm handhold, which is the attainment of your heart to Him. The Prophet (Allah's prayer and peace be on him) will be proud of you before the nations. O you who have believed with your tongue, how long will it be before you believe with your heart? O you who are a believer in your public life, how long will it be before you become a believer in your private life? Combining faith of the heart with striving against the lower self is useful. Combining faith of the tongue with disbelief in your heart is useless. The faith of the hypocrite is the faith of one who is afraid of the sword [of punishment].

✣ O disobedient ones, repent from your disobedience, for your Lord (mighty and glorified is He) is forgiving, merciful! He accepts repentance from His servants and covers the sins and erases them. Repent with your tongues and hearts. O Allah, we repent to you for every sin and guilt and we will never commit them again! "O our Lord, do not condemn us if we forget or make mistake!" (from 2.286). "O our Lord, do not make our hearts deviate after You have guided us!" (from 3.8). O Forgiver of sins, forgive us! O You who cover the shortcomings, draw a veil over our shortcomings! Ask Him for forgiveness, for He (high is He) forgives the sins, accepts the righteous deeds no matter how few they are, and rewards in return with things that are even better, for He is generous and bountiful. He gives rewards without asking for something in return and for no reason, so what if there is a reason?

Deal with Him by means of believing in His oneness, performing good works, being detached from this world and turning away from it, choosing the hereafter and welcoming and wishing for it, and giving up the acts of disobedience and sins and forsaking them. The seeker of the True One (mighty and glorified is He) does not wish for His Paradise and does not fear His Fire, but only wishes to see His face. He wishes for nearness to Him and fears remoteness from Him. You are a prisoner of Satan, passion, the lower self, this world, and lustful desires, but you do not have a clue. Your leg and heart are in shackles, but you are totally unaware. O Allah, deliver him from his captivity and deliver us! Amen.

You must keep the fast, perform the five daily prayers at their prescribed times, and honor all the limits of the Law. After performing the obligatory worship duties, start supererogation. Impose on yourself observing the strictest laws of religion ('azīma) and avoid following the allowed concessions (rukhṣa). If the person resorts to these concessions and gives up observing the strictest laws, it is feared that he would totally lose his religion. Observing the strictest laws is for grown-up men, because it is about enduring what is most dangerous, hardest, and most difficult. Following the allowed concessions is for the youngsters and women because it is the easiest.

⊛ O young man, if you keep to repentance and proper reflection, you will give up all interests in worldly things and become occupied with those that are relevant to the hereafter! You will give up your interest in what belongs to the creatures and become occupied with what belongs to the Creator, and you will give up committing evil and do only good. O you who have relinquished reflection and repentance, you are a loser but you do not have a clue! You are a loser not a winner. Your likeness is as the likeness of a man who sells and buys without keeping account of his expenditure or counting the cash. He will soon find out that his capital has disappeared and what is left with him is bad, pseudo-silver coins. Woe to you! Your capital, which is your lifetime, has gone to waste while you do not have a clue! Everything that you have earned is counterfeit whereas everything that the believers have earned is a gem. The believer will soon fulfill his commitments, whereas you will be taken and thrown in prison. The True One will not accept a single atom of what you have, for the True One (mighty and glorified is He) accepts only sincerity, which you do not have. Have you not heard these words of the Prophet (Allah's prayer and peace be on him): "Call yourselves to account before you are called to account, weigh yourselves before you are weighed, and smarten yourselves up for the greatest parade"?

It has been said that whomever Allah (mighty and glorified is He) wishes to be a knower of Him (mighty and glorified is He), one of His saints, one of His lovers, one of His sought after ones, He assigns an angel to look after him in both his private and public lives, foster his heart and his intention, drive evil away from him, and allow only what is good to reach him. This is similar to what He (high is He) said about Joseph (prayer and peace be on our Prophet and on him): "thus [it was] so that We turned evil and lewdness away from him; [for] he is one of Our chosen servants" (from 12.24). This is what He did for the prophets, the messengers, the saints, and the truthful (Allah's prayer and peace be on all of them).

John (prayer and peace be on our Prophet and on him) was passing by children who were playing who said to him: "Play with us." He replied: "Glory be to Allah, it is not for playing that we have been created." The lower selves of the people of Allah urge them to do good not evil. They have joined their hearts after being subjected to striving. Whenever their lower selves were subjected to strife, they gained comfort and longing for the Highest Companion. Listening to the Qur'an comes to be all their business. Before this, they used to hear only the sound and miss the meaning. Do not listen to or participate in prattle. The Qur'an is the source of life for the hearts and of purity for the innermost beings, and it lays the foundation for neighboring Allah (mighty and glorified is He) in Paradise.

⊛ O young man, you have piled up sins one on top of another, and you are heading toward a vague, ambiguous end which may be good or bad. Pay attention to death as there is no way that you can escape it. Give up indulging in idle gossip and getting involved in matters that are irrelevant to you. Curtail your hopes and reduce your greedy keenness on obtaining worldly things because you will be dead soon. Your death is so close that it may come while you are sitting here. In this case you would have come here on foot but would be carried back to your house in a coffin.

The Mediator

✸ The mediator is essential. Ask your Lord for a physician who can treat the illnesses of your hearts, a healer who can heal you, a guide who can guide you and take you by the hand. Draw near to those whom He has brought near to Him, His elite, the ushers of His nearness, the keepers of His door. You have consented to serving your lower selves and pursuing your passions and natural inclinations. You work hard to fully satisfy and satiate your lower selves in this world, although this is something that you will never achieve. You keep to this state hour after hour, day after day, month after month, and year after year, until you find that death has suddenly come to you and you cannot release yourselves from its grip.

✸ The Prophet (Allah's prayer and peace be on him) is reported to have said: "In every craft seek the expertise of its experts." Worshipping is a craft, and its experts are those whose deeds are righteous; those who are knowledgeable of the Law and have put it into practice; those who have bidden farewell to all creatures after knowing them; those who have run away from their lower selves, their possessions, their children, and everything other than their Lord (mighty and glorified is He) on the feet of their hearts and their innermost beings. Their bodies are in populated places, in the midst of the creatures; but their hearts are in the wilderness and deserts. They keep to this until their hearts grow and their wings strengthen and fly to heaven. Their spiritual aspirations ascended, so their hearts flew up and reached the True One (mighty and glorified is He). Thus, they became among those about whom Allah (mighty and glorified is He) has said: "And in Our sight they are among the righteous elect" (38.47).

You have this world in your hearts. You have acts of disobedience in your hearts. Let me take charge of you to cleanse and purify you with drinks I offer you. The drinks that I give you are pious restraint, renunciation, piety, faith, certitude, knowingness, Knowledge, forgetting everything, and being in a state of extinction with respect to everything. After reaching this state, existence through your Lord (mighty and glorified is He), nearness to Him, and remembrance of Him will come to you. When all of this has become true of someone, he becomes a sun, moon, and guide for the creatures — taking them by their hands from the river of this world to the shore of the hereafter.

Woe to you! You depend exclusively on your opinion and say: "What do I do with the company of the jurisprudents and scholars?" You think you have been created only for earning worldly things, eating, drinking, and having sexual intercourse. Repent and return before the Angel of Death (prayer and peace be on our Prophet and on all prophets and angels) comes to you and takes you while you are amid the worst of deeds. Everyone of you is told to observe the commandments and prohibitions and endure with patience whatever destiny brings.

⊛ Moses (prayer and peace be on our Prophet and on him) came to his people carrying the Torah which contained the commandments and prohibitions. They said to him: "We will not accept what you say unless we see Allah's face and hear His speech." He said to them: "He has not shown His face to me so how would He show it to you?" They replied: "If you do not show us His face and let us hear His speech, we will not accept His words." Therefore, Allah (mighty and glorified is He) revealed to Moses (prayer and peace be on our Prophet and on him) the following: "Tell them if they want to hear My speech, they must fast for three days, and on the fourth day purify themselves and dress up in new, clean clothes, then bring them to hear My speech." Moses told them that, so they did so.

Then they came to the place on the mountain where Moses used to privately converse with His Lord (mighty and glorified is He). Moses had chosen seventy men from the scholars and ascetics of his people. Then the True One (mighty and glorified is He) addressed them, and they were all thunderstruck, with Moses (prayer and peace be on our Prophet and on him) remaining alone. He said, "O Lord! You have killed the elite of my nation," and he wept. Allah responded to his weeping with mercy and revived them. They stood on their feet and said: "O Moses, we do not have the capacity to hear the speech of Allah (high is He), so be the mediator between us and Him!" Thus, Allah spoke to Moses who, in turn, enabled his people to hear Him by repeating His words.

Moses could hear the speech of Allah (mighty and glorified is He) because of the strength of his faith and the realization of his obedience and servitude, whereas they failed to hear Him because of the weakness of their faith. If they had accepted from him what was brought to them of the Torah, had acted with obedience on the commandments and prohibitions, had kept to good manners, had not tried a test, and had not dared to say what they said, they would have been able to hear the speech of Allah (mighty and glorified is He).

Love

❀ The lover has no eyes with which he looks at other than his Beloved.

❀ Woe to you! You claim to love Allah, yet you open up your hearts to others! Because *Majnūn Layla* (the mad lover of Layla) became truthful in his love for Layla, his heart would not accept other than her. One day he came across some people who asked him: "Where have you come from?" He replied: "From being with Layla." They asked him: "Where are you going?" He answered: "To Layla."

Once the heart has become truthful in its love for Allah (mighty and glorified is He) it becomes like Moses (prayer and peace be on our Prophet and on him) about whom Allah (mighty and glorified is He) has said: "And We had caused him to refuse the wet-nurses"[7] (from 28.12). Do not lie; you do not have two hearts but one, so once it is filled with something there is no room for another. Allah (high is He) has said: "Allah has not made for any man two hearts in his breast" (from 33.4) — a heart that loves the Creator and a heart that loves the creatures. There can be no heart in which this world and the hereafter coexist.

❀ Allah (high is He) has said in one of His utterances: "The person who claims to love Me yet goes to sleep once the night has set is a liar." If you were one of the lovers of Allah (mighty and glorified is He) you would not wake up from your sleep reluctantly. The lover is tired, whereas the beloved is at rest. The lover is a seeker, whereas the beloved is sought after. The Prophet (Allah's prayer and peace be on him) is reported to have said: "Allah (mighty and glorified is He) says to Gabriel: 'O Gabriel, wake up so-and-so and put to sleep so-and-so'"! There are two ways to interpret this.

[The first interpretation:] "Wake up such and such person who is a lover and put to sleep so-and-so who is a beloved. The former has claimed that he loves Me, so make him get up and stand in his right position [to worship Me] so that the leaves of his existence with anyone other than Me will fall. Wake him up in order for him to present evidence of his claim and for his love to be confirmed. And put to sleep so-and-so because he is a beloved. He has toiled hard for a long time. Nothing of himself has remained for other than Me. His love has become all for Me. His claim, proof, and adherence to My covenant have been confirmed. His repentance to Me is truthful, and he has kept My covenant. He is a guest, and the guest should not be made to serve or tire. Put him to sleep on the lap of My subtle kindness, give him a seat at the table of My favor, and let

---

[7] After being suckled by his mother, baby Moses did not accept the milk of any other woman.

him feel intimate with My nearness. His love has become true, and when love becomes true the barriers of formality vanish."

The other interpretation: "Put to sleep so-and-so because he worships Me in order to find favor with the creatures; and wake up so-and-so because seeking My favor is the goal of his worshiping Me. Put to sleep so-and-so because I hate to hear his voice, and wake that other person up because I love to hear his voice."

The lover becomes beloved once he has purified his heart of everything other than Allah (mighty and glorified is He), so he will not wish to leave Him for the sake of anyone else. The attainment of the heart to this spiritual station comes about by performing the obligatory worship duties; refraining patiently from prohibited and dubious things; obtaining the permissible and licit things without passion, lustful desire, and engrossment; resorting to curative pious restraint; practicing total renunciation, which is the abandonment of everything other than Allah (mighty and glorified is He); refusing to comply with the lower self, passion, and Satan; and purifying the heart totally of any creature so that praise and dispraise, being given and having things withheld, and gold and clay become all equal. The first stage of this spiritual station is declaring that "there is no God save Allah (*lā ilāha illā Allah*) (from 47.19), Muhammad is the Messenger of Allah (*Muhammadun rasūlu Allah*)" (from 48.29), and its last stage is seeing gold as worthless as clay.

The person whose heart becomes sound and attached to his Lord will see as equal: gold and clay, praise and dispraise, sickness and good health, affluence and poverty, and good and bad fortune in this world. When this has become true of someone, his lower self and passion will die, the fire of his natural inclinations will die out, and his devil will be humiliated before him. His heart will look down on this world and its lords, then he will turn away from them and advance toward his Lord until a path for his heart will appear in the midst of the creatures which it will follow to reach the Creator. The creatures will step aside to the left and right and clear the way for him. They will run away from the fire of his truthfulness and the charisma of his innermost being. At this stage, he will be called "great" in the heavenly kingdom and all creatures will come to be under the feet of his heart and seek protection under his shadow.

Do not be in illusion. Do not claim ownership of what does not belong to you and what you do not have. Your lower self is in total control of you, and the creatures and this world are in your heart greater than Allah (mighty and glorified is He). You are outside the limit of the people of Allah and you are not counted with them. If you wish to attain to what I have referred to, occupy yourself with purifying your heart from everything.

Woe to you! When you are in need for a bite to eat, lose a trivial thing, or one of your worldly affairs fails, it is the end of the world for you! You turn away from your Lord (mighty and glorified is He), release your anger by battering your wife and children, and insult your religion and Prophet (Allah's prayer and peace be on him). If you were sensible and one of the people of wakefulness and watchfulness, you would be silent in the presence of Allah (mighty and glorified is He) and you would see all his actions as favors and caring for you.

⊛ The lovers feel no rest in their hearts even if they enter a million Paradises until they see their Beloved. They do not wish for a created thing but they wish for the Creator. They do not want benefits but they want the Benefactor. They wish for the root not the branch. They have given up all their relationships and have become the individuals of the King. The earth seems too strait for them despite its spaciousness. They have something that keeps them busy and distracts them from the creatures. When their hearts see Paradise while awake or asleep they do not look at it even with a twinkling of an eye. They look at it as they look at lions, shackles, and prisons. They say that it is mere veils, care, and torment. They escape from it as the creatures escape from lions, fetters, and prisons.

⊛ When someone loves Allah (mighty and glorified is He) he loses his will with Him, because the lover has no will above the will of his Beloved. This is known for every lover who has experienced the taste of love. The lover is extinct in the presence of his Beloved, like the servant in the presence of his master. The wise servant who is obedient to his master does not disagree with his master or object to him at all. Woe to you! You are neither a lover nor a beloved, and you have neither experienced the taste of love nor that of being loved. The lover is restless and wary, whereas the beloved is calm. The lover is in hardship, whereas the beloved is in comfort.

You lay claim to love, yet you leave your Beloved to go to sleep! Allah (mighty and glorified is He) has said in one of His utterances: "The person who claims to love Me yet goes to sleep once the night has set is a liar." Some of the people of Allah sleep only out of necessity. Such a person does not fall into deep sleep but he merely dozes off. He sleeps while in prostration. The Prophet (Allah's prayer and peace be on him) is reported to have said: "If the servant falls asleep while in prostration, Allah (mighty and glorified is He) commends him to the angels saying: 'See how his soul is with Me and his body is practicing obedience to Me in My presence'". The person who is overwhelmed by sleep while performing his prayer is considered to be still praying, because his intention was to pray when he was overwhelmed by sleep. The True One (mighty and glorified is He) does not look at the appearance but at the intention and the essence.

⊛ O You who claim to be a seeker, your supposed quest will not be sound as long as you have something that screens you off from your Sought After One! You still say "this is mine" and "this is my property"? The lover has no property, no worldly interest, no treasury, no will, and no house in relation to his Beloved. They all belong to his Sought After One, to his Beloved. The lover is owned by his Beloved and is a humble servant in His hands. The servant and all his property belong to his Master. When the surrender of the lover to his Beloved has become complete, the Beloved returns to him what He received from him and puts him in charge of it. The situation is reversed. The slave becomes free; the humiliated one becomes exalted; the remote one becomes near; the lover becomes beloved. When Majnūn Layla remained patient in his love for Layla, love turned to her and Layla became Majnūn and Majnūn became Layla. The person who is patient and truthful in his love for Allah (mighty and glorified is He), does not run away from His door because of the arrows of His tribulations, and receives them with the front of his heart will become beloved, wanted, and sought after. The person who has experienced this knows it very well. It is indescribable. It is beyond the comprehension of all creatures except a few individuals. These are the most intelligent people. They understand by a mere glance, and by the slightest sign they return [to obedience], acquire good manners, and know what is required of them.

⊛ Woe to you! You claim that you love Allah (mighty and glorified is He), yet you do not obey Him! The love of Allah (mighty and glorified is He) comes only after observing the commandments, refraining from the prohibitions, being satisfied with whatever one gets, and being content with the divine decree. Then you love Him for His favors, after that you love Him for nothing in return, and then you yearn for Him. The lover remembers the True One with his tongue, limbs and senses, heart, and innermost being. When he attains extinction in His remembrance, He commends him to His creatures and distinguishes him from them with unfamiliar spiritual states and sayings. He becomes a truth within a truth. He becomes extinct, as only the First One, the Last One, the Outward One, the Inward One remains. O you who claim to love Him yet complain to the creatures about Him, you are a liar in your claim of love! The person who loves Him in the state of affluence yet complains about Him in the state of poverty is a liar. When poverty comes to a raw heart that has not been strengthened by faith and certitude, that person will undoubtedly end up in the company of disbelief.

⊛ There can be no partnership in love. O you who claim to be in love, the lover is the guest of the beloved! Have you ever seen a guest get his food and drink and look after his needs? You claim to be in love, yet you go to sleep! The lover never sleeps. You are either a lover or a beloved;

there is no third case. If you were a lover then how can the lover sleep? And if you were a beloved then the lover is your guest!

⊛ An inquirer asked me: "Which one is more intense, the fire of fear or the fire of longing?" [I said:] "The fire of fear for the seeker and the fire of longing for one who is sought after. These are two different things. Which of the two fires do you have, O inquirer?"

O you who are reliant on means,[8] your Benefactor and Harmer are one and the same! Your King is one, your Sultan is one, your God is one, and your Creator is one. It is He who made you, and what you do with your hands it is in fact He who does it through your hands. He has created, subsisted, harmed, benefited, and guided you. Why do you rely on something that is created, like yourselves? Why do you worship what cannot cause any harm or bring any benefit to itself? Have you not heard that Allah (high is He) has said: "So let the person who hopes for the meeting with his Lord do righteous deeds and associate no partner in the worship due to his Lord" (from 18.110)? O people, if you are not lovers, serve the lovers, draw near to the lovers, love the lovers, and think well of the lovers!

An inquirer asked him: "Is love by compulsion in the beginning and by volition in the end?" He said: "Love comes by compulsion and volition. For some rare individuals, love comes by way of involuntary compulsion. The True One (mighty and glorified is He) looks at them and loves them, so He transfers them in one moment from one state to another. He does not want to love them after years but He loves them in one moment, so they love Him out of necessity, without delay, without introduction, not gradually, and without any passage of time.

As for the majority of people, love comes by way of choice. The lovers choose Allah (high is He) in preference to His creatures. They see the favors that they have as having come from Him not from anyone else. They recognize His subtle favors, His preparations for them, and His rewards for them so they love Him. Then they choose Him in preference to both this world and the hereafter. They give up all prohibited or legally dubious things, reduce the use of the lawful, and be satisfied with whatever they already have. They abandon the bed and blanket, and sleep and rest: 'Their sides shun their beds' (from 32.16). Neither their night is an ordinary night nor is their day an ordinary one. They say: 'Our God, we have left everything behind the backs of our hearts and hastened to You so that You may be pleased.' They walk to Him sometimes on the feet of their hearts, sometimes on the feet of their innermost beings, sometimes on the feet of their will, sometimes on the feet of their spiritual aspiration,

---

[8] The plural Arabic word *asbāb*, which is translated as "means," denotes the "apparent" causes of things and events. The Qur'an stresses that it is Allah who is the "real" cause of everything that happens and that all "means" are mere instruments in His hand.

sometimes on the feet of their truthfulness, sometimes on the feet of their love, sometimes on the feet of their yearning, sometimes on the feet of their humility and modesty, sometimes on the feet of their nearness, sometimes on the feet of their fear, and sometimes on the feet of their hope. They do all this in love for Him and longing to meet Him.

O you who ask me, are you of those who love Allah (mighty and glorified is He) through involuntary compulsion or through choice? If the answer is neither then be silent and work on correcting your practice of Islam. O you who ask me, if only your practice of Islam and faith are sound! If only you leave the company of disbelievers and hypocrites today and stay away from them in the future! If only you refrain from attending sessions of those who associate creatures and means with God, those who dispute with the True One (mighty and glorified is He)! Repent and do not approach the treasuries and secrets of the kings. Shaikh Ḥammād Ad-Dabbās[9] (may Allah show mercy to him) used to say: 'When someone does not know his status, the decrees of destiny show him his status.' Acknowledging your status is better than denying it, because the ignorant person is ignorant of his own status and that of others. O Allah, do not include us among the pretenders, liars, and those who are ignorant of You and of the elite of Your creatures, and 'give us good in this world and good in the hereafter and protect us from the torment of the Fire'".

⊕ Woe to you! You claim to love Allah, yet you love other than Him! Your claim will be a cause for your destruction. How can you lay claim to love when no sign of it can be seen about you? Love is like a fire in a house with no door or key; its flames come out from the top. The lover keeps his love indoors and conceals it until it shows on him. He has a special language and special speech. He does not wish for anything in addition to his Beloved, which is one of the greatest signs of his truthfulness. O liar, O facetious one, keep silent for you are not one of them! You are neither a lover nor beloved. The lover is at the door, whereas the beloved is inside. The lover is in agitation, movement, and disturbance, whereas the beloved is in tranquility, resting on the lap of the Subtly Kind One, sleeping there. The lover is in tiredness, whereas the beloved is at rest; the lover is a learner, whereas the beloved is a learned scholar; the lover is imprisoned, whereas the beloved is free; the lover has gone crazy, whereas the beloved has become sane.

When a child sees a snake he screams and runs away, whereas the snake-charmer keeps silent at the scene of a snake. When someone sees a lion, he screams and flees in horror, whereas the lion trainer plays with the lions and sleeps with them. Everyone who enters is surprised. Allah

---

[9] Shaikh 'Abd Al-Qadir Al-Jilani accompanied Shaikh Ḥammād Ad-Dabbās for some time.

(high is He) has said: "And be pious to Allah and [then] Allah will teach you" (from 2.282). The lover is pious. He is taught politeness while he is still at the door. His limbs and senses and his heart are taught good manners. Once he has become well-mannered, he enters through the door of nearness. The Law refines the behavior at the door, whereas Knowledge refines the behavior inside. Once the person has acquired good manners through the Law, Knowledge will take care of him, give him authority, make him a commander, enrich him, and enable him to judge properly. The Law is a common door, whereas Knowledge is a special door. When someone behaves with ultimate politeness and obedience at the common door, he will be befriended and brought near, in the inside of the special door. He will join the group of loved ones.

You should not utter a word until you have reached your station, while adhering to reflection and deep thinking, fulfilling servitude, and looking at the deficiencies and shortcomings of yourself. When the person looks at his faults, he accomplishes perfection, but when he looks at his perceived perfection, he reaps deficiency. Reverse your actions in order to succeed.

Trust

❀ O you who associate His means with Him! If you have experienced eating by mere trust you will not deify the means and you will sit at His door full of trust, having total confidence in Him. There are only two ways to make a living: by working while adhering to the requirements of the Law or through trust. Woe to you! Do you not feel ashamed before Allah (mighty and glorified is He) that you have given up making a living through work to beg from people? Making a living through work is the beginning and trust is the end. I do not see a beginning or an end for you. I tell you the truth and I do not feel embarrassed to face you. Listen, accept [what I tell you], and do not dispute. To dispute with me is to dispute with the True One (mighty and glorified is He) Himself. Keep up prayer for it is a link between you and your Lord (mighty and glorified is He).

❀ O young man, when there is an opportunity for action on something you have been commanded to do, be as brave and active as a lion in executing it; when there is an opportunity to do one of the prohibitions, be as inactive as a sick man to avoid it; and when tribulations and decrees of destiny come your way, forget yourself and be calm. The Commander of the Believers (*Amīr al-Mu'minīn*) 'Alī bin abī Ṭālib (may Allah be satisfied with him and ennoble his face) has said: "Be as passive as a dead person in relation to whatever brings benefits to you and prevents evil from you."

The lover hears and sees in relation to the True One (mighty and glorified is He), but he is blind and deaf in relation to the creatures. The longing has taken over his five senses. His body is with the creatures but his essence is with the Creator. His feet are on the earth but his aspiration is up in heaven. His cares are kept hidden in his heart. Therefore, the creatures do not perceive this. They see his feet but they cannot see his aspiration and cares for they are in the safe of the heart which is the safe of the True One (mighty and glorified is He). Where do you stand with respect to this, O liar? You are busy with your property, children, social prestige, and association of creatures and means with God. How can you then claim to be near to the True One (mighty and glorified is He)? Telling lies is a form of wrongdoing, because the reality of wrongdoing is to leave something in the wrong place. Repent from your telling lies before its evil consequences catch up with you.

❀ O you whose hearts are dead, why do you sit here in my presence? O servants of this world and the sultans, O servants of the wealthy, O servants of the rise and fall of market prices! If the price of a grain of wheat becomes as high as one gold coin I would not care. The believer has no concern about his sustenance because of the strength of his certitude and his trust in his Lord (mighty and glorified is He). Do not count yourself among the believers. Put yourself in a different class. Glory be to Him who has made me stand among you!

⊛ Allah (mighty and glorified is He) has already allotted the worldly shares. He would not increase or decrease them by a single atom. The Prophet (Allah's prayer and peace be on him) has said: "Allah (mighty and glorified is He) has completed the creation, the assignment of subsistence, and the appointment of the times of things. The Pen with which He wrote down everything that is to happen until the Day of Resurrection has already run dry." Do not devote energy to obtaining what has already been decided to be yours, for that sort of effort is utter messing about and foolishness. Allah has planned all your circumstances and has appointed for them specific dates. As long as the lower self has not been made calm by striving, it would not believe in this and would not relinquish its greedy keenness and persistence on obtaining things. Before it reaches a state of calmness, the lower self can believe in this only verbally.

Be sensible, and acquire good manners by putting my teachings into practice. Do not devote energy to getting what is predestined, already done, inevitable, and bound to come to you at the time assigned to it in the foreknowledge of Allah (mighty and glorified is He). The Prophet (Allah's prayer and peace be on him) is reported to have said: "Even if the servant says: 'O Allah! Do not provide for me', Allah will provide for him despite his wish." What you earn in return for your work is from Allah (mighty and glorified is He); even earning a single broad bean is from Allah (mighty and glorified is He). The creatures have nothing to do with it.

⊛ O young man, religion in the sight of Allah is Islam, and the reality of Islam is surrender! You have to reach the state of Islam first and then fulfill surrender. Purify your outwards by Islam and purify your inwards by surrender.

Surrender yourselves to your Lord (mighty and glorified is He) and be satisfied with His management of your affairs. Give up your will and accept the destiny that your Lord (mighty and glorified is He) has decreed. Accept all of what destiny brings. Your Lord knows you better than you know yourselves. Accept His words with certitude. Receive His commandments and prohibitions with total acceptance. Receive His religion with all of your hearts, and make it your inner and outer covers. Take full advantage of your lives before your death, before the advent of a "Day from Allah that cannot be turned back" (from 30.43), which is the Day of Resurrection.

⊛ Woe to you! Do not be an idiot, disputing with Allah (mighty and glorified is He) and arguing with Him with your foolishness and ignorance. Otherwise, you will put at peril your capital, which is your religion. Close your eyes, reflect, behave with good manners, know who you are, know your status, and be humble inside. You are a servant, and the servant and all his property are owned by his master. He does not have the right to do with himself as he wishes. The servant must give up his own wishes in favor of his master's, his choice in favor of the choice of his master, and his opinion in favor of his master's.

You behave with impudence with Allah (mighty and glorified is He) for the sake of your own benefit, whereas the people of Allah behave impudently with their Lord only for the sake of the creatures. They appeal to Him on behalf of the creatures and persistently repeat their appeal for their sake. They are those who have already bidden farewell to the creatures and purified their hearts from the creatures so that not a single atom of the creation is left in them. They exist with Him, by Him, and for Him. They are in total relaxation with no tension, total honor with no humiliation, total receiving with no deprivation, total fulfillment with no withholding, total acceptance with no rejection, total happiness with no sorrow, capability with no powerlessness, strength with no weakness, and favor with no anger. They have been vested with clothing of nobility and He handed to the hands of their hearts the authority of delegating power, enabling, and acting with "'be,' and it is" (from 2.117) (*takwīn*).[10] The power to act with "'be,' and it is" has become in their hands an inexhaustible treasure and a river that never runs dry. Whenever they become afraid, He increases their sense of security. Whenever they fall behind, He puts them at the front. Their words are heard, and their intercession [on behalf of others] is accepted. He made over to them the kingdom of this world and the hereafter in a way that is incomprehensible to the creatures. They are called "great" in the heavenly kingdom.

⊛ The believer in the oneness of God does not listen to the sultan or Satan. He has turned away from them, existing by his heart in the presence of Allah. He sees the True One's (mighty and glorified is He) actions of management of him and His creatures. He sees how the leaves of the door of the divine decree and destiny are opened and closed. He sees the creatures as totally powerless, weak, ill, poor, humiliated, and mortal. He has no friend and no foe; no one to offer a prayer of

---

[10] The term *takwīn* refers to the ability to act with the divine power of "'be,' and it is" which God confers on the elite believers, as stated in the following saying of God: "O My servant! Obey Me and then you will be like Me: you will say for anything: "Be,' and it is". The meaning of the Qur'anic term "'be,' and it is'" is made clear in the following verse: "We only say to something We wish: 'Be,' and it is" [16.40].

supplication for and no one to curse. If his Lord (mighty and glorified is He) wishes him to curse someone, he does, and if He wishes him to offer a prayer of supplication for someone, he does. He behaves according to the commandments and prohibitions. His heart has joined the angels whom Allah (mighty and glorified is He) described as follows: "They do not disobey Allah in what He commands them, and they do as they are commanded" (from 66.6). He speaks as the limbs and senses will speak on the Day of Resurrection. When the limbs and senses are blamed by one of those people whom they spoke against, they will answer: "Allah who has made everything speak has made us speak" (from 41.21). The servant who attains to this spiritual station becomes extinct in relation to himself, existing only with respect to his Lord (mighty and glorified is He). O Allah, correct our prayer of supplication to you and "give us good in this world and good in the hereafter and protect us from the torment of the Fire."

⊛ O people, ensure that your children and your family members acquire good manners! Instruct them to worship Allah (mighty and glorified is He), be in ultimate politeness with Him, and be satisfied with Him. Your concern about earning your living must not reach your hearts, but it must be restricted to your effort and work. I can see that most of you have relinquished the education of their children and have become mainly concerned with earning their living. Reverse your actions in order to succeed.

Renunciation

❀ O young man, I am not interested in my speech, you, or the goods, wealth, and presents that you keep in your houses. As long as I remain so, you will benefit from my words, Allah willing. As long as the eye of the speaker is on your turbans, clothes, and pockets, you will not derive any benefit from what he has to say. As long as he frequents the place of the smoke of your cooking and has greedy desires about you, you will not benefit from his words. His speech will be a shell that has no kernel, a bone that has no meat on it, a bitterness with no sweetness, an appearance with no essence. The speech of the covetous person is never free of flattery, and his flattery prevents him from disagreeing with you. The words of the greedy person are as empty as the Arabic word *ṭama'* (covetousness) itself, because the three letters of the word *ṭama'* are all empty and hollow (the way they are written in Arabic): The *ṭā'*, *mīm*, and *'ayn*.

❀ The ascetic has no hands with which he takes the money of people.

❀ The reality of renunciation is giving up this world and giving up the hereafter; giving up all lustful desires and pleasures; giving up one's very existence; giving up seeking spiritual states, rankings, miracles, and spiritual stations, and giving up everything other than the Lord of the creatures so that no one remains other than the Creator (mighty and glorified is He). He is the final destination and He is the ultimate object of all hopes. To Him all affairs belong.

❀ Renunciation is a source of comfort for the hearts of the obedient ones, the ascetics. The burden of renunciation rests on the body, the burden of knowingness on the heart, and the burden of nearness on the innermost being. Practice renunciation, be content, offer thanks, be satisfied with your Lord (mighty and glorified is He), and do not be satisfied with yourself. Think well of others, give up holding a poor opinion of others, and do not hold yourself in high esteem.

❀ When you renounce this world and your asceticism becomes true, this world will appear to you in your dreams in the form of a woman who pays homage to you, saying: "I am a maidservant for you; I have trusts for you, so take them." She will count for you your allotted shares, whether few or many. When your knowingness has strengthened, she will come to you in wakefulness. The first spiritual state of the prophets (prayer and peace be on them) is inspiration and the second is a visionary dream.

When their spiritual states have strengthened, the angel comes to them in wakefulness and says: "The True One (mighty and glorified is He) says to you this and that."

⊛ When someone has genuinely renounced the creatures, they become genuinely interested in him and benefit from listening to his words and looking at him. When the heart's renunciation of the creatures and the innermost being's renunciation of anything other than Allah (mighty and glorified is He), apart from His nearness, have become genuine, nearness becomes his close companion in this world and his entertainer in the hereafter.

⊛ Be sensible, I can see that you do not have hearts or knowledge of the heart. Woe to you! You claim to be an ascetic and put on clothes of ascetics, yet you go knocking at the doors of the kings and the rich, who are the sons of this world, and then return! Your lower self seeks this world and wishes for what those people have. Surely you must have known that the Prophet (Allah's prayer and peace be on him) has said: "Whoever hovers around a prohibited area is very likely to end up encroaching on it." Preoccupation with the affairs of this world obstructs the way of the servants of Allah (mighty and glorified is He), enchants them, and drives them out of their senses. This applies to everyone except those whom Allah (mighty and glorified is He) wills to exclude. These are a few individuals. Allah (mighty and glorified is He) looks after their hearts and deeds and protects them in both their public and private lives. He purifies their food, drink, and clothing by the hand of power. The people of Allah have put into practice what the Messenger of Allah (Allah's prayer and peace be on him) brought with him, so the Master (mighty and glorified is He) took care of them and loved them.

⊛ Woe to you! It is the heart that practices renunciation not the body. O you who are ascetic only outwardly, your renunciation is thrown back at you! You have hidden your turban and shirt, buried your gold in the ground, put on austere woolen clothes, and collected leftovers. May Allah cut off your skin and head if you do not repent. You have opened your shop to sell hypocrisy. May Allah demolish your shop on top of you and kill you under its ruins if you do not destroy it, repent, and cut your waistband[11] (*zunnār*).

Woe to you! The believer has renunciation in his heart and nearness to his Lord (mighty and glorified is He) in his innermost being. This world and the hereafter have both come to his door, inside his treasury, not inside his heart. His heart is empty of anything other than his Master. How can it take in others when it is already filled with Him, His

---

[11] A belt that Christians used to wear.

remembrance, and His nearness? His heart is empty and broken on his Master's account, so no doubt He dwells in it. Allah (mighty and glorified is He) has said in one of His utterances: "I am with those whose hearts are broken on My account." Their lower selves have broken by giving up this world and their hearts have broken on account of their Master. Once this break has taken place, He will come to them and set it. The Physician will come and treat them. This is the true bliss, not the bliss of this world and the hereafter.

⊛ You have to practice pious restraint so that the hand of your heart is never without it. If you give it up then you will be disappointed. When someone gives up the practice of pious restraint, his heart darkens with legally dubious things and impurities. Woe to you! You claim that you are pious yet you do not practice pious restraint! The practicing person abandons many things in fear of falling in prohibited and dubious things, and Allah punishes him on the basis of the lowest allowed concessions.

One day I passed through a village surrounded by fields of corn. I stretched out my hand and picked a corn cane to suck. At that point, two men from the village, each of them holding a stick, came and beat me up until I collapsed to the ground. So I gave a pledge to Allah (mighty and glorified is He) at that moment not to take advantage again of the allowed concessions or avail myself of what is not mine. The Law has allowed the person who passes by fields of cereals and fruit trees to eat as much as he needs without paying anything in return, but it prohibited him from taking away anything. This is a general concession. However, I was not allowed to take advantage of this concession and I was ordered to adhere to the strictest laws. As the person increasingly remembers death, his pious restraint increases, the concessions that are allowed to him decrease, and his adherence to the strictest laws increases.

⊛ Open the eye of your lower self and say to it: "Look at your Lord (mighty and glorified is He) and see how He looks at you. Look how He has destroyed the kings and the rich who lived before you. Remember the deaths of those of bygone times who owned the world and enjoyed its pleasures before it was snatched away from their hands and they were snatched away from it. They are now imprisoned in the jail of torment. Their palaces are deserted, their houses are in ruins, their property is gone, and their deeds have stayed. The lustful desires have gone and their bad consequences have remained."

Do not rejoice, for this is not the time of rejoicing. Do not be impressed by the beauty of your wife's face, by your son, by your house, and by the size of your wealth. Do not rejoice in what the preceding prophets, the messengers, and the righteous (Allah's prayer and peace be on all of them) did not rejoice in. Allah (mighty and glorified is He) has said: "Allah does not love those who are recklessly happy" (from 28.76) with this world and its people and with other than Him. He loves those who rejoice in Him (mighty and glorified is He) and in His nearness.

The thinking and the reflection of the people of Allah are focused on the affairs of the hereafter not on lustful desires, pleasures, and entertainments. O you who are under an illusion, you have not done what He wants you to do! O forgetful ones, in the hereafter there is a severe torment for those who do not obey Allah (mighty and glorified is He)!

Fear

⊛ There is no one on the face of the earth whom I fear or pin my hopes on, be it one of the jinn, human beings, animals, insects, or any other creature. I am not afraid of anyone other than Allah (mighty and glorified is He). The more that He allays my fear the more it grows, for He is "One who certainly works His will" (from 11.107) and "He shall not be questioned as to what He does, but they shall be questioned" (21.23).

⊛ The believer remains in fear until his innermost being is granted the book of safety. He conceals it from his heart and never reveals it to it. This happens to a few individuals only.

⊛ The pious are those who are pious to Allah (mighty and glorified is He) in their public and private lives and watch Him under all circumstances. Their hearts shiver in fear of Him by night and day. They are afraid that tribulations might attack them during the night and cut them off from Him and, with them failing to be patient, they would turn to disbelief. They are afraid that the Angel of Death (prayer and peace be on our Prophet and on him) might come to them while they are doing evil deeds. "They do what they do while their hearts are full of fear" (from 23.60), afraid of being rejected, afraid of the foreknowledge of Allah (mighty and glorified is He) about them.

Al-Fudhayl bin 'Iyādh (may Allah show mercy to him) used to say to Sufyān Ath-Thawrī (may Allah show mercy to him) whenever he met him: "Let's weep over the foreknowledge of Allah (mighty and glorified is He) about us." How excellent these words are! They are the words of someone who is a knower of Allah (mighty and glorified is He) and who is knowledgeable of Him and of His management. As for the "foreknowledge of Allah (mighty and glorified is He)" that bin 'Iyādh referred to when saying "weep over the foreknowledge of Allah (mighty and glorified is He) about us," it is His following saying: "These are to go to Paradise and I do not care, and these are to go to the Fire and I do not care." He mixed them all in one place so one cannot know to which of the two groups he belongs. They did not become conceited because of what became visible of their deeds, because all deeds are assessed according to their final outcome.

The pious are those who give up the acts of disobedience and sins, both the apparent and hidden ones, dissimulation, hypocrisy, and working for the sake of the creatures and worldly purposes. Therefore, today they are in the paradise of obedience and tomorrow they will be in the midst of gardens and springs, sitting among trees that never fade, fruits that never run out, and rivers that never run dry. How could the water dry up when it springs from beneath the Throne? For everyone of them there is a river of water, a river of yogurt, a river of honey, and a river of wine. These rivers will be with them wherever they go, without a cleft in the ground. Everything in this world has an equivalent in the hereafter and more. Everything in Paradise has its prototype in this world. "They receive what their Lord gives them" (from 51.16) (mighty and glorified is He) of bliss that no eye has ever seen, no ear has ever heard, and has never occurred to any human being. "Whose fruits are nigh to cull" (69.23). When one of them reclines on his couch, the fruits come to his mouth and he eats them while resting. The roots of the trees are upward whereas their fruits are downward. Their roots are silver and their branches are gold. When it occurs to one of them to eat some of the fruits, they advance to his mouth, so he picks what he likes and then they return to their places. Everything in Paradise sings for the people of Paradise and entertains them. Their speech is lovely and in the finest sound. This is true even of its rivers, trees, and everything there.

O seekers of this world, this world is ephemeral and tiring! Seek the everlasting Paradise, which is the place of comfort, the place of bliss, and the place of thankfulness. In Paradise there is no ablution, no prayer, no pilgrimage, no obligatory alms-giving, no tribulations to be endured with patience, no illnesses, no chronic diseases, no poverty, and no fear of departure. O people, soon death will call on you and snatch you away! You will be as if you had not been created or seen! Turn your hearts away from your families, children, and property. Renounce all the creatures of your Lord (mighty and glorified is He) and do not rely on anyone of them in trivial or important matters. O Allah, grant us trust in You under all circumstances and awareness of the powerlessness of anyone other than You, and "give us good in this world and good in the hereafter and protect us from the torment of the Fire."

⊛ Give up your wish in favor of His, your preference in favor of His, your decision in favor of His, and your will in favor of His. He is "One who certainly works His will" (from 11.107). "He shall not be questioned as to what He does, but they shall be questioned" (21.23). His company is like the company of lions and snakes, which is why the people of Allah are standing in His presence on the feet of fearfulness and caution. Neither their night is an ordinary night nor is their day an ordinary day. Their eating is like that of the ill, their sleep is like the sleep of those who are drowning, and their speech is out of necessity. The patient feels satisfied with very little of food. He eats while being afraid of his food, unable to tell whether it is good for him or not. The drowning person slumbers only when sleep is irresistible, just to be awakened by the waves of the sea of power, the sea of "One who certainly works His will" not what they will. They are scared of being drowned by the waves and Him sending some animals to eat them. They wish that the waves would throw them ashore and allow them into the palace of His nearness, private conversation, and sightings.

⊛ O young man, the people of Allah have given up everything other than working [for Him], saying that everything else is mere nonsense and a shell. They have sought the kernel, clenched to it, and renounced the shell. They have sought the help of Allah (mighty and glorified is He) in their quest for what is indispensable. The True One (mighty and glorified is He) is indispensable, whereas everything else can be dispensed with. So when He saw and recognized their truthfulness in their quest, He granted them amnesty, well-being, and His nearness: "There, authority is Allah's, the True One" (from 18.44).

Every heart that has no fear is like a town without trees or sheep without a shepherd. Such a town is nothing but ruins and such sheep are doomed to become food for the wolves. When a person is afraid, he keeps wandering throughout the night. He cannot settle in one place so he is always on the move. The destination of the travel of the people of Allah is the abode of the True One (mighty and glorified is He).

Patience

⊛ Endure with patience the harm of the creatures and neighbors, for there is much good in patience. All of you are commanded to show patience and are responsible for yourselves and your flock. The Prophet (Allah's prayer and peace be on him) has said: "Each one of you is a shepherd and responsible for his flock." Be patient with destiny until suffering transforms into bliss. Patience is the foundation of good. The angels were tested with afflictions and they endured them with patience, and the prophets were tested with afflictions and they endured them with patience. You are following in the footsteps of the people of Allah, so emulate their deeds and endure the afflictions with patience.

When the heart has become sound, it will not care anymore for one who disagrees with it and one who agrees with it, one who praises it and one who dispraises it, one who gives it and one who deprives it, one who draws it near and one who keeps it at a distance, one who accepts it and one who rejects it. The sound heart becomes filled with belief in the oneness of God, trust, certitude, faith, and nearness to Allah (mighty and glorified is He). It sees all creatures in light of their powerlessness, humiliation; and poverty, but it does not show arrogance even to the young child. It becomes like a lion at the time of meeting the disbelievers, hypocrites, and disobedient ones — because of its zeal for Allah (high is He); and it shows humility and homage toward the righteous, the pious, those who practice pious restraint. Allah has described the people who have these attributes saying: "Hard against the disbelievers, merciful among themselves" (from 48.29). When the servant becomes like this, he becomes beyond the comprehension of the creatures, outside their domain of control, victorious, and a manifestation of those described in the following words of Allah (mighty and glorified is He): "And He creates what you do not know" (from 16.8). All of this is the fruit of the belief in the oneness of God, sincerity, and patience.

When our Prophet Muhammad (Allah's prayer and peace be on him) endured what came his way with patience, he was raised up to the seventh heaven, where he saw his Lord (mighty and glorified is He) and drew near to Him. This edifice was erected for him after he firmly laid the foundations of patience. All good things are obtainable by patience, which is why Allah (mighty and glorified is He) mentioned it and stressed its importance as the best Speaker said: "O you who believe, be patient, urge each other to be patient, remain steadfast, and be pious to Allah so that you may succeed!" (3.200). O Allah, make us among those who are patient, perfectly following them in word and work, in our private and public lives, in appearance and in essence, in all of our states, and "give us good in this world and good in the hereafter and protect us from the torment of the Fire."

❀ Endure with patience the rulings of the Law so that Knowledge will be unveiled to you. The True One (mighty and glorified is He) has commanded you to be patient, so be patient. He ordered His Prophet (Allah's prayer and peace be on him) in particular and you in general to be patient. The command is for him and for you also. He (high is He) has said: "Then be patient [O Muhammad!] as the messengers of determination were also patient" (from 46.35). [He meant:] "Be patient with Me, O Muhammad, as they were patient with Me and endured My decrees and My destiny about their families, property, and children, as well as the harm that the creatures caused them." They confronted all that with endurance, but how little endurance you have! I do not see among you anyone who would bear a word from his mate or excuse him. Learn from the Messenger (Allah's prayer and peace be on him) his good manners and deeds in the outset so that comfort will come to you in the end.

❀ Woe to you! Remember the hunger of the starving, the nakedness of the naked, the illness of the ill, and the imprisonment of the prisoners and then you will find that your affliction has become easier to bear. Remember the terrifying ordeal of the dead on the Day of Resurrection. Remember the foreknowledge of Allah (mighty and glorified is He) about you, His caring for you, and His foreordination for you and then you will feel a sense of shame in His presence. If you find yourself in anguish, remember your sins, repent from them and say to your lower self: "It is because of your sins the True One (mighty and glorified is He) has distressed you." If you repent from your sins and be pious to the True One (mighty and glorified is He), He will provide for you an outlet from every grief and an exit from every distress. Allah (mighty and glorified is He) has said: "And whoever is pious to Allah He will appoint for him a way out, and He will provide for him from whence he did not expect. And whoever puts his trust in Allah, He will suffice him. Allah will attain His purpose" (from 65.2-3).

The sensible person is one who is truthful and is distinguishable from the liars by his truthfulness. Adhere to truthfulness instead of telling lies, steadfastness instead of running away, advancing instead of backsliding, patience instead of impatience, thankfulness instead of ingratitude, satisfaction instead of dissatisfaction, compliance instead of disputation, and certitude instead of suspicion. If you comply and do not dispute, thank and do not show ungratefulness, be satisfied and do not be discontent, and be calm and do not have doubts then: "Is not Allah sufficient for His servant?" (from 39.36).

❀ O you who are poor, endure your poverty with patience and then affluence will come to you in this world and the hereafter. The Prophet (Allah's prayer and peace be on him) is reported to have said: "The poor who endure their poverty with patience are the companions of Allah (mighty and glorified is He) on the Day of Resurrection." Those who bear their poverty with patience are the companions of Allah, today [in this world] by their hearts and tomorrow [on the Day of Resurrection] by their bodies. As for those who are in need of Allah (mighty and glorified is He) only, who accompany Him with patience, and who are indifferent to anything other than Him, their hearts are reassured, attracted [to Him], and do not accept anyone other than Him. The case is similar to what Allah (mighty and glorified is He) said about Moses (prayer and peace be on our Prophet and on him): "And We had caused him to refuse the wet-nurses" (from 28.12).

⊛ There is no believer who will not, at the moment of death, have the veil removed from his eyes so that he can see what is his in Paradise. The houris and young servants will wave to him and fragrances from Paradise will reach him, so death and its stupor taste good to him. The True One (mighty and glorified is He) will do to him as He did to Pharaoh's wife Āsyā (may Allah show mercy to her). Pharaoh subjected her to all kinds of torture before thrusting iron spikes into her hands and feet. The veil was then removed from her eyes and the doors of heaven were opened wide for her so she saw Paradise and its contents. She saw the angels building a house in Paradise, so she said: "My Lord, build for me a house in Paradise in Your presence!" (from 66.11). She was told: "This is yours," so she laughed. Pharaoh said: "Have not I told you that she is crazy? Do not you see how she laughs in the midst of torture?" The same happens to the believers who see at the moment of death what they have with Allah (mighty and glorified is He). Some of them come to know this before death; they are those who are brought near, singled out, and wanted.

⊛ Woe to you! How can you tell others to endure with patience when you are impatient? How can you tell him to give thanks in return for the favors when you have given up thankfulness? How can you tell him to be satisfied with the divine decree when you are dissatisfied? How can you tell him to renounce this world when you are full of desires about it? How can you tell him to yearn for the hereafter when you have renounced it? How can you tell him to trust Allah (mighty and glorified is He) when you have relied on other than Him? You are hated by the True One (mighty and glorified is He), the angels, and the hearts of the truthful and the righteous of His servants. You must have heard this poetry by one of them:

Do not advise people to avoid a certain action only for you to commit it.

This would be a great shame on you.[12]

You are filled with concerns with the creatures and filled with hypocrisy so no doubt you weigh lighter than the wing of a mosquito in the sight of Allah. You are with the hypocrites in the lowest level of the Fire.

❀ The truthful person offers thanks for the favors he receives, endures with patience the punishments, carries out the commandments, and keeps away from the prohibitions. This is how the hearts are developed. Offering thanks for receiving favors increases them, and enduring with patience the punishments removes and mitigates them. Endure with patience the death of your children and other family members, the loss of property, being dishonored, the failure of worldly interests, and the harm caused by the creatures and then you will receive a great deal of good. When you thank for being in easy circumstances and show patience in hard times, the wing of your faith will become fully fledged and strengthen and your heart and innermost being will fly to the door of your Lord (mighty and glorified is He).

How can you lay claim to faith when you have no patience? Have you not heard this saying of the Prophet (Allah's prayer and peace be on him): "Patience to faith is like the head to the body"? If you do not have patience, then your faith is without a head, so its body is worthless. If you know the One who sends the affliction, you will bear His affliction. If you know this world, you will not fall into disobedience by seeking it. O Allah, guide everyone who has gone astray, forgive every disobedient person, give patience to every afflicted person, and guide to thankfulness everyone who is free of afflictions. Amen.

❀ Be pious and be patient. The head of religion is patience and its body is action. This is why the Prophet (Allah's prayer and peace be on him) has said: "Patience to faith is like the head to the body." No action can be completed without having patience with the decree of Allah (mighty and glorified is He). Be patient, be steadfast, and practice pious restraint. Practice pious restraint both in your public and private lives, renounce the allotted worldly shares of others, and turn away from yours.

❀ O young man, when your standing at the door of the True One (mighty and glorified is He) has lasted long enough, your greed and desires will diminish and your politeness will increase. Patience removes the lustful desires. Patience eradicates the person's habits, eliminates his

---

[12] The poet is Abū Al-Aswad Ad-Dū'lī (608-688) who is credited with being the first one to write the Arabic grammar.

reliance on means, and overthrows the false gods. You are under an illusion. You are ignorant of Allah (mighty and glorified is He), His messengers, His saints, and the elite of His creatures (Allah's prayer and peace be on them). You lay claim to renunciation, yet you long for this world! Your renunciation has no foundations. How can you long for this world and to the creatures but do not yearn for your Lord (mighty and glorified is He)? Think well [of me] and cultivate good behavior so that I may guide you to the door of your Lord (mighty and glorified is He), show you the path to it, strip you of your clothes of arrogance, and vest you with clothing of humility.

Sincerity

⊛ O young man, you must work sincerely for Allah (mighty and glorified is He), in your prayer, fasting, pilgrimage, giving obligatory alms, and all of your deeds. Have a pledge with Him before your arrival to Him. This pledge is nothing less than sincerity, belief in the oneness of God, following the Sunna and the Islamic community, patience, thankfulness, entrusting Allah with your affairs, rejecting the creatures and seeking Him, and turning away from anything other than Him and advancing to Him with your heart and your innermost being. No doubt, He will give you in this world nearness to Him, longing for Him, and loving Him, and in the hereafter He will give you of His nearness and favors what no eye has ever seen, no ear has ever heard, and has never occurred to any human being.

⊛ O sincere one, run away from the association of partners with Allah to the door of your Lord. Stop at it and do not escape when tribulations come. If you stood at His door and tribulations came to you from your rear, cling to the door, for they will be fended off from you by your belief in the oneness of God and the charisma of your truthfulness. When tribulations come to you, resort to patience and steadfastness and recite these words of Allah (mighty and glorified is He): "Allah confirms those who believe with the firm word in the life of this world and in the hereafter" (from 14.27); His (high is He) following utterance: "So Allah will suffice you against them; He is the Hearer, the Knower" (from 2.137); and His following words: "Is not Allah sufficient for His servant?" (from 39.36). Say frequently: "There is no might or strength but by Allah, the High, the Great" (*lā ḥawla wa lā quwwata illā billāhi al-'Aliyī al-'Adhīm*), and frequently ask for forgiveness and glorify the Lord. Remember the True One (mighty and glorified is He). By truthfulness you will be protected from the army of tribulations and the army of the lower self, passion, and Satan. How well I know you, and how little you know me!

"He whom Allah guides is rightly guided" (from 18.17). "And he whom Allah guides will have none to mislead him" (from 39.37). "He whom Allah sends astray there is no guide for him" (from 7.186). Our Prophet Muhammad (Allah's prayer and peace be on him) used to love and wish that those who had gone astray would accept guidance, so Allah revealed this to him: "You do not guide whom you like but it is Allah who guides whom He wills" (from 28.56). So he (Allah's prayer and peace be on him) said: "I have been sent with guidance, but guidance is not under my control. And Satan tempts people, yet temptation is not under his control."

The belief of the followers of the Book and the Sunna of the Messenger of Allah (Allah's prayer and peace be on him) is that the sword does not cut because of its nature, but it is rather Allah (mighty and glorified is He) who cuts with it; that the fire does not burn because of its nature, but it is rather Allah (mighty and glorified is He) who burns with it; that food does not satisfy hunger because of its nature, but it is rather Allah (mighty and glorified is He) who satisfies hunger with it; and that water does not quench thirst because of its nature, but it is rather Allah (mighty and glorified is He) who quenches thirst with it. The same applies to all things of all kinds; it is Allah (mighty and glorified is He) who uses them to produce their effects while they are only instruments in His hand with which He does whatever He wills. When Abraham the Intimate (prayer and peace be on our Prophet and on him) was cast into the fire and the True One (mighty and glorified is He) wanted that the fire would not burn him, He made it "coolness and safety" (from 21.69) to him. It is rightly reported that the Prophet (Allah's prayer and peace be on him) has said: "On the Day of Resurrection, the Fire will say: 'Pass through, O believer, for your light has put out my flames'"! The slave may need to be beaten with the stick, whereas a sign is sufficient for the freeman to understand.

⊛ O you who worship with an absent heart, your likeness is as the likeness of a donkey that has its eyes blindfolded while turning the mill! It thinks that it has walked many miles when in fact it has not left its place. Woe to you! You stand up and sit down in your prayer, and suffer hunger and thirst in your fasting, yet without having a single atom of sincerity and belief in the oneness of God; what benefit would you derive from this? What would you earn other than weariness? You pray and fast while the eye of your heart is on what other people have in their houses, in their pockets, and on their plates. You look at them in the hope that they may present you with gifts, you show them your worship acts, and let them know of your fast and strife.

O you who have made the creatures as partners to Allah, what you have are worthless! Turn back from your attribution of partners to Allah. O hypocrite, O dissimulator, O you who have turned away from the attributes of the truthful, spiritual, godly ones! Have you not realized that I scrutinize you, have authority over you, and ask you for evidence on your claims? The Prophet (Allah's prayer and peace be on him) is reported to have said: "If the claims of people were to be accepted without evidence, some people would claim the blood and property of others. But the evidence must be provided by the claimant and the oath is required of the person who denies it."

How much you talk and how little you act! Reverse your actions in order to succeed. When someone comes to know Allah (mighty and glorified is He), his tongue will stop moving, his heart will start to speak, his innermost being will become pure and serene, and his status will raise in His sight. He will feel intimacy and find comfort with Him and he will find Him sufficient for all his needs, to the exclusion of everyone else.

O fire of the hearts, be coolness and safety! O hearts, get ready for the day on which the mountains will be removed and the earth will be made to appear in full view. The real man is one who, on that day, will stand steadfast on the feet of his faith in his Lord, his trust in his Lord, his love for his Lord, and his longing for his Lord; on the feet of his knowingness of Him in this world before the hereafter. The mountains of the means and the creatures will be removed, whereas the mountains of the Creator of all means will remain in place. The mountains of the kings of the outward and the images will be removed and vanish, whereas the mountains of the kings of the inward will appear and stand firm. The Day of Resurrection is the day of change and replacement. These mountains at whose strength, hardness, and great size you marvel will become like carded wool and will be uprooted. Their hardness will vanish and they will be made to move faster than the clouds. The sky will become like "*muhl*" (from 70.8), which is molten copper. The nature of the earth and the sky will totally change. The bout of this world will be over — that is the bout of the Law, the bout of deeds, the bout of planting, the bout of duties. The bout of the hereafter will come — that is the bout of destiny, the bout of rewarding according to deeds, the bout of the harvest, the bout of rest from duties, the bout of giving every rightful owner what he has the right to, the bout of giving everyone who deserves favors his entitlement. O Allah, grant our hearts and our limbs and senses steadfastness on that day and "give us good in this world and good in the hereafter and protect us from the torment of the Fire."

⊛ You have to practice sincerity. Pray for the sake of Allah not for the sake of His creatures. Fast for the sake of Allah not for the sake of His creatures. Live in this world for His sake not for the sake of His creatures or for the sake of yourselves. When performing any act of obedience, be devoted to Allah not to His creatures.

You will not be able to perform righteous deeds with sincerity unless you practice the curtailment of hopes. You will be able to curtail hopes only by remembering death. You will not be able to remember death unless you see the ruined graves and reflect on their dwellers and what they were involved in. Sit at the destroyed graves and say to yourselves: "Those used to eat, drink, have sexual intercourse, dress up, and amass worldly things. What is their state of affairs now? What benefit would all of that bring them? They do not have with them other than whatever good deeds they did."

There are among you, O people of this town, those who do not believe in the raising of the dead on the Day of Resurrection, adopting the doctrine of *dahriyya*,[13] but they hide their belief in fear of being killed. I know a group of them, but I view you by the Law of Allah (mighty and glorified is He) and conceal what I know about you for the sake of the Knowledge of Allah (mighty and glorified is He). I view you one by one but turn a blind eye to you. O Allah, draw a veil over our shortcomings, forgive us, and grant us guidance, sufficiency, and care! Amen.

---

[13] The term *dahriyya* is derived from the Arabic word *dahr* which means "long period of time." The *dahriyya* believe there is no Creator for this world and that it is the passage of time that causes people to die. Consequently, they do not believe in the Resurrection. This group of disbelievers is mentioned in the Qur'an: "And they say: 'There is nothing but our life in this world; we die and live, and nothing destroys us but time.' They merely conjecture" (45.24).

Truthfulness

✤ O servants of Allah, be truthful and then you will succeed! The truthful person never backslides. The person who is truthful in his belief in the oneness of Allah (high is He) never backslides on the advice of his lower self, passion, or devil. The truthful person never listens to blame and never allows it to enter his ears. The person who is truthful in his love of Allah, His Messenger (Allah's prayer and peace be on him), and His righteous servants never turns back as a result of listening to the words of someone who is hypocritical, hated, and disappointed. The truthful person does not know other than the truthful person and the liar does not know other than the liar. The aspiration of the truthful person is high in the sky. He cannot be harmed by anyone's words. Allah (mighty and glorified is He) has full power over His affairs. If He wants you for a certain purpose, He prepares you for it.

✤ If the truthful person meets all creatures he would not like to look at anyone other than his Beloved. This world does not seem significant to the eyes of his head, the hereafter does not seem significant to the eyes of his heart, and nothing seems significant to the eyes of his innermost being other than the Master. The shouting of the hypocrite comes from his tongue and head, whereas the shouting of the truthful person springs from his heart and innermost being. His heart is at the door of his Lord (mighty and glorified is He) and his innermost being has entered into His presence. It keeps on shouting at the door until it enters the house.

✤ O liars, the truthful person never tells lies. The truthful person never turns back! The truthful person has no back. He is a front with no back, truthfulness with no telling of lies. He is words and action, claim and evidence. He never turns back from his Beloved because of arrows that come to him from Him, but he rather receives them with his breast. Your love for something blinds and deafens you. When one knows what he is seeking, he sees whatever he has to do to be as insignificant. The lover who is truthful in his love always plunges into dangers in the quest for his Beloved. If he faces an inferno, he throws himself right into it. He swoops at what others would not even dare approaching. It is his truthfulness that urges him to do this. It is his love and impatience with being distant from his Beloved that make behave like this. Afflictions reveal the truthful person and the liar and distinguish between them. How excellent this piece of poetry by one of them is:

It is at times of dissatisfaction not at times of satisfaction that the lover becomes identifiable from the hater.[14]

---

[14] This poetry is by the Sufi shaikh 'Ali Bin Wafā Ash-Shādhilī (1359-1405).

Sorrow

⊛ Woe to you! You want to get something in return for nothing? This will never happen to you. Pay the price of something and then take it. One who enjoys himself will never find ultimate happiness, whereas one who exerts efforts will find ultimate happiness. Endure with patience the care and sorrow of this world in order to experience the delight of the hereafter. Your Prophet (Allah's prayer and peace be on him) was in permanent sorrow and continuous reflection. He (Allah's prayer and peace be on him) was given to frequent worship though he had his faults forgiven — both past ones and those that he had yet to commit. He (Allah's prayer and peace be on him) used to reflect on the creatures, in one time, and on the Creator, in another. He (Allah's prayer and peace be on him) used to reflect on what will happen to his nation after him.

When Al-Ḥasan Al-Baṣrī (may Allah show mercy to him) would leave his house, he would look as if he had been dug out of his tomb, with sorrowfulness and sadness showing on his face. Sorrowfulness remains characteristic of the believer under all circumstances until he meets his Lord (mighty and glorified is He). The people of Allah adhere to a state of muteness until they are granted permission to speak to people. They and the righteous seekers are brought together to speak to them and about them and guide them to the One whom they seek, so they develop perfect speech. If their hearts incline toward the creatures, the hand of jealousy pulls in their reins. It closes the door until they apologize and repent. Once their repentance is confirmed, it reopens the door to them and brings their hearts near.

Satisfaction

⊛ Do not be dissatisfied with what destiny brings. No one can turn it back or prevent it from taking place. Everything will come to pass regardless of who is satisfied and who is not. Your involvement in this world requires the right intention, otherwise you will be hated. In all your affairs say: "There is no might or strength but by Allah, the High, the Great (*lā ḥawla wa lā quwwata illā billāhi al-'Alīyī al-'Adhīm*)". Appoint one hour for this world, one hour for the hereafter, one hour for yourself, one hour for your family, and all of the remaining hours for your Lord.

⊛ O poor ones, O you who are tested with afflictions, remember death and what is after it and then you will find that your poverty and afflictions have lost their importance to you and that detachment from this world has become easy! Accept this advice from me for I have experienced this path and have followed it. The people of Allah do not wish for anything apart from the face of Allah (mighty and glorified is He). They have given up sleep to stand in the presence of the Creator of sleep. "Their sides shun their beds" in their quest for His face and satisfaction. Their hearts have been detached from their property. The commandment of their Lord came to them, closed their shops, and made them live in the deserts and unpopulated areas, with no fixed place to settle in. Neither their night is an ordinary night nor is their day an ordinary one: "Their sides shun their beds." Their hearts become like grains in a hot pan, trying to pop out and run away from it. Their hearts are grains on the frying pan of the reflection on the reckoning, interrogation, and trial [of the Day of Resurrection]. They are the sensible ones; the intelligent ones; the astute ones, ones who have known this world, its people, its schemes, its bewitching, its perfidy, and its slaughter of its sons. Their hearts were called upon, so their hearts shunned their beds. Their essences heard [the call] after their bodies. The birds heard [the call] as did the cages. They heard what the True One (mighty and glorified is He) revealed in one of His utterances: "The person who claims to love Me yet goes to sleep once the night has set is a liar." They felt a sense of embarrassment and shame in this company so they stood in His presence in the darkness of the night, lining up their feet in His presence, and letting their tears run down their cheeks. They spoke to Him through their tears, entered into His presence with the feet of their hearts, and stood in front of Him on the feet of fear and hope: fear of rejection and hope for the safety of acceptance.

O people, serve the manifest Law! Act according to the Book of Allah and the Sunna of His Messenger (Allah's prayer and peace be on him). Be sincere in your deeds and then look what you will see of His subtle favors, generosity, and the loveliness of His private conversation.

O deprived ones, O runaway slaves, O backsliders, come forward, O you escapers! Come back and do not run away from the arrows of tribulations for this is nothing other than a testing illusion. Stand firm and then you will be protected from their effect and evil. Stand steadfast for nothing that is destined for others will come your way. Their shield is the breasts of the truthful. You are not the kind of people who know how to treat them. They are not for you and you are not for them. You are people who watch the battle from a distance, without taking part in it. You are thoughtless followers. You frequent the gatherings of common people, and anyone who frequents gatherings of common people is one of them.

⊛ O You who have wishes, make every effort to come to have none! One of the people of Allah was once asked: "What do you long for?" He replied: "To long for nothing." Everything depends on being satisfied with the divine decree, giving up the very act of wanting, and casting down the heart in the hands of its Transformer. O Allah, include us among the Muslims who have thrown themselves prostrate in the hand of Your destiny and "give us good in this world and good in the hereafter and protect us from the torment of the Fire."

⊛ How little your belief in the oneness of God is! How little your satisfaction with Allah (high is He) is! There is no home, except those excluded by Allah, in which disputation and dissatisfaction do not exist. How frequent you associate the means and creatures with God! You have taken this and that as gods instead of Allah (mighty and glorified is He). You consider them the source of harm and benefit, and giving and withholding. Do not do that. Return to your Lord (mighty and glorified is He). Empty your hearts for Him, supplicate to Him, and ask Him to provide for your needs. Turn to Him in all of your serious problems. You do not have another place [to turn to], you do not have another door [to knock at]. All doors are locked except His. Go to unpopulated places to be alone with Him and speak and talk to Him with the tongues of your faith. When the family of each of you has gone to sleep and the creatures' voices have fallen silent, let him purify himself and place his forehead on the ground, draw near [to Allah], repent, apologize, confess his sins, beg for His favor, ask Him for his needs, and complain to Him about everything that is causing him grief. It is He your Lord (mighty and glorified is He), not someone else. It is He your God, not someone else. It is He your King, not someone else. Do not escape from Him because of the arrows of His tribulations. He has treated all your predecessors with affliction, adversity, hardship, and prosperity so that they may come to know Him, thank Him, be patient with Him, and repent to Him. Punishments are for the common people; expiations for the pious believers; and the spiritual degrees for the righteous, the certain, the seekers, the truthful.

Piety

❀ O you who have a noble pedigree! Forget about your pedigree and come here. The truly noble pedigree is that of piety. The Prophet (Allah's prayer and peace be on him) was asked: "Who are your family, O Muhammad?" He (Allah's prayer and peace be on him) replied: "Every pious person belongs to the lineage of Muhammad."

Do not come to me on the feet of your pedigree but come to me on the feet of your piety. Be sensible, you will not get what Allah has by virtue of your ancestral pedigree, but only when you deserve the pedigree of piety. The Invincible One has said: "The noblest of you in the sight of Allah is the most pious to Allah of you" (from 49.13).

Striving Against the Lower Self

☸ O young man, do not occupy yourself with washing the clothes of your body while leaving the clothes of your heart dirty! Wash the heart first and then wash the clothes. Combine both acts of washing, both acts of purification. Wash your clothes clean of dirt and wash your heart clean of sins. Do not be overconfident about anything, for your Lord is a "doer of what He wills."

It has been reported that one of the righteous people once paid a visit to his brother in Allah (mighty and glorified is He) and said to him: "O my brother, let's weep over the foreknowledge of Allah (mighty and glorified is He) about us!" How excellent the words of this righteous man are! He was a knower of Allah (mighty and glorified is He) and had heard the following words of the Prophet (Allah's prayer and peace be on him): "One of you may act as the people of Paradise act until nothing remains between him and between it other than the distance of a cubit or a span, then the divine decree comes to pass and he acts as the people of the Fire do and therefore enters it. One of you may act as the people of the Fire act until nothing remains between him and between it other than the distance of a cubit or a span, then the divine decree comes to pass so he acts as the people of Paradise do and therefore enters it."

O young man! The foreknowledge of Allah about you will be unveiled to you if you return to Him with all your heart and your aspiration; stay at the door of His mercy; build a barrier of iron between yourself and lustful desires; keep the grave and death under the eyes of your head and heart; be watchful of the gazes of the True One (mighty and glorified is He) at you, His foreknowledge about you, and His presence near you; feel content with poverty; be satisfied with bankruptcy; and be content with little while adhere to the limits of the Law, which means to abide by the commandments, observe the prohibitions, and endure with patience whatever destiny sends your way. If you keep to this you will meet your Lord and enter with your innermost being into His presence. At this point, things will be unveiled to you.

☸ The people of Allah doze off only out of necessity. Among them, there is one who deliberately puts himself to sleep for one hour in the night to be able to keep vigil for the rest of the night. He grants his lower self some of its needs so that it calms down and does not hurt him. One of the righteous people used to force himself to sleep some nights and prepare for sleep without real need for it. When he was asked about this practice he replied: "My heart sees my Lord (mighty and glorified is He)". He has uttered the truth because the true dream is an inspiration from

Allah (mighty and glorified is He). The delight of his eye was in his sleep.

As for the person who is brought near to Allah (mighty and glorified is He), there are angels dedicated to looking after him all the time. When he sleeps they sit at his head and feet to protect him from any danger that may come in front of him or behind him, while Satan stands away from him and does not dare to come near him. He sleeps under His protection, gets up under His protection, and moves and stops under the protection of Allah (high is He). O Allah, put us under Your protection in all circumstances and "give us good in this world and good in the hereafter and protect us from the torment of the Fire."

⊛ The believer draws satisfaction when his lower self is hurt and says to it: "I have advised you but you did not heed the advice. I have warned you of this, O ignorant one, O disbeliever, O enemy of Allah!" Anyone who does not call his lower self to account, put it to trial, and exhort it will not succeed. The Prophet (Allah's prayer and peace be on him) has said: "If the person does not act as a preacher to his lower self, no preacher's advice will ever benefit him." The person who seeks success must exhort his lower self, teach it renunciation, and strive against it. Renunciation means giving up what is prohibited, then giving up what is legally dubious, then giving up what is permissible, and then giving up what is absolutely lawful, under all circumstances, until nothing to be given up is left.

⊛ Give up the lustful desires for this leads to healing and the purification of the hearts. Gratifying the desire for lawful things blinds and intoxicates the heart, so what of satisfying the desire for unlawful things? This is why the Prophet (Allah's prayer and peace be on him) has said: "A proper diet is the source of healing, while filling one's stomach with food and leaving the body to eat what it is used to are the source of disease." The Prophet (Allah's prayer and peace be on him) has summarized in this saying the science of the human body. Filling the stomach with food puts out the light of intelligence, the lamp of wisdom, and the light of sainthood. As long as you are in this world and among the creatures you must remain on a diet because you are in a hospital. When your heart attains to the True One, your affairs will become His business. He will take charge of you while you are in isolation from yourself. How could not He look after you when you have become genuinely worthy of His company? The Invincible One has said: "My guardian is Allah who sent down the Book, and He guards the righteous" (7.196).

Work on purifying your heart first for this is an obligatory duty and then move on to the acquisition of knowingness, because if you miss the root your engrossment with the branch will not be accepted of you. What benefit would the purity of the limbs and senses have when combined with impurity of the heart? Purify your limbs and senses with the Sunna and your heart by applying the Qur'an. Protect your heart so that your limbs and senses will be protected. Every vessel exudes its contents. Whatever is in your heart will ooze out to your limbs and senses.

❈ Do not ask for what you will not get. Congratulations to you, if you put into practice this black-on-white while you are Muslims. Blessed are you, on the Day of Resurrection be in the company of the Muslims not in the company of the disbelievers. Blessed are we! We sit on the ground of Paradise and at its door and not be with those confined to the depths of Hell.

❈ No good will come of you, O lad, O young man, O old man, O seeker, if you do not purify your morsel of what is unlawful! Many, in fact most, of you eat food that is contaminated with manifestly unlawful things. When someone eats unlawful food, his heart darkens, and when someone eats dubious food, his heart becomes impure. Your lower selves and passions belittle to your eyes any misgivings you may have about eating unlawful food. The lower self and passion join forces in seeking lustful desires and pleasures and they practice no pious restraint whatsoever in their efforts to obtain them. If you have accustomed your lower self to eating oat bread but it asks you for honey, you must feed it barley bread until its only wish becomes that you return it to eating oat bread. If the lower self does not practice pious restraint in its diet, the likeness of it will be as the likeness of a hen that feeds from the garbage dumps, eating both pure and defiled food. So the person who wants to eat its meat or eggs must isolate it, feed it pure food, and only then eat it. Prevent yourself from eating forbidden food, and feed it pure, lawful food until all its flesh that had grown from unlawful food disappears. Then make it avoid eating forbidden and dubious food, then make it stay away from eating lawful food with passion.

O my sons! When any of you is asked: "Do you wish to die while you are doing this kind of deeds?" he answers: "No." Yet when he is told: "Then repent and improve your deeds," he replies: "If Allah (mighty and glorified is He) enables me I will do!" He argues citing destiny when his repentance is concerned but he does not use destiny as an argument when his lustful desires and pleasures are concerned, while standing on the foot of procrastination, hesitating between "yes" and "no." If death will come to him while he is enjoying his comfortable life and bliss, it will snatch him away from his powerful position and state of honor; it will snatch him away from his shop and earnings. Death will take him by surprise while his will is still unwritten, his accounts are still unregistered, and he has endless hopes.

It is right thinking that makes the righteous move away from inhabited regions and come nearer to unpopulated places, removes their happiness, and perpetuates their sorrow. When a person comes to know Allah (mighty and glorified is He), his sorrow and fear increase. He comes to have a speaker that speaks to him and an engrossment that keeps him busy. He wishes not to hear the speech of any creature and not to meet anyone. He wishes to be freed from his family and his property. He wishes that his allotted worldly shares be transferred to others. He wishes to change his natural inclination and attributes to angelic attributes. Whenever he wants to get rid of all those limitations, the Law prevents him and the Controller restrains him by the foreordination and Knowledge and guards his night and day. He then forsakes this world to be alone with His Lord (mighty and glorified is He), then his knowingness takes him over so He protects him outwardly and inwardly. Al-Fatḥ Al-Muṣillī (may Allah show mercy to him) used to say in his private conversation: "O Allah, how much longer will You reject me and imprison me in this world? When will You transfer me to You so that I get relieved from this world and the creatures?"

The likeness of your case is as that when Noah (prayer and peace be on our Prophet and on all prophets) said to his son: "'O my son, embark with us and do not be with the disbelievers!' He replied: 'I shall take refuge in a mountain that will protect me from the water'" (from 11.42-43). The preacher is saying to you: "Come, board with me the ship of salvation," yet you reply: "I shall take refuge in a mountain that will protect me from the water." Your mountain is your far-reaching hopes and your greedy keenness on this world. The Angel of Death will soon come and drown you on your mountain.

Come, O servants of Allah! Leave your homes of ignorance for you have erected the walls of your religion without foundations. You have set your broken religion without a base. This is something that requires demolishing and resetting.

⊛ The people of Allah worship the True One (mighty and glorified is He) day and night, standing on the foot of fear and hope. They are afraid of facing an evil end. They are ignorant of the foreknowledge of Allah about them and their end, so they keep day and night to sorrow, sadness, and weeping, while keeping up the prayer, fasting, making the pilgrimage, and performing all works of obedience. They remember their Lord (mighty and glorified is He) with their hearts and their tongues. Therefore, when they reach the hereafter, they will enter Paradise and Allah (mighty and glorified is He) will direct His bountifulness to them, so they will thank Him and say: "Praise be to Allah who has put sorrow away from us" (from 35.34).

⊛ O young man, take your place in the front row for it is the row of men and the brave! Leave the last row for it is the row of cowards. Put this lower self to work and make it used to observing the strictest laws because the heavier load you put on it the more it can carry. Do not take the stick away from it, otherwise it will fall asleep and throw down the loads. Do not show it the white of your teeth and the white of your eyes because it is a bad servant that will not do its duties unless it gets the stick. Do not satisfy its appetite unless you are sure that this will not make it transgress the limits and that it works in return for having its appetite satisfied. One of the righteous people (may Allah show mercy to him) used to keep on eating until his appetite is fully satisfied, and then he would recite the following piece of poetry before starting a long spell of worship:

> Satisfy the appetite of the slave and make him work hard
> because the slave is like a donkey.

Someone has said: "I saw Sufyān Ath-Thawrī eat so much that I disliked him, then I saw him pray and weep so much that I felt compassion for him." Do not emulate Sufyān in eating so much but emulate him in the plentifulness of his worship, for you are not like Sufyān. Do not satisfy the appetite of your lower self as he used to do to his for you are not in control of yours as he was of his.

Once this heart has become sound, it will become a tree with branches, leaves, and fruits. It will have benefits for the creatures: the human beings, jinn, and angels. If the heart is unsound then it will be like the hearts of animals: an appearance with no essence, a vessel with no water, a tree with no fruit, a stone with no ring, a cage with no bird, a house with no inhabitant, a treasure of gold and silver coins with no one to spend them, and a body with no soul. It will be like the Jewish priests who were transformed into apes and swine, making them an appearance with no essence.

⊛ The lower self is ignorant, so educate it. It lacks polite behavior, so teach it that. It is unable to distinguish between the disease and the medicine, the lawful and the unlawful, and what mends and what ruins. It keeps on disputing with its Lord. Do no feed it even a morsel of lustful desires and pleasures and do not give it more than what it deserves, which is bread alone — that is, with no seasoning. Then when it has got used to that move it to eating green vegetables until returning it to the bread becomes all that it wishes for. Then when it has got used to that, calmed down, and its evil has gone, its allotted worldly shares will come; the seal will come from your Lord: "And do not kill yourselves. Allah is Merciful to you" (from 4.29). Allah has said: "O tranquil soul! Return to your Lord well-pleased and well-pleasing" (89.27-28). Its allotted worldly shares will become clear to it and the foreknowledge will order it to take them. So it will take them while keeping to steadfastness and true renunciation toward them. At this stage, it will not be harmed by taking its allotted worldly shares. Instead, taking them will turn into expansion in the breast and light and purity in the heart.

The case will be like that of a patient whose physician prevents him from eating certain kinds of food and feeds him instead medicines that suit him, be they food or drinks, until he attains good health. After that he orders him to eat food, moving him from one kind of food to another so that eating food becomes a medicine for him and strengthens his body. This is the situation with the ascetic. When he takes his allotted worldly shares after his attainment, they become a source of welfare for his religion and a light in his heart and his innermost being. O Allah, include us among those who renounced everything other than You! Make us seek You under all circumstances and "give us good in this world and good in the hereafter and protect us from the torment of the Fire."

⊛ O people, acquire faith and strike your lower selves with the stick of strife. Hand it over to the trainer of faith. It is an unreliable horse. Your lower selves are untamed, untrained, and full of arrogance and pride. On the way of Allah (mighty and glorified is He) there is no room for saying "I," "with me," and "mine." This way is all about extinction and obliteration. In the beginning, when faith is still weak, [the person says]: "There is no God save Allah (lā ilāha illā Allah)" (from 47.19), but at the end, when faith has become strong, [the person says]: "There is no God save You (lā ilāha illā Anta)" (from 21.87), as he addresses One (mighty and glorified is He) who is present and seen. This is a hidden matter, total secret, one of His favors. Therefore, the Prophet (Allah's prayer and peace be on him) has said: "There are days in your lifetime in which Allah (mighty and glorified is He) confers favors, so avail yourself of them."

⊛ The believer must strive against his lower self in order to improve his behavior and force it to adhere to good manners. He must also strive to force it to do all required works of obedience, for it has taken arrogance, anger, and abasing people as habitual practices. Strive against it until it calms down. Once it has calmed down, it will become modest and humble, it will become well-mannered, it will know its status, and it will be patient with others. Before being subjected to striving, the lower self is as arrogant as a Pharaoh.

Blessed is anyone who came to know his lower self, treated it as an enemy, and opposed it in all that it ordered him to do! Make remembering death and what follows it incumbent on it as this humbles it and refines its character. Prevent it from getting what it wants and give it the duties that it must do, so that it will become humble and well-mannered and come to know its status. By way of contemplation, enter it into the Fire and Paradise to see their contents, as this will humiliate it and amend its behavior. Think of the Day of Resurrection and experience it before it takes place. The Day of Resurrection is a happy day for some people and a sad one for others, celebration for some people and funeral for others. It is the day of the righteous; the day on which they dress up, wear jewels, ride on thoroughbreds, and on which their knowledgeable scholars and eminent ones appear. Their deeds become images whose light appear on their faces.

⊛ Make it binding on your lower selves to behave with humility to Allah (mighty and glorified is He) and the believers among his creatures. Order them to fulfill the duties that Allah (mighty and glorified is He) has imposed on them. Interrogate them and call them to account as the righteous people do. When the night has set, 'Umar bin Al-Khaṭṭāb (may Allah be satisfied with him) used to say to his lower self: "What have you done for your Lord? What service have you shown to Him?" He would then pick a stick and hit his thighs and interrogate his lower self for everything it did. He would require of his lower self Allah's (mighty and glorified is He) rights and ask it for more service to Him, although he was one of the great truthful, the righteous, those who are drawn near [to God], those who transmitted the sayings of the Prophet, and those who have been granted paradise. The righteous call their lower selves to account despite their righteousness and obedience, yet you do not call yours to account! No doubt, you will not benefit from them. O Allah, give us power over our lower selves, passions, and devils! O Allah, include us among Your party and with Your party! Bring our hearts near to You before death and grant us the special meeting [with You] before the general meeting [at the Resurrection], Amen.

Luqmān the Wise (may Allah show mercy to him) used to say to his son: "O Son, how can a person feel safe from the Fire when he has to pass through it? How can he feel safe in this world when he has to leave it? How can he feel secure from death when he has to die? How can he forget death when death will not forget him?" All of you will have to pass through the Fire and no one will come out unscathed save those who are pious to Allah (mighty and glorified is He). Passing through the Fire successfully is a journey that requires piety as provision. It does not seem to me that you have acquired any piety.

⊛ O young man, leave the lower self to this world, the heart to the hereafter, and the innermost being to the Master, and never feel secure in this world. It is an adorned snake that uses its finery to attract people then destroys them. Turn totally away from it. You must be sincere in worshipping your Lord (mighty and glorified is He), accompanying and serving your righteous brothers, and avoiding lustful desires. Believe truly in the oneness of the True One (mighty and glorified is He) until not even a single atom of any creature is left in your heart, until you do not see a house or an inhabitant. Do not have any wish other than the wish to have genuine belief in the oneness of God because it kills off everything else in the heart. The belief in the oneness of God and turning away from the love of this world are the ultimate remedy. There will be no good in you until you come to know your lower self, prevent it from getting what it wants, and allow it only what it deserves. At this point it will feel secure with the heart, the heart will feel secure with the innermost being, and the innermost being will feel secure with the True One (mighty and glorified is He).

Do not take the stick of striving away from your lower selves, do not be deceived by their tricks, do not be fooled by their pretended neglect of you, and do not be taken in by the apparent sleep of the beast, for it gives you the impression that it is asleep when it is in fact waiting to pounce on the prey. Beware of it when it is asleep as you are on your guard when it is awake. Beware of your lower selves. Do not take the arm away from the neck of your lower selves. The lower self puts on an appearance of calmness, humility, modesty, and compliance with what is good, yet it conceals inside the exact opposite. Watch out for what it does after that.

Increase your sorrow and decrease your happiness for this business is based on sorrow and sadness. This is how the preceding prophets, messengers, and righteous persons (Allah's prayer and peace be on them) were. The Prophet (Allah's prayer and peace be on him) was in continuous sorrow and in permanent reflection. He would never laugh but merely smile and he would only ever pretend to be joyful. The sensible person among you will never feel happy with this world, the children, family, property, food, clothing, vehicles, or women. All of this is an illusion. The believer feels happy with the strength of his faith, his certitude, and the attainment of his heart to the door of nearness to his Lord (mighty and glorified is He).

✸ When the heart of the servant treads the right path, he bids farewell to everything and leaves them behind the back of his heart. He sees the kingdom of this world as totally negligible and that the kingdom of the hereafter is all that matters. He advances to the fire and lions, mixes with the beasts, escapes from the creatures, surrenders his lower self to the thirst and hunger of wildernesses, destroys it, and says: "O Guide of the bewildered ones, guide me to You!"

O young man, make sure that you have only one concern. This comes about only after renouncing the unlawful, then renouncing the permissible, and then renouncing the absolutely lawful. Try your best that you live your night and day without having even a single atom of the creatures in your heart. I can see that you are full of lustful desires, pleasures, interest in the creatures, concerns with this world, and reliance on the means.

✸ This business [of attaining to God] can come true in one of two ways. First, through striving, suffering, and enduring the heaviest and most arduous burdens. This is the way of the majority of the righteous people. Second, through a gift that requires no effort. This rare way is open only to a few creatures.

⊛ Where do you stand with respect to those whose plentiful worship has been described by Allah (mighty and glorified is He) in His noble Book: "They slept only a small part of the night. And at dawn they prayed for forgiveness" (51.17-18)? When He recognized their truthfulness in worship He assigned to them someone to wake them up and make them get off their beds. The Prophet (Allah's prayer and peace be on him) has said: "Allah (mighty and glorified is He) says to Gabriel: 'O Gabriel, wake up so-and-so and put to sleep so-and-so'"! When the footsteps of the hearts of the people of Allah have led them to Allah (mighty and glorified is He), they start to see in sleep what they do not see when they are awake. Their hearts and innermost beings see things that they do not see in wakefulness. They fast, perform prayer, strive against their lower selves, practice detachment from worldly matters, and spend the day and night performing all sorts of worship acts until they are given Paradise. But once they have been given Paradise, they get told that this is not the real way, but it is seeking the True One (mighty and glorified is He). Thus, their deeds start to originate from their hearts, and upon reaching Him they grow and become firm in His presence.

When the person comes to know what he is seeking, he will see whatever energy and effort he has to spend in obeying Allah (mighty and glorified is He) as being negligible. The believer remains in tiredness until he meets his Lord (mighty and glorified is He). This is why the Prophet (Allah's prayer and peace be on him) has said: "When a [faithful] man dies, enters his grave, and successfully answers the questions of the angels Munkar and Nakīr, his soul is given the permission to ascend to Him (mighty and glorified is He) and to prostrate to Him with a group of angels. So He receives it, and what had been kept hidden from it is revealed to it. It will then be carried to Paradise where the souls of the righteous are. They will receive it and ask it about its state of affairs and about the affairs of this world. It will answer them with what it knows. They will then ask it: 'What about so-and-so?' It will say: 'He died before me.' They will reply: 'He did not arrive to us. There is no might or strength but by Allah, the High, the Great! He must have been thrown in the bottomless pit.' Then the soul will be put inside the craw of a green bird that feeds on the plants of Paradise and resorts to a lamp that is suspended beneath the Throne." This is the description of the encounter of the majority of believers (Allah's peace and greetings be on them). O Allah, include us among them and make us live as they live and die as they die! Amen.

⊛ Woe to you! Your lower self is sick, so protect it from the food that is unsuitable for it until it is restored to the good health of nearness by its Lord (mighty and glorified is He). Woe to you! How could you wish for the nearness to Allah (mighty and glorified is He) when prohibited things have infiltrated your body through your food, drink, sex, and all your behavior? How could you wish for the nearness to Allah when your lower self is in charge of you, your passion is guiding and steering you toward lustful desires and pleasures, and the fire of your natural inclination is burning out your piety and religion? Be sensible, this cannot be the behavior of someone who believes in death and is certain of it. This is not the behavior of someone who looks forward to the encounter with the True One (mighty and glorified is He) and fears His calling him to account and His interrogation. You have no reason, no prudence, no piety, no proper thinking, and no repose. You indulge night and day in amassing things from this world, thinking of it, accompanying its people, and paying homage to them. The people of Allah detach themselves from this world, the hereafter, and from emulating the creatures. Each one of them is like a man who has dispatched his trade camels caravan to Khurāsān[15] and sat here with horses waiting for the caravan to move and for the leader to come out. His body is present, while all of his heart is occupied with his house. The believer has sent all his property to the hereafter. He has built there a palace with which he is charmed and he has furnished it with all that he needs. All of his heart is occupied with the nearness to the True One (mighty and glorified is He). Therefore the Prophet (Allah's prayer and peace be on him) has said: "This world is the prison of the believer."

---

[15] Located today in the east of Iran, the north of Afghanistan, and some parts of the former Soviet Union.

The Blessings of Remembrance [of Allah]

✪ O you who are dead at heart! Keep to remembering your Lord (mighty and glorified is He), reciting His Book and the traditions of His Messenger (Allah's prayer and peace be on him), and attending sessions of remembrance. This will quicken your hearts like the earth is revived by the falling rain. Keeping to remembrance is a means for the continuation of good in this world and in the hereafter. When the heart becomes sound, remembrance becomes permanent in it and gets inscribed on its sides and all over it. His eyes will sleep while his heart will continue to remember his Lord (mighty and glorified is He). He inherits this state from his Prophet, Muhammad (Allah's prayer and peace be on him). One of the righteous (may Allah show mercy to him) had a rosary for performing remembrance. One day, as he was remembering Allah, he felt asleep while the rosary still in his hand. He then woke up to find the rosary still moving in his hand, without him trying to move it, and his tongue remembering Allah.

✪ O young man, how can your heart acquire knowledge and your innermost being attain purity when you are still associating creatures with Allah? How can you succeed when every night you choose someone to call on to complain to and beg from? How can your heart become pure when it is empty of the belief in the oneness of God, without a single atom of it? The belief in the oneness of God is light, whereas associating partners with Allah is darkness. How can you succeed when your heart is empty of piety, without a single atom of it? You are screened off from the Creator by the creatures. You are screened off by the means from the Creator of all means, screened off by trust in the creatures and having confidence in them. You are a false, trivial claimant. The claims you make will not be accepted without evidence.

✪ Where do you stand in relation to the belief in the oneness of God, O idolatrous worshipper? Where do you stand in relation to purity, O impure one? Where do you stand in relation to satisfaction, O dissatisfied one? Where do you stand in relation to patience, O you who complain to the creatures? Your current behavior is not the religion of the righteous predecessors. I get angry when I hear someone say "Allah, Allah" while he sees someone other than Him. O you who perform remembrance, remember Allah (mighty and glorified is He) while you are in His presence! Do not remember Him with your tongue while your heart is with someone else. Escape from the creatures to His door. Evict from your heart this world, the hereafter, and anything other than Him, then remember Him with the tongue of your heart, innermost being, and essence, and then with the tongue of your outward.

Woe to you! How often you say "Allah is Greater (*Allahu akbar*)" while you do not really mean it and you are only telling lies! Bread is greater in your sight, the seasoning of the bread is greater in your sight, meat is greater in your sight, the wealth that you have amassed in your life is greater in your sight, the watchman on your street and the ruler of your town are greater in your sight, and the ruler of your city is greater in your sight. You fear all of those, pin your hopes on them, flatter them, and conceal your real state from them. Your clothes cover you up. Yet you challenge your Lord with all kinds of detestable deeds! You rely on those people in your serious problems and consider them the source of harm and benefit, and giving and withholding. If I investigate you, you will turn out to be bankrupt of religion and will be no more Muslims or believers.

Remoteness from Allah keeps things concealed from the person, whereas nearness to Allah discloses them to him. Things are revealed to the person who has been drawn near, but he conceals them and does not disclose anything unless there is an irresistible necessity. So glory be to the One who conceals the faults of His servants. Glory be to the One who reveals to the elite of His creatures the real states of His servants and then orders them not to expose them.

⊛ O you who are proud of your affluence and purity, soon your purity will turn into impurity, your affluence into poverty, and your ease into hardship! Do not be conceited about whatever state you are in. You must keep on attending sessions of remembrance, thinking well of the practicing shaikhs, listening to them, and accepting their words.

⊛ O young man, in my eyes, you are Satan's mate and his representative! You have entrusted yourself to him and you have befriended him while he is devouring the flesh of your religion and your piety and wasting your capital, but you have no clue. Woe to you! Ward him off and force him to escape from your vicinity by continuously performing remembrance, for remembrance destroys him, defeats him, and disperses his soldiers. Remember the True One (mighty and glorified is He) with your tongue at one time and with your heart at another. Change your food and drink. Practice pious restraint under all circumstances. Seek help in defeating Satan by saying: "There is no might or strength but by Allah, the High, the Great (*lā ḥawla wa lā quwwata illā billāhi al-'Alīyī al-'Adhīm*). What Allah wills will happen (*mā shā'a Allah kāna*). There is no god save Allah, the King, the Manifest True One (*lā ilāha illā Allah al-Maliku al-Ḥaqqu al-Mubīn*). Glory be to Allah and praise be to Him (*subḥāna Allah wa biḥamdih*). Glory be to Allah, the Great, and praise be to Him (*subḥāna Allah al-'Adhīm wa biḥamdih*)". This way he will be overthrown, his power will be broken, and his soldiers will be defeated. Satan's throne is on the sea and he sends his soldiers to the land. The most respected of his soldiers in his sight is the most capable of seducing the son of Adam.

❀ The Prophet Muhammad (Allah's prayer and peace be on him) is reported to have said: "These hearts get rusty, and the polish they need is the recitation of the Qur'an and attending sessions of remembrance." Joining the sessions of practicing knowledgeable scholars polishes, cleanses, and promotes the hearts and removes their hardness. A man complained to Al-Ḥasan Al-Baṣrī (may Allah be satisfied with him) about the hardness of his own heart, so he said to him: "Keep on remembering Allah."

Those who remember Allah, those who are knowledgeable of Him, those who are His saints, are the kings of the truth. They have known the King, so they proceeded toward Him, therefore he made them kings. They have seen the hereafter, so this world lost its significance in their hearts; and they have seen the True One (mighty and glorified is He), so the creatures became of little importance to them. Honor is obtained by obeying Allah (high is He) and giving up all acts of disobedience.

❀ O disobedient ones, do not despair of the mercy of Allah (mighty and glorified is He)! Never lose hope of Allah's (mighty and glorified is He) clemency. O you who are dead at heart, keep on remembering your Lord (mighty and glorified is He), reciting His Book and the traditions of His Messenger (Allah's prayer and peace be on him), and attending sessions of remembrance. This will quicken your hearts like the earth is revived by the falling rain. When the heart makes remembering Allah (mighty and glorified is He) common practice, it will earn knowingness, Knowledge, belief in the oneness of God, and trust in Him, and it will turn away from anything other than Him. Continued remembrance of Allah is a means for the continuation of good in this world and the hereafter.

As long as you are given to this world and to the creatures, you will continue to be sensitive to both praise and dispraise, because you are living through your lower self, passion, and natural inclination. When your heart attains to your Lord (mighty and glorified is He) and He takes charge of you, your sensitivity to praise and dispraise will go away, thus you will be relieved of a heavy burden. If you work for this world while relying on your might and strength, you will lose, be torn apart, tire, and be dissatisfied. Similarly, if you work for the hereafter with your strength you will be cut off. If you work for the True One (mighty and glorified is He), open the door to livelihood by the hand of His strength and trust in Him and open the door of the works of obedience by the hand of His guidance. Once you have attained to the spiritual station of seeking Him, ask Him for strength as well as truthfulness in asking for strength and help from Him. Place the feet of your heart and your innermost being firmly in His presence and give up all preoccupations with this world and the hereafter.

The Works of the Heart

⊛ When the heart acts in accordance with the Book and the Sunna, it draws near. Once it has become close, it will come to know and see its credits and faults, what belongs to Allah (mighty and glorified is He) and what belongs to others, and what belongs to the truth and what belongs to falsehood.

⊛ When this heart becomes pure and sound, it will hear the call of the True One from its six directions. It will hear the call of every prophet, messenger, saint, and truthful person (Allah's prayer and peace be on all of them). At this stage, it will draw near to Him so that its life will mean nearness to Him and its death will mean remoteness from Him. Its satisfaction will be in having private conversation with Him. It will become totally content with that to the exclusion of anything else. It will not care if this world turned its back to it and will not care about hunger, thirst, nakedness, and all diseases.

⊛ Woe to you! All what you are about and all what you are involved in are illusion within illusion which Allah will pay no attention to. This business is not achieved by deeds of the body but by works of the heart. Our Prophet Muhammad (Allah's prayer and peace be on him) has said: "Renunciation is here, piety is here, sincerity is here," and he pointed to his breast.

⊛ This heart will not be sound and will not attain success until it gives up every beloved, cuts off every object of attachment, and renounces every creature. Give up and you will be rewarded with much better than what you abandoned. The Prophet (Allah's prayer and peace be on him) has said: "When a person gives up something [for the sake of Allah], Allah compensates him with something better." O Allah, wake our hearts up so that they attend to you, awaken us from our forgetfulness of You, and "give us good in this world and good in the hereafter and protect us from the torment of the Fire."

⊛ When this heart has become sound and planted its feet firm at the door of the True One, it will fall in the wilderness of "'be,' and it is," in its valleys, and in its sea. It will exist there sometimes with its words, sometimes with its aspiration, and sometimes with its sight. It will start to behave as commanded by Allah (mighty and glorified is He) and it isolates itself from any detachments; it will become in a state of extinction, and only He will remain. Only a minority of you believe in this; the majority do not. Believing in this is sainthood and putting it into practice is attainment. No one denies the spiritual states of the righteous people other than a hypocritical impostor who is riding on his passion.

This business is based on having sound belief and applying the outward of the Law which will cause the person to inherit knowingness of Allah (mighty and glorified is He) and Knowledge of Him. The Law will come to be between him and the creatures, whereas Knowledge will be between him and his Lord (mighty and glorified is He). His outward deeds will be as little as an atom in comparison with the mountain of his inward deeds. His limbs and senses will rest but his heart will never do. The eyes in his head may doze off but the eyes of his heart will never sleep. His heart will work unceasingly and remember Allah while he is asleep. When will you know this world so that you give it up and divorce it?

⊛ Wayfaring is the wayfaring of the hearts and attainment is the attainment of the innermost beings. When the innermost beings achieve attainment they become kings and the limbs and senses become followers and an entourage. When the heart arrives at the door it asks for permission for the innermost being to enter. The innermost being enters and then the heart follows.

⊛ O young man, consult the Book and the Sunna in all of your affairs. When you find a certain matter of your religion confusing say: "What do you say about it, O Book of Allah? What do you say about it, O Sunna? What do you say about this problem, O Messenger of Allah (Allah's prayer and peace be on him)? What do you say about it, O my shaikh who has shown me the way to the Messenger (Allah's prayer and peace be on him)? What do you say about it, O Messenger of Allah (Allah's prayer and peace be on him) who has shown me the way to the Sender?" If you do this, your problem will be solved and the darkness you are in will disappear. When anything poses a problem for you, ask about it outwardly the people of the Law and inwardly your heart. The Prophet (Allah's prayer and peace be on him) once said to a righteous man: "Consult your heart even if the legal experts have offered you advice." See what your inward says even though you have sought the opinions of legal experts. See what is in your heart and what it suggests even if the legal experts have offered you their opinions. Seek the advice of the ushers, doorkeepers, and ministers then enter into the presence of the king and see what he has to say. If the heart agreed, this is a welcome agreement, but if it disagreed, follow its ruling and ignore the ruling of anyone else.

⊛ Among the signs of wretchedness of the servant is the hardness of his heart, dryness of his eyes, wideness of his hopes, his niggardliness about his property, giving little importance to the commandments and prohibitions, and his dissatisfaction when tribulations strike. When you see someone of this description, be aware that he is wretched. The person with a hard heart does not show mercy to anyone and his eyes never turn moist with tears at times of happiness or times of sadness, for the dryness of his eyes is due to the hardness of his heart. How could his heart not be hard when it is full of wishes, acts of disobedience, sins, wide hopes, desires to obtain things that are not destined for him, envy for their owners, and stinginess with the obligatory alms? Additionally, he does not pay the dues of expiations, does not fulfill his vows, does not pay attention to the needs of his relatives, does not settle his debts despite his ability to do so, and even tries to delay them in the hope of avoiding payment altogether, and hates to give anything by way of charity or in fulfilling the obligatory duties. All these and the likes are signs of wretchedness. The Invincible One has said: "Has the time not yet come for the hearts of those who believe to submit with humility to the remembrance of Allah and to the truth that has come down?" (from 57.16).

⊛ The heart inside which belief in the oneness of God and nearness has developed grows bigger everyday. As it grows bigger, greater, and higher it will not see any more on the face of the earth and in heaven other than Allah. All creatures will submit to its command and there will be a secret between it and its Lord (mighty and glorified is He). Once it has reached this stage, it will gain access [to Him], attain to Him, and become the absolute ruler of its time. It will become capable while complying with the divine decree, destiny, the Law, and Knowledge. The low ranking angels will serve it. O people, believe the words of Allah (mighty and glorified is He), His Messenger (Allah's prayer and peace be on him), and the righteous among His servants! He is truthful because He has said: "And who is truer in speech than Allah?" (from 4.122). The truthfulness of the Messenger and the righteous is derived from His truthfulness.

⊛ When you stand at the door of the True One (mighty and glorified is He), you will witness something wonderful, or rather many wonders. Forget your food, drink, clothes, existence, and the praise and the dispraise of people. All these are works of the hearts. This heart will then turn into an orchard that contains trees and fruits. It will have deserts and unpopulated spaces, seas, rivers, and mountains. It will become the gathering place of human beings, jinn, angels, and spirits. This is beyond the comprehension of the creatures. O Allah, if what I am talking about is true, confirm it for the seekers, but if it is false, obliterate it! If I am following the truth, erect my edifice, raise it high, and speed up the guidance of the creatures through me. O Allah, raise our hearts to you! How long will this tiredness last? When will the cares of the heart end? When will we enjoy the banquet on the roof of the palace of nearness, looking from its balconies at Your creation? "And Allah strikes parables for people" (from 14.25).

When the heart becomes sound, it forgets everything other than the True One (mighty and glorified is He), the One whose existence has no beginning, the Perpetual One, the Eternal One. Everything else has been created at a certain moment of time. Once this heart has become sound, the words that originate from it will be a truth that no one can refute. The heart will speak to the innermost being, the innermost being to the private life, the private life to the essence, the essence to the kernel, the kernel to the consciousness. At this stage, its speech to the hearts will be like seeds that are sown in a land that is good, soft, and not saline, so they will grow into green plants.

The Knowledge of Saints

❀ The saints of Allah (mighty and glorified is He) have someone who awakens them, a teacher who teaches them. The True One provides for them the means of learning. The Prophet (Allah's prayer and peace be on him) has said: "Even if a believer was on the top of a mountain, Allah (high is He) will appoint for him a knowledgeable scholar to teach him."

Do not borrow the good words of Allah, pretend that they are yours, and utter them. Borrowed things cannot be concealed. Clothe yourself from what you have, not from what you have borrowed. Plant the cotton with your hand, water it with your hand, and cultivate it with your effort, then weave the cotton, sew it, and wear it. Do not be happy with someone else's property and someone else's clothes. If you borrow someone else's words and utter them pretending that they are your own, the hearts of the righteous people will detest you.

❀ Listen, O objectors, O disputers, O you who are ill-mannered! Listen to me, for I am one of the callers of the nation of prophets and one of their followers and brokers. I adjudicate by the Book and the Sunna and then by the heart. Anyone whose heart has been brought near to Allah (mighty and glorified is He) will not fail to recognize what I say. Only a few individuals among the servants of Allah (high is He) renounce the company of the creatures and derive intimacy from reading the Qur'an and the words of the Messenger (Allah's prayer and peace be on him). No doubt, they will come to have hearts that feel intimacy with the True One (mighty and glorified is He), are close to Him, and with which they see themselves and others. The eyes of their hearts open so nothing of what you are involved in can be concealed from them. They speak about what you think of and tell you what you keep in your homes. Woe to you! Be sensible, do not compete with the people of Allah with your ignorance.

❀ The believer has three eyes: the eye of the head with which he looks at this world, the eye of the heart with which he looks at the hereafter, and the eye of the innermost being with which he sees the True One (mighty and glorified is He). The eyes of the head expires in this world, the eyes of the heart expires in the hereafter, and the eyes of the innermost being remains with the True One (mighty and glorified is He) in this world and in the hereafter because it is focused on Him in this world and in the hereafter. If the believer who has this quality happens to be in a populated area, he will be a mercy to its people. Were it not for him, that area would have been made to sink into the ground and the buildings would have collapsed on its inhabitants. Accept this and believe it. Do not choose to be with the ignorant people who killed the prophets and messengers (Allah's prayer and peace be on all of them). Do not be with those who became enemies of their Lord (mighty and glorified is He), those who have been placed at a distance, screened off, and expelled. O Allah, forgive us and forgive them! Amen.

⊛ When you know the creatures through Allah's Knowledge and know them through His knowingness, their attributes will disappear from you. Any nature of the human beings, jinn, and angels will vanish from you. Your heart will acquire new attributes and so will your innermost being. The shell of your existence will be removed from you. This is the shell of the habitual practice of the children of Adam (prayer and peace be on our Prophet and on him). The Law will come and be a garment on your body, so you will become clothed with your own affairs and with the attributes of your Lord (mighty and glorified is He) and His commandment. Then the Divine, Lordly Knowledge will come and be a garment on your heart and innermost being.

⊛ The reality of Islam is submissiveness. The people of Allah have thrown themselves prostrate before their Lord (mighty and glorified is He) and have forgotten asking "why" and "how" and saying "do" and "do not." They perform all kinds of works of obedience while standing on the foot of fear. This is why the True One (mighty and glorified is He) has described them as follows: "They do what they do while their hearts are full of fear because they will return to their Lord" (23.60). [He means]: "They carry out My commandments and observe My prohibitions. They endure with patience My affliction and offer thanks for My rewards to them. They surrender themselves, their property, their children, and their worldly affairs to the hand of My foreordination, while their hearts are afraid, fearful of Me."

⊛ O servants of Allah, be sensible and work hard to know the One whom you worship before death comes to you! Ask Him by day and night to supply all your needs. Asking Him for something is an act of worship. Whether He gives you what you ask for or not, do not accuse Him, rush Him, or get bored of asking Him. Ask Him while standing on the feet of humility. If His answer was delayed, do not object to Him for He knows your best interests better than you. Listen to these words, understand them, and act in accordance with them. These are words of a straight way. They are the words of someone who is experienced, an expert. Alas for you that you should die before you know your Lord (mighty and glorified is He). Woe to you! How could you come to One whom you have not known or dealt with, whose hospitality you have not enjoyed, and whose remembrance of entertainment you have not eaten from? Do business with Him and you will see that your business has become profitable.

Make sure that you will have favor for you with Him before arriving in His presence. Be generous to the poor and the needy and console them with some of your wealth. Thus you will have made sure that you will have favor for you with Him. If you do that, He will confer on you rewards and treat you with kindness in this world and the hereafter.

⊛ When the knower renounces the hereafter he says to it: "Get out of my way for I am seeking the door of the True One (mighty and glorified is He). You and this world are one and the same in my eyes. This world used to screen me off from you and you screen me off from my Lord (mighty and glorified is He). You are unworthy of respect as you try to screen me off from Him." Listen to these words because they are the essence of the Knowledge of Allah (mighty and glorified is He) and the kernel of what He wishes from His creatures and wants to happen in His creation. This is the spiritual state of the prophets, messengers, saints, and righteous (Allah's prayer and peace be on all of them).

⊛ When Pharaoh disputed destiny and wanted to change Allah's foreknowledge, He destroyed him, drowned him in the sea, and made Moses and Aaron inherit him. When the mother of Moses (prayer and peace be on our Prophet and on them) feared the butchers whom Pharaoh appointed to slaughter every newborn child, Allah inspired her to cast him into the sea. She became afraid for his safety, so she was told: "Do not fear or grieve. We shall return him to you and make him one of Our messengers" (from 28.7). [He meant]: "Do not be afraid. Let your heart be assured and your innermost being be at rest. Do not be afraid that he may drown and die. We shall return him to you and turn through him your poverty into affluence." So she prepared an ark, put him inside it, and threw it into the sea. It floated on the surface of the water until it reached Pharaoh's house. When it went past it, Pharaoh's maidservants and Āsyā received it. They opened the ark and found a child inside it. They all loved him, and compassion for him grew in their hearts. They anointed him and changed his underwear and clothing with new ones. He became among the closest creatures to Āsyā and her maidservants. Everyone of Pharaoh's people who saw him loved him, which is the meaning of His (high is He) words: "And I cast love from Me over you" (from 20.39). It has been said that anyone who looked him in the eye loved him. Then He returned him to his mother and brought him up in Pharaoh's house against Pharaoh's will and Pharaoh could not kill him.

How could one whom the Lord created and reared for Himself be killed and slaughtered? How could the water drown him when he is protected and spoken to [by Him]? How could anyone hate one whom the True One (mighty and glorified is He) loves? How could anyone fail one whom He supports? How could anyone impoverish one whom He enriches? How could anyone demote one whom He promotes? How could anyone depose one whom He appoints as a ruler? How could anyone keep remote one whom He brings near? O Allah, open for us the door of Your nearness! Include us among the people who obey You. Include us among your few individuals and soldiers. Give us a seat at the mat where Your favor is served, give us a drink of Your intimacy, and "give us good in this world and good in the hereafter and protect us from the torment of the Fire."

⊛ O young man, be sound in order to be eloquent! Be sound in your private life and then you will be eloquent in your public life. If you are sound in this world you will be eloquent in the hereafter when you will speak in the presence of Allah (mighty and glorified is He). You will be allowed to intercede and you will be asked to intercede on behalf of others. He will cause you to intercede on behalf of whomever He chooses of His creatures. After His permission and issuing the command, He will accept that from you to honor you and reveal your status in His eyes. Be sound in your relation with Him and then you will be eloquent in teaching His creatures. You will become a teacher and an educator who teaches them polite behavior. Woe to you! Having sat in this place to preach to people, how could you laugh with them and tell funny stories? No doubt, neither you nor they will succeed. The preacher is a teacher and an educator who teaches polite behavior, whereas the listeners are like children. The child learns only when treated with roughness and faced with seriousness and frowning. Only a few of them learn without the need for that but through a gift from Allah (mighty and glorified is He).

O people, this world is ephemeral! This world is mere shackles, sorrows, cares, grieves, and a veil between you and your Lord (mighty and glorified is He). Look at it with the eyes of your hearts not the eyes of your heads. The eye of the heart looks at the essence, whereas the eye of the head looks at the appearance.

The believer totally belongs to Allah (mighty and glorified is He). There is not even a single atom of him that belongs to Allah's creatures. He is with Him in both his outward and inward. He does not move except for His sake and does not come to rest but for His sake. So, he exists in Him, from Him, and for Him. The allotted worldly shares of the believer in Allah come to him and knock at his door while he is forgetful of them. They come to him and stand at his service.

⊛ O people, remember and remind others, for "only those with sound reason remember" (from 13.19)! It is the people of Allah who are the ones with sound reason. They have properly understood this world so they renounced it. Then they understood the hereafter so they entered into it. Once its trees have sprouted for them, its rivers have flowed for them, and they have become in possession of it in wakefulness and sleep, the love of the True One (mighty and glorified is He) came to them, so they abandoned the hereafter, traveled away from it, and left it. They tightened the girdles of their hearts and headed to their Lord (mighty and glorified is He). They became among those who seek His face and wish for nothing other than Him. Seek blessings from these people, seek them out, serve them, get to know them, and behave with ultimate politeness in their company. O Allah, grant us good behavior with You under all circumstance and with the righteous of Your servants and "give us good in this world and good in the hereafter and protect us from the torment of the Fire."

⊛ Once the wing of Knowledge has grown long, the scissors of the Law clip it. Accept my words and my good advice to you as I teach on account of my belief in the oneness of God and listening to the words of the truthful and the saints. Their words are like revelations from Allah (mighty and glorified is He). They speak on His behalf, and He commands them in a way that is beyond the comprehension of the common man. You are in illusion! You compose your speech from the books and then deliver it. What would you do if your book is lost? What if your books are burned? What if your lamp went out? What if your jar broke and the water inside spilled? Where are your flint, matches, and the fuel that you see with?

⊛ Someone asked: "I want to be one of those who seek His face, for my heart has glanced at the door of nearness and was shown the lovers entering and coming out dressed in clothes that the King has conferred on them. What is the price of entering into it?" We said to him: "Sacrifice the whole of you. Give up your lustful desires and pleasures. Be extinct in Him that you cease to exist to yourself. Bid farewell to Paradise and its contents and leave it. Abandon the lower self, passion, and natural inclination. Give up the lustful desires of this world and the hereafter, bid farewell to everything, leave them behind your back, and then enter, for you will see what no eye has ever seen, no ear has ever heard, and has never occurred to any human being."

O young man, say "Allah." "Say 'Allah' then leave them alone" (from 6.91)! Say: "[He] who created me, so He guides me" (26.78). O you who have renounced this world! When your heart has gone out of it seeking the hereafter, say: "[He] who created me, so He guides me." And you, O seeker of the True One, who are longing for Him, who have renounced everything apart from Him! When your heart leaves through the door of Paradise seeking its Master, say: "[He] who created me, so He guides me." Seek His guidance to overcome the rugged parts of the road. O people, answer my call for I am a caller of Allah (mighty and glorified is He)! Return to your Creator with your hearts. All of you will soon be dead. Work to open the door of repentance to Him and forgiveness in His presence. You must watch Him and you must know that He is overseeing, watching, and witnessing you. Have you not heard Allah's (high is He) following words: "There cannot be a private conversation between three but He makes the fourth, or between five but He makes the sixth, or between fewer or more but He is with them, wherever they may be" (from 58.7)?

Eat from the food of His remembrance and drink from the drink of His intimacy. His nearness should be all that you need. O you who are dead at heart, O you who are seated in dissimulation, stand up before you are paraded! Stand up before you die. O you who are seated in the place of ebb, stand up before the tide reaches you! Stand up for the water has run beneath you. Get up off the ground of your polytheism and move to the ground of your belief in the oneness of God. O our Lord, set us up in a trade that makes You satisfied with us! "Do not make our hearts deviate after You have guided us" (from 3.8). Do not deviate our hearts from the truth. Do not turn them away from following Your Book and the Sunna of Your Messenger Muhammad (Allah's prayer and peace be on him) and acting in accordance with them. Do not cause us to deviate from following in the footsteps of the prophets, messengers, martyrs, and righteous (Allah's prayer and peace be on all of them). Place our souls with their souls. Let us enter the house of Your nearness in this world before the hereafter. Amen.

If, on the Day of Resurrection, the lovers can find a way not to enter Paradise then they will not enter it, because they will say: "What have we to do with made things? We wish for the Maker. What have we to do with Paradise? We wish for the Creator. What have we to do with what is done? We wish for the Doer. What have we to do with things that are new? We want the Old One." This will be the state of the heart when it becomes sound, so no doubt it will be drawn near to the True One (mighty and glorified is He). If its abandonment of this world and the creatures proves genuine, it will deserve nearness.

Woe to you! I have been standing at the door of the True One (mighty and glorified is He) from my childhood, whereas you have not seen it at all. Your heart has not seen the door or its Owner. You are in the East and what I am referring to is in the West. Be sensible. I have been educated and so I am teaching now. I have not tried to comprehend everything with my intellect while I am standing at His door with the elite of His servants. Say: "The trustworthy one has spoken the truth," and suspend your intellect. O friend of Joseph, talk about what you have and talk about what you know! O young man, speak from your heart and truthfulness, otherwise shut up. Spend from your coins, your treasure, and what you have in your home, otherwise do not steal to spend. Feed the people from your plate and let them drink from your spring. The believer who has become a knower gives drinks and drinks from a spring that never runs dry — a spring that he has excavated with the mattocks of his strife and truthfulness.

⊛ The people of Allah have deeds that compare to mountains of goodness, yet they consider them worthless. They behave with humility and force their lower selves into submission. Behave with a similar humility, caution, and fear of the One who must be feared, of the loss of the purity of the innermost being, and of causing strain in it and in the breast. If you continue like that, you will be awarded safety by Allah (mighty and glorified is He) and it will be sealed on your heart and innermost being and be written on the walls of your private life. Your private life and your limbs and senses will come to have signs, languages, glorification, and remembrance of Allah whose wonders your heart will hear yet which your mouth will not utter a word about. Your outward and the creatures will not hear a single word about it. This will be something that will not be revealed for someone else. It will be a favor that you get used to and talk about within yourself: "And of the favor of your Lord do speak" (93.11). [It means]: "O saint, do talk about these inward favors within yourself! And O Prophet, do talk to the creatures about the favors of your Lord (mighty and glorified is He) and His generosity to you!" It is a condition on the saint to conceal and on the Prophet to disclose. The saint's disclosure is an action of Allah (mighty and glorified is He). If he discloses his favors he gets afflicted and deprived of his spiritual state. But if his disclosure is caused by Allah's (mighty and glorified is He) action, he does not get subjected to rebuke and reproach because that was not his action. Someone once said to me: "I have noticed that everyone who is given a spiritual state conceals it, yet you disclose it!" I replied: "Woe to you! We have not disclosed anything. It shows up involuntarily, not intentionally. Whenever my basin becomes full I reduce it. But when the flood comes it spills out all around without my choice; what can I do?"

Woe to you! You go into seclusion to receive revelations! What have you to do with the retreat when the creatures have filled your heart? You have to take to the deserts and wildernesses. After you find the treasure of nearness there return to sit with the creatures. At that stage, you will become a medicine for them. May Allah show mercy to anyone who believes in what I say, tastes what I say, and puts what I say into practice in both his private and public lives.

⊛ Among the saints are those who, during their sleep, eat from the food of Paradise, drink from its drinks, and see all its contents. Among them are those who become free of any need for food and drink, retreat from the creatures, become invisible to them, and live on the earth without dying, such as Ilyās and Al-Khidhr (may Allah be satisfied with both of them). Allah (mighty and glorified is He) has a large number of them on this earth hidden behind a veil. They can see people, but people cannot see them. The saints among them form a majority but the elite represent a minority. They are a few, isolated individuals to whom everyone comes and draws near. It is through their agency that the earth becomes full of plants, rain falls from the sky, and affliction is removed away from the creatures. The food and drink of the angels is the remembrance of Allah, the True One (mighty and glorified is He), glorification, and recitation of "there is no God save Allah (lā ilāha illā Allah)". There are a few saints for whom this comes to be their food. How much disadvantaged you are, O you who are healthy, you who have free time! The Prophet (Allah's prayer and peace be on him) is reported to have said: "Two favors that many people fail to appreciate: good health and free time."

⊛ Many servants work diligently by night and day in worshipping Allah, yet with ignorance of Knowledge, the divine decree, and destiny. They speak about the truth without making any reference to the Law. No doubt, therefore, they end up as infidels. This is why it has been said: "Every truth that is not supported by the Law is mere infidelity," meaning that the Law should be perfected first and this will be the foundations on which the edifice should be erected afterward.

⊛ O young man, rely on Allah and get up and have determination! I do not see a beginning or an end for you. You have not been genuine in saying "there is no God save Allah (lā ilāha illā Allah) (from 47.19), Muhammad is the Messenger of Allah (Muhammadun rasūlu Allah)" (from 48.29), and you are not fulfilling its conditions. In addition, you are not one of the elite so that gold and clay would be one and the same in your sight. What are you then exactly? How could we remember you and count you when you do not belong to the former or the latter? You would like me to praise you for something that you do not have so that your lower self would be happy and you would be pleased with me and give me presents! You are unworthy of respect! I speak the truth and do not fear the criticism of anyone. I am in attack and retreat between the creatures and the Creator, between the One who does not forget and those who forget, between the One who acts with precision and those who do not. You are ignorant, what have you to do with me? Do not be my enemy, otherwise you will perish. Do not be one of those who show enmity to what they are ignorant of. You have been ignorant of what I am involved in so you became my enemy. But I do not care at all about you and your enmity.

⊛ Among the people of Allah is one who once he has come to need only Allah (mighty and glorified is He), to the exclusion of all creatures and everything on the earth, He tires him with children and with the task of providing for them to cause him to return to the creatures and accept things from them so that taking from them will be a mercy to them. His poverty will be outward, whereas his affluence will be inward. His affluence will be secret, whereas his poverty will be public. Allah exposes them (these people) to whatever states He wishes while they keep silent, adhering to ultimate politeness. He shows them first the Book and the Sunna, so they put them into practice and become pious. Then He shows them the Messenger (Allah's prayer and peace be on him) in their dreams who tells them to do this and that and to refrain from doing this and that. They then see their Lord (mighty and glorified is He) in their dreams and He orders them to carry out certain things and refrain from doing others. They are then promoted from one degree to another, from one book to another, from one abode to another, and from one form of remembrance to another.

The believer sees all creatures as one person who is ill, powerless, and unable to bring benefits to himself or drive any harm away from it. He hates those creatures that disobey Him and loves those who obey Him. He complies with His Lord (mighty and glorified is He) in his love and hatred. He does not love the creatures for their giving and does not hate them for their withholding. He does not love and hate for the sake of his lower self and passion. He is detached from his lower self. He does not comply with it except in matters that are works of obedience to Allah (mighty and glorified is He). He keeps this world away from his heart. He is always committed to the religion of His Lord (mighty and glorified is He), observing its laws and supporting it.

⊕ O young man, when the servant knows the True One (mighty and glorified is He), He draws his heart completely near, rewards him with everything, confers on him the ultimate intimacy, and bestows on him the ultimate honor. Once he gets used to these, He takes them away from him, leaves him empty-handed, sends him back to his lower self, and establishes a veil between Himself and him in order to test him and see how he will respond: Will he escape? Will he deviate or remain steadfast? If he stands firm, He removes the veil from him and returns him to his previous situation. Have you not seen how the father puts his son to the test? He sends him out of his house, locks the door in his face, and waits to see what he does. If he finds that his son kept to the doorstep, did not go to his neighbor, did not complain about him, and did not abandon polite behavior, he reopens the door, allows him in, embraces him, and honors him more than before.

Anyone who does not act with sincerity will not earn a single atom of the nearness to Allah (mighty and glorified is He). Allah (mighty and glorified is He) has said in one of his utterances: "I release the partners that are attributed to Me from all obligations of this partnership. If someone dedicates an action to Me and to a partner that he associated with Me, I leave it for the alleged partner as I do not accept anything other than what was for the sake of My face." The Prophet (Allah's prayer and peace be on him) is reported to have said: "The hypocrite will be told on the Day of Resurrection: 'O perfidious one, O infidel, ask for the reward from whom you have dedicated your work to'"! O worshippers of other than your Lord (mighty and glorified is He), have you not heard His (high is He) following words: "I have not created the jinn and the human beings but to worship Me" (51.56), these words of His (high is He): "And they were commanded to worship one God only" (from 9.31), and His (high is He) following saying: "And they were only commanded to worship Allah, devoting religion sincerely to Him" (from 98.5)?

Every servant must worship his Lord (mighty and glorified is He) seeking His face and His satisfaction, not for the sake of a certain purpose or for receiving rewards. Anyone of you who fails to be sincere to Allah in his public life, let him worship privately, so that no eye of a creature will see him and no ear will hear his recitation [of the Holy Qur'an] and his glorification of Allah. Dissimulation is a grave matter. It is reported that one of the people of Allah has said: "If a person prayed in a dark house but was seen by a powerless, poor slave who is unable to do anything whatsoever, it would be as if he performed his prayer to impress the slave and, therefore, he would have performed it without any sincerity."

O you who refrain from charitable spending! Have you not heard His (mighty and glorified is He) following words: "And [those who] spend of what We have bestowed on them" (from 2.3)? He means spending their money on the family, the children, and the poor. The niggard is deprived, expelled, and distant from the creatures and the Creator. Ask your Lord to provide for you from His favors. Ask Him for help whether He answers you or not, for asking Him for help is in itself an act of worship. Asking Him for help takes the form of calling in the case of remoteness, the form of private conversation in the case of nearness, and the form of silent gesture in the case of love. The person who is at a distance asks for help, crying out: "O King, give me, bring me near!" One who has come close and attained to Him converses with Him privately in a low voice at difficult times for he is near to Him. And one who has sat beside Him is overwhelmed by His majesty so he guards his tongue and speaks only by signs. The Muslim is in a state of remoteness, so he calls out and shouts; the believer who has become a knower is in a state of nearness, so he privately converses with Him with utter politeness; while the beloved, whose heart has arrived at the chamber of nearness, speaks only through silent gesture. May Allah bestow mercy on anyone who comprehends what I am saying, puts it into practice, removes from his heart any doubt about me and about my words, and submits to his Lord (mighty and glorified is He) what he does not understand and is beyond his knowledge.

The people of Allah have faith, believe, put their knowledge into practice, work with sincerity, and spend their money in the service of the righteous. In order to spend their money on good causes, they bring forth arguments to silence their objecting lower selves. They spend their money sometimes as obligatory alms, sometimes as a voluntary charitable

selfless concern

donation, sometimes altruistically, sometimes in fulfillment of vows, and sometimes by swearing an oath to donate money. They do all this as a means to draw near to Allah (mighty and glorified is He) due to the strength of their hearts and certitude and their subjugation of their lower selves. Some of them are ordered to donate some of what they have, so they obey the command of Allah (mighty and glorified is He), whereas others hand out rewards without being aware of what they are doing. The saints are commanded to give to the poor and needy, whereas the spiritual substitutes have their money taken from their hands while they are completely unaware. It is related that one of the people of Allah was one day praying in a desert when one of a group of passing travelers took his cloak and then put it back on his shoulder. When the man finished his prayer, the traveler who took his cloak said to him: "Forgive my guilt in taking your cloak and annoying you." The man replied: "By Allah, I did not feel anything when you took it or when you returned it. If you want to take it, go ahead and take it."

The people of Allah are unaware of anything other than what they are involved in. When they stand in the presence of their Lord (mighty and glorified is He), they become totally unaware of anything other than Him. The essence becomes absent and only the appearance remains present; the heart becomes absent and the body remains present. When one of the people of Allah — Muslim bin Yassar[16] (may Allah show mercy to him) — would enter his house, his children used to stop behaving joyfully and become well-behaved so that no one of them would even laugh. He recognized their state of restraint, so whenever he wanted to pray he used to say to them: "Do what you like and give up your restraint for I will not be aware of what you do." So, when he starts praying they play, relax, and laugh, while he is totally unaware of what they did. One day he was praying in the mosque when a column of the building and parts of the roof that it supports collapsed beside him but he did not realize what happened. On another occasion, a fire broke out in his house while he was praying, so people gathered and put it out but he did not take notice of what took place.

The people of Allah totally belong to the True One (mighty and glorified is He). They are wholly devoted to helping the creatures, and the Creator supports them. They spend of the worldly property that they have in their hands and of the Knowledge in their hearts. They have found the greatest treasure so this world lost its importance in their eyes. They have seen the greatest kingdom, so the kingdom of this world has become worthless in their view. They have renounced every created thing, so their hearts have been given the favor of "'be,' and it is."

---

[16] A famous jurist (died 718). He was originally from Mecca but lived in Basra.

As long as this outward thing is in your hand and your heart is embracing it, you will have nothing of the favor of "'be,' and it is." One of the people of Allah was asked: "Where do you obtain your food from?" He replied: "From the big threshing floor." It was asked: "What is the big threshing floor?" He replied: "'be,' and it is."

When it comes to worldly matters, look to those who are inferior to you, whereas with matters of the hereafter look up to those who are superior to you. It is reported about one of the people of Allah that on the day of celebration (*Eīd*) he bought broad beans and sat to eat them. He said: "Could there be anyone in a situation similar to mine, on such a day eating only broad beans without even oil or salt?" He then turned his head just to see someone eating the peels that he was throwing aside. So he wept and apologized to Allah (mighty and glorified is He) about what he said.

⊛ How few those who seek the face of the True One (mighty and glorified is He) and His nearness are! Seeing Him is the delight of the eyes of the knowers and the lovers. Seeing Paradise, living in it with the houris, eating, and drinking are consolation for the eyes of the ascetics. What a huge difference there is between the two groups! How far they are from each other! O you who wish for this world, you have wasted your lifetime on nothing! And O you who wish for Paradise, the houris, and the youths of Paradise, you have wished for something other than your Lord (mighty and glorified is He) and you have chosen something other than Him! If you had any knowledge you would not have enjoyed being absent from His presence even for a single moment. Woe to you, You do not know! Woe to you! The joy of one look at the True One (mighty and glorified is He) encompasses all of the youths, pleasures, lustful desires, and bliss of Paradise put together, so what of the delight of so many looks for hours?

⊛ Give up your illusion. This business [of attaining to Allah] cannot be achieved by pretense, wishful thinking, and tongue-wagging. If you are sitting in front of this plate and at this spring, then eat and drink, and feed and offer drink to others. But if you have only heard of it, then keep silent. Do not talk about something you have not seen. Do not invite people to someone else's party. Do not invite people to an empty house because they would laugh at you. Shoot for us an arrow from your own quiver. Spend on us from your earnings, from what you earn by the sweat of your brow. Do not feed us from the yield that you have stolen from your neighbors. Do not offer us clothes that you have borrowed. We do not accept the gifts from a borrower, usurper. The belief in the oneness of God is a scorching fire. "O fire, be coolness and safety!" (from 21.69). O Allah, grant us the goodness of this day and protect us from its evil, and grant us the same for all nights and days! Amen.

⊛ Do not argue with Him citing His destiny. Work hard, be diligent, dedicate yourselves to Him, ask for His help, weep, ask for intercession, behave with submissiveness, stand firm at the door, and do not run away. All matters are in Allah's (mighty and glorified is He) hand. He is the One who awakens, grants success, and gives warning. He is the One who awakens you, and he is the One who puts you to sleep. When our Prophet Muhammad (Allah's prayer and peace be on him) heard the private conversation of the True One (mighty and glorified is He): "O you covered [in the mantle!]. Arise and warn" (74.1-2), he got up from bed and went out wandering, searching for Him. Similarly, when the believer hears the private conversation of the True One (mighty and glorified is He), he responds to Him, wanders searching for Him, and longs for Him. He awakens the hearts and shows them the way to Him.

When Allah (high is He) wants you to do something, He prepares you for it. This is an inward matter. It is what is referred to by destiny, foreordination, and foreknowledge. We are not allowed to depend on this and use it as an argument against making serious efforts, but we have to work hard, be diligent, do not pretend to be ill, and do not be lazy. O Allah, make us satisfied with Your decree, grant us patience with Your affliction, and enable us to thank You for Your favor! We ask You to give us Your full favor, the permanence of well-being, and steadfastness in love.

Ibrāhīm ibn Adham[17] (may Allah, high is He, show mercy to him) is reported to have said: "Once I stayed up all night praying to Allah (mighty and glorified is He) with all kinds of supplication and was weeping. When the dawn was about to break, my eyelids drooped. While asleep, I saw Allah (mighty and glorified is He) who said: 'O Ibrahim, you are not praying to Me in the best way! Say: "O Allah, make us satisfied with Your decree, grant us patience with Your affliction, and enable us to thank You for Your favor! We ask You to give us Your full favor, the permanence of well-being, and steadfastness in love"'. Then I woke up while I was repeating it."

The servant who has truly accomplished servitude is one who is content with his Lord to the exclusion of all creatures, satisfied with his spiritual state to the exclusion of the spiritual states of others, and content with his Prophet (Allah's prayer and peace be on him) to the exclusion of all other prophets (Allah's prayer and peace be on all of them). He becomes in need of nothing, whereas things need him. The people of Allah do not ask Allah (mighty and glorified is He) for other than Allah Himself. They ask for the Benefactor not the benefit, the Creator not the creature. They run away from food, drink, clothes, sexual

---

[17] A well-known Sufi (ca. 718-778). He was born in Mecca when his parents came from Khurāsān for pilgrimage.

intercourse, and the strife for worldly things. They escape to Him from those things. They worship Him for His sake not for the fodder of their lower selves. They do not worship Him for the abode of the Day of Resurrection. They say: "We do not find happiness in mercy. We do not wish for mercy, but we wish for solitude with the Beloved with no mercy."

✹ O young men, do not cut yourselves off from the bliss that I have explained to you by running after your allotted shares of this world! Give up running after them and then they will start chasing you. This is something I have experienced and seen and has been seen by others who followed this path. Do not rush things for nothing that has been allocated to you will miss you. The Prophet (Allah's prayer and peace be on him) is reported to have said: "The soul will not leave this world until it has obtained all its allotted sustenance. So, be pious to Allah (mighty and glorified is He) and do not be greedy when you ask Him for what you need." Stop! Do not be over keen on obtaining what you want. Do not run after things but be steadfast. Be careful when you ask for something, if you really have to ask. If you turn away from the door of the kings, a door that will never be locked will be opened to you. This is the door of the innermost being, the door of the inward which will be opened for you without the intervention of your might, strength, or thinking.

The believer is one who left the house of his lower self, natural inclination, and passion, heading to his Lord (mighty and glorified is He). While he is in this state, tribulations that hit him, his family, and his property will obstruct his way. He will first stop in confusion. Then he will look back at his sins and impolite behavior in violating the limits of the Law of his Lord (mighty and glorified is He), so he will repent, give up asking "why" and "how," stop protesting and disputing outwardly and inwardly, surrender, fall prostrate, and refrain from trying to tackle the barrier that is in front of him with only his own effort and toil. He will not seek to remove it with anything other than his Lord (mighty and glorified is He). He will focus completely on remembering Allah, returning to Him, remembering his sins, asking for them to be forgiven, and blaming his lower self. Once he has done all of that, he will refer to the destiny that his Lord (mighty and glorified is He) has preordained and say: "The destiny of Allah, His decree, and His foreordination about me will have to pass." He will then return to submission and reliance by the heart not the tongue. While he is in this state, with his eyes closed in reflection, he will open his eyes suddenly to find that the barrier has gone, the door is open, favors have replaced the tribulations, affluence has replaced hardship, well-being has replaced illness, and kingship has replaced destruction. All this confirms Allah's (mighty and glorified is He) following saying: "And whoever is pious to Allah He will appoint for him a way out, and He will provide for him from whence he did not expect" (from 65.2-3).

The true servant continues to respond to the favors with thankfulness and to affliction with compliance, admitting his crimes and sins and blaming the lower self, until the footsteps of his heart lead him to his Lord (mighty and glorified is He). He keeps on walking with the steps of good works and repentance from bad deeds until he arrives to the door of his Lord (mighty and glorified is He). He continues to step forward with thankfulness on the favors and patience on afflictions until he arrives to the door of his Lord (mighty and glorified is He). Once he is there, he will face what no eye has ever seen, no ear has ever heard, and has never occurred to any human being. When the heart of the servant arrives at the door of his Lord (mighty and glorified is He), the bout of good works, bad deeds, thankfulness, patience, tiredness, and hardship comes to an end, like the footsteps of the traveler come to a halt when he arrives to his destination and house. What remains after that is the sitting together, intimacy, conversation, direct seeing, and viewing the secrets. When the lover arrives to his Beloved (mighty and glorified is He), could there still be any tiredness? Tiredness turns into comfort, remoteness into nearness, absence into presence, and the hearing of news into direct seeing. He will come to view His secrets. He will take His servant on a tour in His house and He will open for him His treasures and show him His garden. Can you not comprehend this? "And Allah strikes parables for people" (from 14.25). It is the people of signs who understand the signs.

⊛ When I was a little boy, I used to go alone to unpopulated places where I would sometimes hear a voice without seeing a figure. The voice would utter: "O you who are blessed, you are good and you will meet goodness!" I used to stand and roam the place around me without discovering where the voice was coming from. With all praise due to Allah (mighty and glorified is He), I did enjoy blessings in all of my circumstances.

Among the servants of Allah (mighty and glorified is He) are those who say for something "be,' and it is," but you cannot see them, and if you see them you would not recognize them and you would lock your doors shut in their faces and tighten your purses and pockets so that you do not give them anything.

⊛ When the believer who has become a knower closes the eyes of his head, the eyes of his heart open wide, so he sees the reality of the creatures. When the eyes of his heart close, the eyes of his innermost being open wide so he sees the True One (mighty and glorified is He) and His management of the creation. When the Creator becomes present, the creatures leave. When the hereafter becomes present, this world leaves. When truthfulness becomes present, the telling of lies leaves. When sincerity becomes present, polytheism leaves. When faith becomes present, hypocrisy leaves. Everything has an opposite.

The sensible person looks at the ultimate consequences and does not look at this world and its adornment for it will soon pass away. This world is continuously changing and is ephemeral. You will pass away and then it will disappear after you. Do not run away from the company of your Lord (mighty and glorified is He) because of the tribulations that He subjects you to, for He knows about your best interests far better than you.

⊛ As for the exceptions, they are a few individuals among His creatures. He created them for something that is beyond the limits of the normal. He created them for a purpose that He knows. He created them for His company, deputyship, ambassadorship, and guidance of His creatures to Him. He sends them to the East, West, and sea. They address the creatures in their own languages. He appointed them as His deputies among the creatures. They do not wish for life or death, for they are totally extinct in Him that they have no will of their own. Their wills have died, their lower selves have come to rest, their passions have been broken, the fires of their natural inclinations have died out, their devils have been defeated, and this world has surrendered in submission to them and lost any influence on them. In other words, they have left nothing to be blamed for. These are the rarest of the rare. No love for anyone other than Him is left in their hearts. They are the beloved of the True One (mighty and glorified is He) and the ones He chose from His creatures.

⊛ The people of Allah have inherited the spiritual states of the prophets (Allah's prayer and peace be on them). They have inherited their spiritual stations, not their names and titles. They have inherited the qualities and virtues that they had. The saints and spiritual substitutes are restricted to a certain number that does not increase or decrease. Among them is one who attains his spiritual status early in his life, whereas another attains his spiritual status in the latter part of his life. Before the attainment of the latter, his states continuously change, although he is a confirmed saint of Allah (mighty and glorified is He) in Allah's (mighty and glorified is He) foreknowledge, for infallibility is not a prerequisite for spiritual substitution and sainthood. There is no infallibility after the time of the prophets as infallibility is one of their unique attributes (Allah's prayer and peace be on them). It is reported that the Prophet (Allah's prayer and peace be on him) has said: "When one of the saints of Allah (mighty and glorified is He) disobeys Allah, the angels (Allah's prayer and peace be on our Prophet and on them) laugh and say to one another: 'Look at this saint of Allah, see how he is disobeying Allah (mighty and glorified is He)'"! How could not they be astonished at his disobedience, disbelief, remoteness, and hypocrisy when they know that in a few days he will become a beloved saint; one who is drawn near, honored, and purified; an intercessor; a guide; and an heir?

✸ I have renounced you, my lower self, and my allotted worldly shares. Blessed I am! I do not eat, drink, dress up, have sexual intercourse, or show off. Blessed I am! I have been made to stand aside from you and I have taken advice from signs without the need for verbal instructions. I hate seeing the hypocrites, disobedient ones, and those who associate partners with Allah, but I have to see them. They are ill people and I have been made a healer. The believer who is still a beginner in faith cannot look at anyone of these people or share with him a moment of time. When he happens to see a hypocrite, disobedient person, or polytheist he becomes angry at him and if it was in his power, he would kill him. One of the people of Allah (may Allah show mercy to him) used to become so angry to the point of falling to the ground when he sees a disbeliever. He used to pass out as a result of the enormity of his undivided loyalty to Allah (mighty and glorified is He) and his anger for His sake that one of His servants should fail to believe in Him. No doubt, this believer was a novice, because the start is characterized by weakness and the end by strength.

One of the people of Allah (may Allah show mercy to him) is reported to have said: "No one laughs in the face of a hypocrite other than the knower." The knower recognizes the graveness of the illness of the hypocrite and knows his treatment, so he smiles in his face saying: "Yes, your medicine is with me; so come." He speaks to him with nice words in order to attract him, make him work with him, and make him feel close to him. Once he has become in charge of him, he cures his illness. He introduces him to Islam and faith and describes them to him. He introduces him to the words of his Lord (mighty and glorified is He) and guarantees to him reconciliation with Him. Day after day, his disbelief, hypocrisy, and disobedience melt away. The illness of his heart dissolves, his wounds heal, and his lower self is discarded. Both his outward and inward reform, without any quarrel or dispute, without a stab or blow.

Jesus, the son of Mary, and John, the son of Zechariah, (prayer and peace be on our Prophet and on them) used to glorify the Lord in the wilderness. When the night sets, John would go to the village of the believers, whereas Jesus would go to the village of the disbelievers. John approached the believers because of the weakness of his spiritual state, whereas Jesus went near to the disbelievers because of the strength of his spiritual state, so that he could preach to them, warn them, and take them by the hand to the door of their Lord (mighty and glorified is He). One liked to pray and fast in the midst of believers, whereas the other liked to summon the people to Allah (mighty and glorified is He) and His worship. The knower is a reminder and his worship is to call the creatures to Allah (mighty and glorified is He). His relation with Allah (mighty and glorified is He) remains on this basis. The Muslim is a worker, and the believer is a foreman; the knower is a builder, and the person who is knowledgeable of Allah (mighty and glorified is He) is a roads engineer.

⊛ If you are not among the people of Allah, then serve them, accompany them, sit in their presence, draw near to them, make your money available for their use, and follow them by emulating their works, not by quoting, applauding, and expressing astonishment at their words. Make sure that your heart not your clothes is the abode of your righteousness. Dress as common people do but do not do what they do. Monasticism is not to be defined with relation to food, clothing, and sex. Allah (high is He) has said: "And monasticism they invented — We did not ordain for them" (from 57.27). The Prophet (Allah's prayer and peace be on him) has said: "There is no monasticism in Islam."

As for those who are sincere in their belief in the oneness of God, their cells are their hearts. Their austerity is imposed on their lower selves, passions, and natural inclination. The fruit that they enjoy is loneliness and the visions they see. Their feeling of intimacy with their Lord (mighty and glorified is He) lies in the private conversation with Him. The True One (mighty and glorified is He) informs you about the spiritual state of the righteous through me in order for you to join and emulate them. So do not only hear these words. He uses my tongue to inform you in order for you to inform one another, so pay heed to the good advice. He calls you through me, so respond to His caller. He calls you to purity. He calls you to renounce His creatures and to wish for Him. He calls you to remember Him so that you become remembered in His presence. The servant who is truthful in seeking his Master (mighty and glorified is He) continues to remember Him outwardly and inwardly, in both his private and public lives, by night and day, in hardship and prosperity, in bliss and agony, until he becomes remembered in His presence. He hears his remembrance of Him (mighty and glorified is He) around him and in his heart.

You are in a deep sleep, unaware of the bliss of the people of Allah. O you who are forgetful of the bliss, you are unaware, absent, and unconscious! While you are knowledgeable in dealing with the affairs of this world, you are totally ignorant about the affairs of the hereafter. You are bogged down in mud, so the more you move the more you sink. Stretch out your hands to Allah (mighty and glorified is He) while being truthful in your seeking Him, repentance, and apology so that He will rescue you from your situation.

I am calling on you to stand firm against your lower selves, passions, natural inclinations, and lustful desires and to endure with patience the loss of worldly things. Respond to my call and then you will sooner or later come to see the results. I am calling you to the red death in the name of Allah. Who will attack? Who will advance? Who will dare? Who will take the risk? It is death that is followed by an everlasting life.

Do not escape. Force patience on yourselves when you are still impatient, and when you have become patient, endure with patience. Courage is an hour's patience. Equip yourselves with the patience required for compliance with your Lord (mighty and glorified is He). When any of you carries the burden of the divine decree with satisfaction, Allah (mighty and glorified is He) will relieve him of it and write his name in the record of the brave. Anyone who takes risk with himself will gain certitude. When one knows what he is seeking, he sees whatever he has to do as being insignificant. O servant of God, stand firm in your places and do not rush! Come on the foot of truthfulness to knock at the door of the True One (mighty and glorified is He) and do not leave until the door is opened for you and processions have come out to welcome you. Be impudent when asking Him to provide your needs, for this is better in His eyes than your asking with impertinence your kings, your sultans, and the rich among you. Emulate your predecessors in their quest for their Lord (mighty and glorified is He) and their extinction in Him.

O Allah, You are our Lord and their Lord, our Creator and their Creator, our Provider and their Provider, so treat us as You treated them! Bring us out toward You. Make us pin no hopes on the kings and the servants, the sultans and their subjects, the rich and the poor, the elite and common people, the rise and fall of market prices, and abundance and scarcity. Remind us of Your remembrance, be kind to us in Your actions, draw us close to your nearness, and make our hearts feel Your intimacy. Protect us from the evil of Your countries and Your servants, and from the evil of every moving creature that You hold by the forelock.[18] Protect us from the evil of the evildoers and from the scheming of the infidels. Include us among Your party who is traveling to You, seeking the way to You, calling others to You, submitting with humility to You, and treating with arrogance those who are arrogant with You and with the believers of Your creatures. Amen.

⊛ If you learn for the sake of this world you will end up working for this world, and if you learn for the sake of the hereafter you will end up working for the hereafter. The branch is an outcome of the root. You will be rewarded according to your behavior. Every vessel exudes its own contents. You fill your vessel with tar, yet you expect rose water to ooze out of it! You are unworthy of respect! You work for this world in this world, yet you wish that the hereafter will be yours tomorrow! You are unworthy of respect! You work for the sake of the creatures, yet you hope that tomorrow you will have the Creator on your side, have His nearness, and enjoy looking at Him! You are unworthy of respect! This is the

---

[18] This is a reference to this verse: "I have put my trust in Allah, my Lord and your Lord. There is no creature that crawls but He takes it by the forelock. Certainly, My Lord is on a straight Path" (11.56).

obvious rule that applies to most people. However, if He wishes to give you His rewards out of His generosity not in return for work you did, then it is up to Him.

Listen to me and comprehend what I have to say, for I am a servant of the predecessors. I serve in their presence, spread out their goods, and call on people to view them. I do not betray them or claim that the goods are mine. I praise their words. Allah (mighty and glorified is He) has qualified me for this through the blessing of my following of the Messenger (Allah's prayer and peace be on him) and my filial devotion to my father and mother (may Allah, high is He, show mercy to them). My father renounced this world despite his ability to earn a lot in it, and my mother agreed with him on that and was pleased with his action. They were among the people of righteousness, religion, and compassion for the creatures. However, I am not concerned with them or with the creatures. I am only concerned with the Messenger of Allah (Allah's prayer and peace be on him) and the Sender. It is through them that I gain my goodness. My favors are with them and in their presence. I do not wish for anyone of the creatures other than Muhammad (Allah's prayer and peace be on him), and I do not wish for any lord other than my Lord (mighty and glorified is He).

Putting Knowledge into Practice

☸ After reading books you got up to the preaching platform to preach to people! After the blackness of the ink has smeared your clothes and your hand, you got up to speak to people! This is a business that requires commanding the outward and inward, and then attaining extinction in Him to the extent of being non-existent in relation to everything else. O you who are unaware of what will be done to you! Remember the private resurrection and the universal resurrection. The private resurrection is the death of each one of you, whereas the universal resurrection is what is promised by Allah (mighty and glorified is He). Recite and remember these words of Allah (mighty and glorified is He): "The day when We will gather the pious to Allah as a good delegate and drive the guilty to hell thirsty" (19.85-86). The good delegate of the pious will be in groups and riding, and the guilty will be brought thirsty. The pious will be gathered together, whereas the criminals will be driven by force. May Allah bestow mercy on any servant who remembers that Day. The person who accompanies the pious today will be gathered with them on that Day. O you who have given up piety! On the Day of Resurrection, the pious will be taken to Him riding in a goodly company while the angels around them giving their deeds various appearances. They will ride on thoroughbreds. The thoroughbred of everyone will be his works; his ornament and turban will be his deeds. The works take on beautiful or ugly appearances [according to their nature].

☸ The seeker is stationed under the shade of his repentance, whereas the one who is sought after is stationed under the shade of the care of his Lord (mighty and glorified is He). The seeker is walking, whereas the one who is sought after is flying. The seeker is at the door, whereas the person who is sought after is inside, in the chamber of nearness. When the seeker works with diligence he becomes sought after. Seeking nearness without working toward that goal is an illusion. This statement applies to the majority of cases not the rare ones. When did Moses (prayer and peace be on our Prophet, on him, and on all prophets) become near? Was not that after experiencing hardships and strivings? After escaping from Pharaoh's house and working hard for years tending sheep, he experienced what he experienced. How long it took him before he was brought near! After suffering hunger, thirst, and living in exile, his essence was purified and He married him to the daughter of Shu'aib. Goodness came to him through his wife, because she was the cause of his serving her sheep. Hunger had hit him hard, yet when he gave water to her sheep, He caused him to withdraw alone under the tree and prevented him from asking for a wage in return for his work. Foreordination guided his action, the divine care enabled him to see, and the glances of the True One (mighty and glorified is He) made him prudent and caused him to ask his Lord (mighty and glorified is He) to provide for his needs so he said: "O My Lord, I am in need of whatever good You send down to me!" (from 28.24).

While he was in that situation, Shu'aib's daughter came and took him to her father. Shu'aib asked him about his circumstances, so he told him everything. Shu'aib then said: "Do not fear, you have escaped from the wrongdoing people" (from 28.25). He married him to his daughter and employed him to shepherd sheep. Moses then forgot the kingdom of Pharaoh and the affluence that he was in. He put on shepherds' clothes and spent the night and day with the sheep, with those that do not speak. In the wilderness, he learned renunciation and solitude, so his heart was purified, and he matured in those years. The Pharaoh's kingdom departed from his heart, and this world and all its contents left his innermost being.

By fulfilling the term that he had agreed with Shu'aib (prayer and peace be on our Prophet and on him), Moses fulfilled the obligation on his outward, but his obligation to Allah (mighty and glorified is He) and the covenant that He has in his heart and innermost being remained to be fulfilled. Moses bid farewell to Shu'aib and took his wife with him. After walking for three parasangs[19] away from Madian the night set in. At this point, his pregnant wife began to feel the pains of labor. She asked him to provide her with some light so she could see. He tried unsuccessfully to produce a spark with the flint stick. Then the night got even darker and he found himself overwhelmed by confusion. The earth seemed too strait despite its spaciousness. He was left as a stranger and lonely man on an unfamiliar road, with his wife in that distress. So he stood on a high spot and looked right and left, forward and backward, trying to hear a sound or see a fire in the distance. He caught sight of a fire at the side of mountain Ṭūr, so he said to his wife: "Calm down, for I have seen a fire that I might be able to bring you light from, or ask the people who started it about the road." "So when he came to it, he was called from the right bank of the valley" (from 28.30). When he came close to the fire and wanted to take a firebrand from it, the situation completely changed, as the familiar state of affairs disappeared and reality became manifest. He forgot his family and their welfare, but someone came to his wife, treated her with honor, looked after her, and provided for her needs. He was called by a Caller, addressed by an Addresser, and spoken to by a Speaker, who is the True One (mighty and glorified is He). This happened without any intermediary, "from the right bank of the valley, in the blessed spot from the tree" (from 28.30). The tree came to be in front of him. He said: "O Moses! I am Allah, the Lord of the worlds" (from 28.30). He meant: "I am not an angel, jinn,

---

[19] An ancient Persian unit of distance that is equal to about 3.5 miles (5.6 km).

or human being, but the Lord of the creation. Pharaoh has lied when he said: 'I am your Lord, the most high' (from 79.24) and claimed divinity. It is only I, Allah, who is the Lord. Pharaoh and the other creatures — jinn, human beings, angels, and all creatures from beneath the Throne to beneath the surface of the earth; the world of your time and the world of the times to come, until the Day of Resurrection — are all created things."

Woe to you, O innovator! No one can say "I am Allah" (from 28.30) other than Allah. Allah (mighty and glorified is He) does speak. He is not mute. This is why Allah (mighty and glorified is He) confirmed the verity of His speaking faculty by saying: "And Allah did speak to Moses; He spoke to him" (from 4.164). He (high is He) has speech that can be heard and understood. When Moses heard the words of Allah (mighty and glorified is He), his soul almost left his body and he fell on his face as a result of hearing a kind of speech that he had never heard before. The speech fell on the weakness of the human nature so it shattered it. Allah then sent an angel who enabled him to stand on his feet. The angel put one of his hands on Moses' breast and the other behind his back until he was able to stand and restored his full strength. He caused his heart to be present so that he could comprehend and understand His words. Moses qualified for this after experiencing what seemed to him like his Day of Resurrection and after the earth seemed too strait to him despite its spaciousness.

He was ordered to go to Pharaoh and his people and be a messenger to them, so he said: "O my Lord! 'And loose the knot of my tongue, that they may understand my words' (from 20.27-28) and support me with my brother!" He had a stutter so he was unable to speak fluently. This was because of what happened to him with Pharaoh (may Allah curse him) when he was a little boy. Whenever he wanted to say a word to Pharaoh he stuttered and struggled to pronounce its letters for such a long time that another person would have uttered seventy words. This impediment resulted from what happened to him in Pharaoh's house when he was a child. Āsyā, Pharaoh's wife, brought baby Moses to him and said: "He is 'a delight of the eye for me and you. Do not kill him. May be he will be useful to us or we may take him for a son'" (from 28.9). She brought Moses near to Pharaoh to kiss the baby, but the baby grabbed Pharaoh's beard, so Pharaoh said: "This is the newborn baby at whose hands my kingdom will be destroyed; he must be killed." She replied: "This is a young child who does not understand what he is doing." Then she ordered that a vessel containing red-hot coals and another containing pearls be brought and put in front of him and said: "Let's leave both vessels in front of him. If he will know the difference between them and stretch his hand toward the pearls and avoid the fire, put him to death. But if he will not be able to tell the difference between them and will stretch his hand toward the fire, do not kill him." They agreed to carry out this test and left both vessels in front of the baby. He stretched his hand to the fire, picked up a piece of the red-hot coal, and put it in his mouth, so he wept. She said: "Did not I tell you that he does not recognize what he is doing? Did not I tell you that he did not do that to you deliberately?" So Pharaoh spared him death. Thus, Allah (mighty and glorified is He) brought him up in Pharaoh's house. Glory be to Him who prepared for him his affairs and provided for him an outlet and exit from every care, grief, and hardship. The Invincible One has said: "And whoever is pious to Allah He will appoint for him a way out, and He will provide for him from whence he did not expect. And whoever puts his trust in Allah, He will suffice him" (from 65.2-3).

✷ O servants of Allah! Observe the five daily prayers at their prescribed times. Perform them with total adherence to their conditions and requirements. Do not perform them while you are absent-minded. Have you not heard these words of Allah (mighty and glorified is He): "So woe to those who pray while being unmindful of their prayer" (107.4-5)? Ibn 'Abbās (may Allah be satisfied with both of them) has said: "By Allah, they did not abandon the prayers but delayed them to later than their prescribed times."

Repent, so that Allah will show mercy to you. Satisfy the Forgiver by your repentance. Repent, O disobedient ones! Repent, O you who have delayed the prayers beyond their appointed times! O you who embrace Satan's justification and deceitful argument, O you who are cheated by his guile! Do not disobey! You will not have salvation from the punishment of the Fire. Do not underestimate the One who punishes in this world with blindness, deafness, disability, poverty with the lack of patience, and the need to the creatures despite the hardness of their hearts; and in the hereafter with the Fire. All this is the result of the evil omen of the acts of disobedience and sins. We seek refuge in Allah from His revenge, punishment, striking, and anger. O Allah, pardon us and treat us with Your patience and Your generosity not Your justice! Give us the sustenance of complying with You. Amen. The Prophet is reported to have said: "Allah will create in Hell myrmidons with whom He will exact revenge on His enemies: the disbelievers. When He wishes to punish a disbeliever, He says to the myrmidons: 'Seize him,' whereupon seventy thousand myrmidons immediately move toward him. As soon as he falls in the hand of one of them, he melts like fat does when exposed to fire, so nothing of him remains in the hand of the myrmidon other than the drippings. Then Allah (mighty and glorified is He) re-creates him and the myrmidons will shackle and fetter him with fetters of fire, tie his head to his legs, and throw him in the Fire."

✷ O young man! You will not come close to the True One (mighty and glorified is He) through hypocrisy, fluency, eloquence, turning your face away from people in contempt, ignorance, and patching up your frayed garment. All that comes from your lower self, devil, associating creatures with Allah, and begging for worldly things from them. Think well of others and hold a poor opinion of yourself. Treat yourself with contempt and conceal your status. Maintain this practice until you are told: "Speak about the favor that Allah has conferred on you." Ibn Sam'ūn[20] (may Allah show mercy to him) used to say about any miracle that occurred through him: "This is a trick from Satan." He kept this practice up until he was told: "Do not you know who you are and who your father is? Speak about Our favor".

O lovers, O seekers! Beware of losing the True One (mighty and glorified is He), for if you lose Him, you will have lost everything. Allah (mighty and glorified is He) inspired Jesus (prayer and peace be on our Prophet and on him) with the following: "O Jesus, beware of losing Me, for if you lose Me, you will have lost everything, and if you do not lose Me, you will have lost nothing." Moses (prayer and peace be on our Prophet and on him) said in the course of his private conversation with his Lord (exalted and high is He): "O my Lord, advise me!" So He (exalted and high is He) said to him: "I advise you to be concerned with Me and to seek Me." Moses repeated his request four times and every time He gave him the same answer. He said to him: "Do not seek this world or the hereafter." It is as if He said to him: "I advise you to obey Me and give up disobeying Me. I advise you to seek My nearness. I advise you to believe in My oneness and to work for My sake. I advise you to turn away from everything other than Me."

⊛ O people, remember death and what is after it! Give up your keenness on collecting the goods of this ephemeral world. Curtail your hopes and decrease your greedy keenness. Having great expectations and greedy keenness is most harmful to you. The Prophet (Allah's prayer and peace be on him) is reported to have said: "When the son of Adam dies and enters his grave, four angels come to it. One angel stands at his head, one angel to his right, one angel to his left, and one angel at his feet. The one at his head will say: 'O son of Adam, all property has gone and only the deeds have remained!' The angle to his right will say: 'O son of Adam, the appointed times have expired and only the hopes have remained!' The one to his left will say: 'O son of Adam, the lustful desires have gone and only their consequences have remained!' The one at his feet will say: 'O son of Adam, blessed are you, if you have earned your livelihood lawfully and ended up a righteous one'"! O people, take advice from these exhortations — in particular, the exhortations of Allah (mighty and glorified is He) and the exhortations of His messengers (Allah's prayer and peace be on them). O Allah, bear witness for me that I am trying my best to preach to Your servants, exerting strenuous efforts to reform them!

---

[20] A famous Sufi Shaikh from Baghdad (912-998).

⊛ O young man! When you firmly establish your faith, you will reach the valley of knowingness, then the valley of Knowledge, then the valley of extinction to yourself and to the creatures, and then the existence only through Him, not through yourself or through them. At this point, your fear will disappear, preservation will be at your service, protection will surround you, guidance will stand in respect before you, angels will walk around you, spirits will come to salute you, the True One (mighty and glorified is He) will commend you to the creatures, and His glances will look after you and draw you to the abode of His nearness, intimacy, and private conversation.

⊛ The heart that has turned away from Allah and disbelieved in him is metamorphosed, which is why Allah likened it to stones, when the Best Speaker said: "Then, your hearts hardened after that and became like stones or even harder still" (from 2.74). When the Children of Israel did not put the Torah into practice, Allah (mighty and glorified is He) turned their hearts into stones and expelled them from His door. The same applies to you, O Muhammadans! If you do not apply the Qur'an and follow its laws to the letter, Allah will metamorphose your hearts and dismiss them from His door. Do not be like those each of "whom Allah has knowingly sent astray" (from 45.23).

If you acquire knowledge for the sake of the creatures you will end up serving them, and if you acquire knowledge for the sake of Allah (mighty and glorified is He) you will serve Him. The deeds of obedience are the work of the people of Paradise and the deeds of disobedience are the work of the people of the Fire. Other than that, it is up to Him whether to reward one of us without good work or to punish one of us without bad work. All that is up to Him: "[He is] One who certainly works His will" (from 11.107) and "He shall not be questioned as to what He does, but they shall be questioned" (21.23).

⊛ O young man, you are nothing other than a lower self, natural inclination, and passion! You spend time with strange women and young boys then you say: "I am not interested in them!" You are a liar. Neither the Law nor reason agree with what you say. You add fire to fire and firewood to firewood, so there is no doubt that the house of your religion and faith will catch fire. The Law's disapproval of this behavior is universal, exempting no one.

Acquire faith, knowingness of Allah (mighty and glorified is He), and strength of nearness first and then open up a clinic and be a physician for the creatures, acting on behalf of the True One (mighty and glorified is He). Woe to you! How can you touch and handle snakes when you have no expertise in snake handling and have not taken the antidote? You are blind, so how can you cure the eyes of people? You are mute, so how can you teach people? You are ignorant, so how can you practice religion?

How can the person who knows no usher bring people to the door of the king? You have no right to utter a single word until you experience a resurrection and witness wonders.

Be sincere in your actions; otherwise, do not lay claims. Once you have cut off all relations and closed the doors and ways, the direction of the True One and His nearness will open to you, the way to Him will be paved for you, and the finest, best, and noblest things will come to you. This world is ephemeral, evanescent, and vanishing. It is the abode of tribulations, afflictions, grieves, and cares. No one will have a perfect life in this world, especially if he is a wise man. As the saying goes, "the wise man who remembers death will never find the delight of his eye in this world." As for the person who has a lion whose mouth is wide open standing next to him, how can he settle and how can his eyes drop off to sleep? O unaware ones, the mouth of the grave is wide open, the mouths of the lion and the snake of death are wide open! The executioner of the sultan of destiny is carrying the sword in his hand, waiting for the command. Only one in a million is in this state of wisdom — wakeful and free of unawareness. The vigilant person has renounced everything, saying: "O my God, You know what I want! You have favored your creatures with these plates, but I wish for a morsel from the plate of Your nearness. I want something from a thing that belongs to You."

⊛ The Prophet is reported to have said: "When the believer starts the prayer and his heart enters into the presence of His Lord (mighty and glorified is He), tents of light get erected around him, angels stand around him, righteousness descends on him from heaven, and the True One (mighty and glorified is He) becomes proud of him." Among the praying people is one whose heart is snatched and taken to the True One (mighty and glorified is He) like the bird is snatched from the cage and like the child is snatched from the arms of his mother. He is taken from what is familiar to him, from what is known to him, and from his abode and is made to become unaware of himself to the extent that if he were to be torn apart and pierced throughout, he would not be aware of that. It has been reported that a righteous man from the honorable people of Allah, who was one of the followers of the companions of the Messenger (Allah's prayer and peace be on him), namely 'Aurwa bin Az-Zubayr bin Al-'Aawwām, a nephew of 'Āisha (may Allah be satisfied with her), had a gangrenous leg and was told that his leg must be amputated or he would die. He said to the physician: "Amputate it after I have started praying." The physician cut it off while he was in prostration so he did not feel the pain of the operation.

You are in illusion in comparison with those who lived before you. You are words with no action, an appearance with no essence, a scene with no substance. Woe to you! Do not be misled by what people say about you.

You know very well what you are involved in and what you are up to. Allah (high is He) has said: "No, the human being will be a proof against himself" (75.14). How good you are in the eyes of the common people and how ugly you are in the sight of the elite! A shaikh said to the seekers who follow him: "If you are wronged, do not do wrong. If you are praised, do not be happy. If you are dispraised do not be saddened. If you are accused of telling lies, do not get angry. If you are entrusted with something, do not show betrayal. If you are saddened, do not be sad." How good these words are! He ordered them to slay their lower selves and passions. This derives from the Prophet's (Allah's prayer and peace be on him) following saying: "Gabriel (peace be on him) once came to me and said: 'The True One (mighty and glorified is He) says to you: "Pardon the person who wrongs you, maintain a connection with the person who cuts you off, and give to the person who deprives you"'". Reflect on the signs of Allah (mighty and glorified is He), His acts, and His management of His creatures.

⊛ How can you talk about the spiritual states of the righteous people and claim to have attained these states yourself? Do not talk about the spiritual state of someone else and do not spend from the purse of another person. You read books and extract their words which you then use, misleading the audience into believing that these are the fruit of your own thinking and your powerful spiritual state and that they are utterances of your heart. Woe to you! Put their sayings into practice first and then speak so that your speech will be a chick of your deeds and the fruit of the tree of your works. This business is not achieved by merely visiting righteous people and memorizing their words, but by putting what they say into practice, behaving with ultimate politeness in their company, and thinking well of them, in all circumstances. The layperson is rewarded in proportion to the steps he takes with his feet, whereas one of the elite is rewarded in proportion to his spiritual aspiration. When all of the person's concerns become one single concern, the True One (mighty and glorified is He) will be One for him. If he turns his heart away from anyone other than Him, He (high is He) Himself will guard him. The Invincible One has said in His Book: "My guardian is Allah who sent down the Book, and He guards the righteous" (7.196).

⊛ O young man, while your faith is still weak you have to be concerned with your own affairs. Do not be concerned with your family, your neighbors, and the people of your town and county. When your faith has strengthened, come out to your family and children and then to the creatures. Do not emerge to them before protecting yourself with the armor of piety, covering the head of your heart with the helmet of faith, having in your hand the sword of the oneness of God and in your quiver arrows of answering the Caller, riding the horse of good guidance, and learning the art of attack and retreat, fight and thrust. If you attack the enemies of the True One (mighty and glorified is He) at this point, support and aid will come to you from your six directions: right and left, above and below, and in front and behind. You will snatch creatures from the hands of Satan and carry them to the door of the True One (mighty and glorified is He). The person who attains to this spiritual station will have the veils removed from the eyes of his heart. Whenever he turns to one of his six directions, his sight penetrates the veils and nothing remains screened from it. When he raises the head of his heart, he sees the Throne and the heavens, and when he lowers his head in reflection, he sees the levels of the earth and all its inhabitants of jinn, human beings, and wild beasts. Once you have attained to this spiritual station, you can summon the creatures to the door of Allah (mighty and glorified is He). Before this happens, you can achieve nothing. If you call the creatures when you are not at the door of the Creator, your call to them will be disastrous to you. Whenever you move, you go down; whenever you seek promotion, you get demoted. You have no clue about the righteous. You are tongue-wagging with no heart, an outward with no inward, a public life with no private life, and a tour with no attack. Your sword is made of wood and your arrows are matchsticks. You are a coward with no courage. The smallest arrow can kill you and send you to the Day of Resurrection. O Allah, strengthen our practice of religion, faith, and bodies with your nearness and "give us good in this world and good in the hereafter and protect us from the torment of the Fire."

⊛ When the servant becomes extinct to his lower self, passion, will, and the creatures, he will be in the hereafter by his essence and in this world only by his body. He will come to be in the Knowledge and grasp of Allah (mighty and glorified is He), swimming in the sea of His power. When the fear of this fearful person intensifies and his heart is about to be torn to pieces by fear, the True One (mighty and glorified is He) will draw him near, make Himself known to him, give him good news, and reassure him. The situation will be similar to how Joseph (prayer and peace be on our Prophet and on him) treated his brother Benjamin. He saw his brothers sitting together behind him, so he invited them to sit and eat in one place, but he gave to Benjamin a seat beside him and ate with him. When they finished eating he confided a secret to him: "I am your brother, Joseph," so he became very happy. Then Joseph said to him: "I would like to publicly implicate you in a theft and accuse you of stealing, so endure the test with patience." Benjamin's brothers were astonished at what happened between him and Joseph and they envied him as they previously envied Joseph. After he made Benjamin's robbery and disgrace public, Joseph conferred honor on him and drew him close to himself. The same applies to the believer. When Allah (mighty and glorified is He) befriends him He tests him with afflictions and tribulations, so if he endures them with patience, He confers on him honor and nearness.

⊛ O young man, do righteous works and take in return the nearness to the Lord of the worlds. As for the people of Paradise, "they shall be safe in the chambers" (from 34.37). They will be safe from the tribulations of this world, from having to endure poverty with patience, the death of children, illnesses, diseases, grieves, and cares. They will live safe from death, from drinking its glass again, and from the questioning of the angels Munkar and Nakīr. They will enter Paradise and the doors will be locked behind them. They will not leave Paradise, staying there forever. The real comfort of the people of Paradise is entering it.

⊛ If any of you work for the sake of Paradise, he should not count this as work. Work for the sake of the face of Allah. Do not lose your commitment to fasting, praying, and doing all kinds of good works, while being sincere in all. Master this outward matter, for putting it into practice carries you to the valley of Knowledge. Walk to the door of your Lord (mighty and glorified is He) with steps of faith and certitude. Then, you will see what no eye has ever seen, no ear has ever heard, and has never occurred to any human being. O hearts, listen! O eloquent ones, listen! O sensible ones, listen! The True One (mighty and glorified is He) did not address the children, but He addressed the mature adults — those with reason. He did not address the lower selves, but He addressed the hearts. The believers listened to His words, whereas the polytheists met His address with deafness. O Allah, awaken us from our sleep and draw a veil over our shortcomings in all circumstances! Draw a veil over our good and evil things. Do not involve us in dealings with anyone other than You, neither in praise nor in scandals; neither at the time of commendation, in which case we would become boastful, nor at the time of a scandal, as our shortcomings would be made public; let it be neither this nor that. Amen.

⊛ The people of Allah sought the neighbor before buying the house, the companion before traveling the way. What is this neighbor? It is drawing near to the True One (mighty and glorified is He), knowing Him, believing in Him, trusting Him, and having confidence in His promise. Their hearts have understood, so they shunned the abode of this world and the abode of the hereafter and stood aside from them. O unaware ones! The thing that I have explained comes about only through action and submerging into it, at times with the limbs and senses and at others with the heart. Speak sometimes, then be silent at others. Work sometimes, but give up action at others. Be embarrassed and close the eye of the heart so that it does not see your deeds. If you achieve this, you will be mobilized by Allah (mighty and glorified is He). It will be said to you: "move, advance, open your eyes, and see with the eyes of your head and the eyes of your heart what has come to you from Allah (mighty and glorified is He), through the hand of His destiny." The people of Allah always behave with humility and humbleness. They continue to do so until the One for whose sake they have humbled themselves raises them up.

⊛ Acquire knowledge for there is much good in it. Acquire knowledge and put it into practice in order to benefit from it. Knowledge is like the sword and action is like the hand. A sword without a hand cannot cut anything, and a hand without a sword also cannot make any cut. Acquire knowledge outwardly and work sincerely inwardly. You will not be given the smallest reward without sincerity. Listen to the Qur'an and apply it for the True One (mighty and glorified is He) revealed it in order to be used as a means for attaining to Him. It has two ends, one in His hand and one in our hands. If you grab it firmly, He will elevate your hearts to Him. He will snatch your hearts and place them in the abode of His nearness while you are still in this world, before the hereafter. If you wish to attain to Him, renounce this world and the creatures. Renounce yourself, your family, your property, your lustful desires, your dubious things, and the love for receiving praise, applause, and attention from the creatures. When you have genuinely renounced all these things, you will not need them. Your stomach will be fully fed, your belly will have sufficient water, your inward and your private life will prosper, your heart and your innermost being will become lit, and your lower self will calm down. All of this will result from the blessings of your putting the Qur'an into practice. This Qur'an is an illuminating sun so keep it in the houses of your hearts to light for you. Woe to you! If you put out the lamp, how can you see in the darkness of the night what is in front of you?

⊛ As for you, O preachers, you have got up to the position of the prophets (Allah's prayer and peace be on all of them) without credentials! You have advanced to the first row, yet you do not know the art of attack, retreat, and battle. Get down, learn, work, act with sincerity, and only then get up. This business comes about by striving against the lower self, passion, natural inclination, Satan, this world, and lustful desires; and by giving up any interest in the creatures and not viewing them as the source of harm and benefit. When you have overcome all these and overpowered them by the strength of your faith, certitude, and belief in the oneness of God, the True One will descend on your heart and your innermost being, allow them access to the house of His nearness, give them the authority to command His creatures, and send them back to the creatures. At this stage, you will have learned the art of attack and retreat which you will need when you mix with people and set yourself as an example for them. O Allah, employ us in what pleases You with us and "give us good in this world and good in the hereafter and protect us from the torment of the Fire."

⊛ O young man, practice pious restraint in relation to this world and the hereafter under all circumstances and then you will succeed. If you practice pious restraint, no argument against you will remain and Allah will be pleased with you. A righteous man was seen in a dream after his death and was asked: "What has Allah done to you?" He replied: "My Lord has forgiven me." He was asked: "On what account has Allah (mighty and glorified is He) done that to you?" He said: "One day I performed the ablution in a public bath and headed to the mosque. When I approached it I noticed on my leg a spot the size of a sliver coin that had not been touched by the water. So I returned and washed that area. The True One (mighty and glorified is He) said: 'I have forgiven you for your respect of My Law'".

Where do you stand in relation to the people whose "sides shun their beds" and who cannot sleep? How could they sleep when fear is disturbing them and wiping sleep from their eyes? They sleep only when they are overwhelmed by sleep while in prostration. So, glory be to Him who sends to them that favor of irresistible sleep so that their bodies can take a moment of rest. "Their sides shun their beds." Their beds reject their sides, and their sides cannot settle down on their beds — sometimes because of fear, sometimes because of hope, sometimes because of love, and at others because of longing. How little your fear of your Lord (mighty and glorified is He) is despite how little your obedience is! How great the fear of the righteous ones is despite how great their obedience to Him (mighty and glorified is He) is! When our Prophet Muhammad (Allah's prayer and peace be on him) used to pray, a whizzing in his breast like that of a kettle was heard. As for Abraham (prayer and peace be on our Prophet and on him), the humming of his breast when he prayed was heard from the distance of a mile, which equals three parasangs. They were in fear despite being truthful, prophets, intimate friends [of Allah], and lovers, and having their prayers answered. Tell me, what is exactly your state of affair? I can see that you have turned away from the middle and left the column, your feeling of intimacy with obedience has decreased and your sense of alienation with it has increased, and you have become content with earning very little good, while much of this world is too little to satisfy you. This is not the behavior of someone who knows that he will die, meet his Lord (mighty and glorified is He), and have his works paraded before him on the Day of Resurrection. This is not the behavior of someone who fears the reckoning and interrogation. This is not the behavior of someone who will descend into his grave having no idea whether it is one of the pits of the Fire or one of the gardens of Paradise.

The people of Allah fast during the day and spend the night in worship. When they feel exhausted they lay on the ground to rest. "Their sides shun their beds" so they wake up and resume their works. "They pray to their Lord in fear and hope" (from 32.16). They are afraid of rejection and hope for acceptance. They say: "O our Lord, our deeds are not righteous. They are imperfect. They are not done with sincerity. They are not devoid of self-admiration and vanity." Therefore, they are afraid of rejection and hope that their works be accepted for they know that He is generous, accepts what is little but gives very much. He accepts what is bad and counterfeit yet gives what is good. He accepts little, defective goods yet gives in full measure. Being afraid is a form of observing the strictest laws of religion, whereas being hopeful is a form of resorting to the special concessions. The people of Allah swing between fear and hope, at one time in this, at another in that; at one time with the outward, at another with the inward; at one time in a state of purity, at another in a state of impurity; at one time in a state of honor, at another in humiliation; at one time in a state of being given, at another in a state of having things withheld from them. They continue in this situation until the prescribed term is fulfilled and their hearts attain to their Creator. From then on, they will no more make use of the special concessions or have impurity but instead they will observe the strictest laws of religion and have total purity. The property will follow you to the door, your family will follow you to the grave and then return, whereas your works will accompany you, go down with you to the grave, and will not leave you.

⊛ Serve this King, the Creator, the Provider, the Benefactor, the One who "made the sun for a brightness and the moon a light" (from 10.5) and made the night for stillness. He drew your attention to favors and reckoned them so that you may thank Him for them. Then He said to you after reckoning them: "And if you reckon the favors of Allah you will never count them" (from 14.34). Anyone who comes to know the reality of the favors of Allah will find himself unable to be thankful for all of them and will be stunned by them. This is why Moses (prayer and peace be on our Prophet and on him) said: "O Allah, I thank You through my inability to thank You!" How little your gratitude is and how frequent your protest is! When you come to know Him, your tongues will be silent in His presence and your hearts and your limbs and senses will adhere to ultimate politeness under all circumstances. This is why the Prophet (Allah's prayer and peace be on him) has said: "When someone comes to know Allah, his tongue becomes exhausted." The knower acts as if he were mute and does not disclose the secrets that he knows except with His permission.

O young man, entrust yourself, your limbs and senses, your family, and your property to the True One (mighty and glorified is He) whose trusts are never lost. Move with your heart to Him for you will find with Him all that is good. Pay due respect to the Law, please the Prophet (Allah's prayer and peace be on him), follow in his footsteps, then enter into the presence of your Lord (mighty and glorified is He) on the feet of your Knowledge of Him, then enter into the presence of your Lord (mighty and glorified is He) on the feet of your deeds and your knowingness of Him. Accompany the Law until you reach the door. Once you have arrived, stop the Law there, ask it to pray for your safety and good fortune, and then enter to the house of your innermost being and essence. One of the righteous people is reported to have said: "Earning my livelihood by playing the drum and the pipe is closer to my heart than making a living by selling my religion."

⊛ How diverse your knowledge is, yet how few your works are! You have restricted your share of knowledge to memorizing and relating narratives and biographies. It would not benefit you at all to memorize certain Prophetic sayings and not put a single letter of them into practice. This will be evidence against you not in your favor. He says: "My shaikh is so-and-so," "I have accompanied so-and-so," "I have learned under the supervision of so-and-so," and "I have said such-as-such to the learned scholar so-and-so." All of this without action is worthless. The person who is truthful in his deeds bids farewell to the shaikhs, goes past them, and points out to them: "Stay in your place and I will go to the place that you showed me the way to." The shaikhs are a door, so is it any good that you remain at the door and never enter the house? "And Allah strikes parables for people" (from 14.25).

⊛ O you who claim to possess what you do not have, you will know the consequences of this in a while. You will know sooner or later the punishment for your claim! O learned scholars, O learners, knowledge is not in itself the goal but the aim is its fruit! What use is the tree that does not bear fruit? What is the fruit of knowledge other than works and sincerity? The Book and the Sunna are both tools to be used, so what is to be hoped of a tool if left unused? The workman earns his wage only after he has done his work and exerted efforts. You are not allowed to say anything unless you return from your journey into this world, the universe, and the creatures. When you arrive to Him, He will explain, disclose, and reveal to you. Allah (high is He) has said: "And be pious to Allah and [then] Allah will teach you" (from 2.282). And He (high is He) has said: "And whoever is pious to Allah He will appoint for him a way out, and He will provide for him from whence he did not expect" (from 65.2-3). Piety is the foundation of every good and the means for the arrival of worldly rewards, wisdom, and various kinds of Knowledge and for acquiring purity of the hearts and innermost beings.

⊛ The Prophet (Allah's prayer and peace be on him) is reported to have said: "The person who acquires knowledge, puts it into practice, and teaches others will be called 'great' in the kingdom of heaven." Reflect on what you are involved in and what you are up to. If you find that it is pleasing to Allah (mighty and glorified is He), adhere to it, but if you find that it is contrary to His pleasure, give it up. Practice pious restraint with respect to your food, drink, wife, house, speech, action, and inaction.

O young man, conceal the favors that you have. If you had to reveal them because of the intervention of someone else, this would be out of your control, but if it was you who revealed them, you would be punished. Ultimate politeness dictates that the teller should be someone other than you. Among the righteous there is one who sits in privacy, in a cell in the wilderness, on his shore, watching with his head and innermost being the emptiness of his stomach, feeling intimacy with his Lord (mighty and glorified is He). Then a righteous believer from the human beings, jinn, or angels passes by and says to him: "May Allah (mighty and glorified is He) comfort you, may Allah confer intimacy on you, may Allah bless you with His remembrance, O purified one, O preferred one, O pious one, O sincere one, O distinguished one, O favored one!" He will not raise his head to look at him and will not become conceited because of what he heard from him with his heart. He hears those words time after time, yet he behaves as if he never did. Should this man, and anyone like him, return to the creatures, he will become a physician for them in the hospital of this world. His medicines will be beneficial and effective. His medical kohl will stop the running of the tears of the eyes of the hearts and cure their diseases. He is healthy, so good health can be restored by him. He is alive, so life can be given by him. He is a light, so he is sought for illumination. He is food, so hunger can be satisfied by him. He is a drink, so thirst can be quenched by him. He is an intercessor, so his intercession will be accepted. He is a speaker, so his speech will be heard. He is a commander, so his commands will be obeyed. He is one who has the authority to forbid, so His prohibitions will be honored.

The people of Allah conceal what is in their hearts. They keep secret the various kinds of knowingness and Knowledge they have. The doors of their hearts are open in the direction of the house of nearness to their Lord (mighty and glorified is He) by night and day. They enjoy the hospitality of the guest-house of the hearts. Their hearts and innermost beings remain, by night and day, in the heaven where rewards descend from the True One (mighty and glorified is He). When the heart has become sound, it will become prefect — raises above everything, turns into a jewel, becomes pure, raises above all, becomes the gathering place of all good things, and becomes like the staff of Moses (prayer and peace be on our Prophet and on him) in which all sorts of good things were gathered for him. It has been suggested that Gabriel (prayer and peace be on our Prophet and on him) picked it from the plants of Paradise and handed it to Moses when he escaped from Pharaoh. It has also been suggested that Jacob (peace be on him) handed it to someone and it later reached Moses. Allah made the staff a miracle for the creatures, a source of strengthening and affirmation of the prophethood of Moses, and a means that brings to him various things. When Moses (prayer and peace be on our Prophet and on him) felt tired, the staff carried him and his belongings like a riding animal. When he came up against a river, it turned into a bridge for him to cross over. When an enemy of Moses appeared, it fought the enemy on his behalf. One day Moses (prayer and peace be on our Prophet and on him) was tending his sheep in a desolate wilderness, alone with no intimate companion other than his Lord (mighty and glorified is He), when sleep overcame him. He woke up to find a trace of blood on the end of his staff. Looking around, he found a huge dead serpent. He thanked Allah (high is He) for protecting him from its harm.

When Moses (prayer and peace be on our Prophet and on him) became hungry, the staff immediately turned into a tree and produced fruit for him to eat until he felt satisfied. When he became thirsty, it turned into a river so he drank from it until his thirst was quenched. When the heat of the sun became too intense for him, he placed the staff by his side so its shade protected him. This is what happens to the servant when his heart becomes sound and suitable for his Lord (mighty and glorified is He). It becomes endued with benefits for the creatures in general and for him in particular: general benefits and special benefits. Those that become manifest are for the creatures, whereas the hidden ones are for him. Those that are public are for the creatures, whereas the secret ones are for him.

The onset of this business is [the recitation of] "there is no God save Allah (lā ilāha illā Allah) (from 47.19), Muhammad is the Messenger of Allah (Muhammadun rasūlu Allah)" (from 48.29), and its final stage is seeing as equal: praise and dispraise, good and bad, benefit and harm, acceptance and rejection and people's attention and neglect. Rectify your practice of the first stage so that your practice of the second will become right. If you do not put your foot firm on the first step of the ladder, how can you climb up to the second? The works are judged by their final outcomes. Your declaration that "there is no God save Allah (lā ilāha illā Allah), Muhammad is the Messenger of Allah (Muhammadun rasūlu Allah)" is a claim, so where is the evidence [that you do believe in it]? The evidence is the belief in the oneness of God, sincerity, and applying the Law properly and giving it its due.

⊛ Woe to you! Do not attend the sessions of nonpracticing scholars! Do not vomit in their places what you drink in my presence, for that drink will not benefit you. These scholars are like laymen in comparison with those who act on their knowledge. The scholar who does not put his knowledge into practice is a layman, even if he has memorized all kinds of knowledge. Anyone who fails to come to know Allah (mighty and glorified is He) is a layman. Anyone who does not fear Allah (mighty and glorified is He) and does not have hope in Him is a layman. Anyone who is not pious to Him in his private and public lives is a layman. The truth of your spiritual states is as clear to me as this sun. You cannot find the right path. You are young men messing around and seeking to satisfy your lustful desires. You are slaves to the creatures, slaves to their giving and withholding, and slaves to their praise and dispraise. Do not try to conceal your faults from me, for I do not have any doubt. What is inside the door and outside it are one and the same to me. Everything in your hearts has left traces and marks on your faces. Glory be to the One who has placed me in front of you and set for me the test of preaching to you.

⊛ Woe to you! You have not perfected your practice of Islam, so how can you get up to this position and preach and teach the creatures? Get down, otherwise I shall take you down and make you land on your head. Religions differ from one another. The True One (mighty and glorified is He) defends His religion, separates between truth and falsehood, and deposes the hypocrite from his governing position, brings him down from his pulpit, and prevents him from lecturing to people. O hypocrites, have you not known that I have a comprehensive authority and that I am in charge of the affairs of religion? O all you creatures, by virtue of my reliance on Allah (mighty and glorified is He), I do not need you. Wealth is under my command, despite the fact that I do not possess a single atom of this world. If any creature gives me something, I see it as mere prattle for him to claim it to be his favor to me. I accept that thing as given to me from the hand of Allah (mighty and glorified is He). I see it as a favor from Allah not from him and I thank my Lord (mighty and glorified is He). And when I give someone a gift, I see it as a gracious enablement from Allah (mighty and glorified is He), that He has caused that gift to be given by means of my hand, so I see Allah (mighty and glorified is He) as the Giver not myself. You are given gifts in proportion to your aspiration, and gifts are withheld from you also in proportion to your spiritual aspiration. It is for this reason that the Prophet (Allah's prayer and peace be on him) has said: "Allah (mighty and glorified is He) loves the noblest of things and hates the lowest of things."

Spending on the Poor

⊛ Woe to you, O rich one! You must not think that offering thanks for your wealth is to merely say: "Praise be to Allah, the Lord of the worlds." The real giving of thanks is comforting the poor by giving them some of what you have. You must pay to them the obligatory alms, then you must console them by giving them further as much as you can. You must give them without reminding them that you are doing a favor to them, for this harms the hearts and makes the donation impure. Many of the poor would rather endure the fire of poverty than bear the fire of being reminded of the favor. Give the gift without deliberately reminding the receiver of your present, otherwise do not give at all. Have you not heard the following words of Allah (mighty and glorified is He): "O believers, do not make your alms void by reminding the recipient of your favor and causing harm" (from 2.264)? The nullification of alms means that they merit no reward, so the donor who reminds the recipient of his favor loses his money and reward and his heart becomes tarnished, because the donor's reminder to the recipient of his favor is an act of associating partners with Allah. The believer gives and does not give a reminder of his favor but he rather offers thanks to Allah (mighty and glorified is He) for enabling him to give alms. He believes that Allah (mighty and glorified is He) is the giver not himself. He believes that He is one with no partner, who takes from him and gives to others. He believes that it is He who gave him what he has and it is He who takes from him and gives to others.

O rich people, O You who have been granted affluence! Do not be misled by your wealth, do not boast of it, and do not use it to show arrogance to the poor, for this will cause your fall into poverty! And you, O young people, do not be misled by your youth and might over the poor, using your youth and might in acts of disobedience to Allah (mighty and glorified is He)! The works of disobedience are poison for the bodies of your religions. They are a beast that devours the flesh of your religions, good health, and wealth. How good this piece of poetry by one of them is:

If you were in a state of favor, take care to maintain it,
for the acts of disobedience remove the favors![21]

Come to me while thinking well of me and having no doubts about me. When you go back to your homes, remember this talk and do not forget it. Remember death and what is after it. You must keep up praying during the night and ensure that your mind is focused while you are in His

---

[21] This poetry is attributed to Muhammad Ash-Shāfiʿī (766-820) who is the founder of one of the major schools of Islamic law.

presence. Keep the fast for it enlightens the heart, particularly when you break your fast with lawful food. You will not earn anything without giving something. The men of knowledge and the men of wisdom are agreed that the state of bliss has to come to an end and that the real bliss can be attained only by renouncing bliss. One righteous man is reported to have spent forty years without sleep except when in prostration while praying. His prostration was his mattress, cover, and pillow. This is the state of affairs of someone who has renounced this world, wished for the hereafter, feared death and afflictions, renounced the creatures and what they have, wished for the Creator, knew what He has, and came to know Him, so he worshipped Him and fought against his lower self for His sake. The person who comes to know Allah (mighty and glorified is He) loves Him, and the person who loves Him obeys Him.

⊛ The believer exerts strenuous effort to give charitable donations from his possessions and prefer others to have them, for he knows that these charitable donations will be kept hidden for him should he need them. He exercises pious restraint and does not assume that everything he gets is pure and hence lawful. He, therefore, avoids many things in order to get one thing the root and branch of which he knows well. He tries hard to find reasons for donating anything in his possession to give to charity. He does not touch what he inherits from his father and mother saying to himself that they may have earned them while not exercising pious restraint, so he donates them to the poor and the needy.

⊛ O son of Adam, how stingy you are to yourself! Has He not asked you for a loan yet you refuse to lend Him? Have you not heard His (mighty and glorified is He) following words: "Who is he that will lend to Allah a good loan" (from 2.245)? If you give Him a loan through the hands of the poor, Allah will multiply it for you manifold and will give you, today and on the Day of Resurrection, much more than what you gave. Do business with Him and then you will make profit. Go ahead and do business with Him without putting Him to test first. When Imām Ja'far Aṣ-Ṣādiq (peace be on him) would find himself in need of five hundred gold coins while he had only fifty, he would donate the fifty gold coins so that a few days later five hundred gold coins would come his way. If the money would not come, however, he would not have doubts about his Lord (mighty and glorified is He), protest against Him, or accuse Him of niggardliness.

The people of Allah are accustomed to dealing with their Lord (mighty and glorified is He) according to His Book and the Sunna of His Messenger (Allah's prayer and peace be on him), with certitude in their hearts. It is reported that one day a righteous man had only three eggs when a beggar came to him asking for help. He said to his maidservant: "Give him those eggs." However, she gave the beggar only two and hid the third away. An hour later, a friend of the righteous man presented him with twenty eggs, so he turned to his maidservant asking: "How many eggs did you give to the beggar?" She replied: "I gave him two and left one for you to break your fast with." He said to her: "O you of little certitude, you have made us lose ten eggs!" The Prophet (Allah's prayer and peace be on him) is reported to have said: "The person who relies on a created thing like himself is under a curse."

O miserable one, when a poor person comes asking for a loan, go ahead and lend him and never say: "Who is going to give me?" You must disagree with your lower self and give him a loan, and after a while make it a donation to him. Among the poor is one who disapproves of begging for alms, preferring to ask for a loan, with every intention of paying it back. He has confidence in Allah (mighty and glorified is He), and on the basis on this confidence he borrows. So, if he approaches you for a loan, O wealthy one, lend him and never face him with a request to pay back, for this would further humiliate him. If a long time past without you receiving any repayment, go to see him, ask him to accept that loan as a gift, and absolve him of his obligation. Thus, you will be rewarded for his first joy [when you gave him the loan] and for his second one [when you turned the loan into a gift.] The Prophet (Allah's prayer and peace be on him) has said: "A beggar at the door is a gift from Allah (mighty and glorified is He) to his servant."

Woe to you! How can the beggar not be a gift from Allah (mighty and glorified is He) when he takes from your share in this world to add to your share in the hereafter? He saves for you something that you will find when you need it. The amount that you give him will vanish and disappear anyway, yet on account of giving it to him you will be promoted by several degrees in the eyes of Allah (mighty and glorified is He). Woe to you, O servants! Do not you feel ashamed that you worship your Lord so that He gives you Paradise, houris, and young servants? Paradise is the abode, but where is the Neighbor? One who seeks the face of Allah (mighty and glorified is He) is different from one who seeks Paradise, different from one who seeks this world, and different from one who seeks the creatures.

⊛ O people, you have to comfort the poor and give them preference over yourselves! When faith is still weak, you have to prefer them over yourselves. When faith is strong, you have to comfort them and prefer them over yourselves while smiling. Receive the poor with generosity or send them away in the kindest way when you have nothing to give. The Prophet (Allah's prayer and peace be on him) is reported to have said: "A beggar at the door is a gift from Allah (mighty and glorified is He) to his servant." Woe to you! You hate Allah's gift, reject it, and do not accept it? You will soon find out. Poverty will come to you, drive out your affluence, and replace it. Disease will come to you, drive out your good health, and replace it. Do not jeopardize the capital of favors that your Lord (mighty and glorified is He) has given you. The believer knows that the True One (mighty and glorified is He) sent the beggar to him so that He will give him from the favors that He has kept for him. He will find out that when he gives him, treats him with respect, and accepts to loan Allah through him, He will reward him with something that is more and better than his gift, both in this world and in the hereafter.

O backslider, you build relations with the sultans, the princes, and the rich seeking power and further worldly things, yet you do not do business with the King of kings, the Wealthiest of the wealthy, the One who never dies, the One who never becomes poor, the One who repays your loan to Him multiplied manifold! He gives you ten silver coins in return for everyone in this world, apart from your reward in the hereafter. He gives you blessings in this world and rewards you in the hereafter. Have you not heard that He (high is He) has said: "And what you spend He replaces it" (from 34.39)? O Allah, grant us [the favor of] working for You! Make it pleasant for us to serve You and stand at Your door among Your servants and "give us good in this world and good in the hereafter and protect us from the torment of the Fire."

⊛ Woe to you! If you shut your doors in the faces of the poor, Allah (mighty and glorified is He) will shut things up in your faces, and if you open your doors to them, Allah (mighty and glorified is He) will open up things for you. If you spend your wealth for the sake of the face of Allah (mighty and glorified is He), He will replace them for you, and if you spend them for the sake of the creatures, He will impoverish you. Spend and do not be stingy, for generosity is from Allah (mighty and glorified is He) and niggardliness is from Satan. Allah (high is He) has said: "Satan promises you poverty and orders you to commit indecency" (from 2.268). Allah (high is He) has promised you reimbursement of any expenditure as He (high is He) has said: "And what you spend He replaces it" (from 34.39).

Woe to you! You lay claim to Islam, yet you disagree with the Messenger (Allah's prayer and peace be on him) and introduce into his religion what your passion desires! You have lied about your embracement of Islam. You are not a follower but an innovator. You are not compliant but discordant. Have you not heard that the Prophet (Allah's prayer and peace be on him) has said: "Follow and do not introduce heretical innovations for you have been provided with all that you need" and: "I have left you on a clear, unambiguous way"? You reject his sayings and contradict his words yet claim that you follow him?

⊛ Worshipping is the relinquishment of habitual practice. Worshipping abrogates habitual practice. The Law abrogates habitual practices and removes them. Adhere to the Law of your Lord (mighty and glorified is He) and give up your habitual practices. The learned person stands on the side of worshipping, whereas the ignorant one stands on the side of habitual practices. Accustom yourselves, your children, and your family members to doing what is good and to continue doing so. Accustom your hands to charitable spending of material things of this world and accustom your hearts to renouncing them. Do not behave with niggardliness, withholding them from those who need them. Do not turn down the request for help, otherwise Allah (mighty and glorified is He) will reject your plea for help. How would not He turn down your request when you have turned down His gift? The Messenger of Allah (Allah's prayer and peace be on him) has said: "A beggar at the door is a gift from Allah (mighty and glorified is He) to his servant."

Woe to you! Do not you feel ashamed that you are sure of the poverty and hunger of your neighbor yet you deprive him of your help because of a false assumption? You say: "He has hidden gold but pretends to be poor!" You lay claim to faith, yet you go to sleep while your neighbor is starving, and you have a lot to spare but you do not give him anything! Your wealth will soon be snatched from your hand. Your feast will be taken from your hand. You will be humiliated and impoverished, and this world, which is your beloved darling, will abandon you. Give up this world by your own will not out of coercion.

Look at your allotted worldly shares, not at the shares of others. Be content with as little food as you need for survival and as little clothing as you need to cover your private parts. If anything else was destined for you, it will certainly come your way at the appointed time. This is how the intelligent and experienced people conduct themselves. They have relieved themselves of the burden of greed and humiliation. The ascetics have come to know this world. They have given it up on account of knowingness and experience. They have known that it comes forward then turns its back, gives then takes, enthrones then dethrones, loves then hates, fattens then devours, and raises to the top of the heads then lowers to the ground. Give it up with your hearts and your essences. Never drink from its breast. Never sleep in its lap. Never wish for it because of its ornament, the softness of its skin, its clothes, its nice speech, and the sweetness of its food, for its food is poisonous. It is deadly, charming, cunning, and perfidious. It is not the abode of permanent residence and honor. Look at what happened to those before you who went along with this world and how it treated them. Do not kill yourselves in your attempts to seek more things from this world, for it cannot give you more than your due. Give up seeking more. Hold up your tongue, behave politely, be content, and say: "Allah has spoken the truth concerning His promise, and the Messenger (Allah's prayer and peace be on him) has spoken the truth when he said: 'Your Lord has completed the creation, the assignment of subsistence, and the appointment of the times of things. The Pen with which He wrote everything that is to happen until the Day of Resurrection has already run dry,' and in saying: 'When Allah created the Pen He said to it: "Write!" It said: "What shall I write?" He (high is He) said: "Write down My decree about My creatures until the Day of Resurrection""".

Seclusion

⊛ Do not retire to your cell in the company of ignorance, for seclusion with ignorance is a total loss. This is why the Prophet (Allah's prayer and peace be on him) has said: "Acquire knowledge and then you may retire." It is not right for you to retire to a cell when you still have on the face of earth anyone whom you fear or pin hopes on. You must have only One whom you fear and only One whom you pin your hopes on: Allah (mighty and glorified is He). Worshipping means the relinquishment of habitual practice until the former replaces the latter. Do not seek attachment to this world, the hereafter, or the creatures, but be rather attached to the True One (mighty and glorified is He).

Do not try to pass off your counterfeit coins for the assayer is an expert. He will not accept any coin from you without testing it first with the touchstone. Throw away any counterfeit coins and consider them worthless. The assayer will not accept from you your metal before it has been put into the bellows and purified of the impurities, so do not think that it is an easy business.

Most of you lay claim to sincerity when in fact they are hypocrites. Were it not for the test, the claims would have been even more. When someone claims to be patient, we test him with exasperation. When someone claims to be generous, we test him with demands. When someone lays claim to something, we test him with its opposite. When the servant detaches himself from this world, the hereafter, and anything other than Allah and places his heart in the abode of His nearness, favor, and subtle kindness, He will not trouble him with providing his food, drink, or clothes or looking after his interests. His heart will be purified of any involvement in that.

⊛ This world is the abode of tribulation, and the greatest tribulations are the lustful desires of the belly and of the genitals. What benefit would the unmarried man derive from breaking his fast during the daytime, wandering in the marketplaces, indulging in lustful desires and pleasures and spending time in the company of human devils, by whom I mean bad mates? It is like starting the fire of lustful desire in the firewood of the lower self. O Allah, strengthen us to strive against our lower selves, grant us sustenance, and guide us so that we guide people! Enlighten our hearts and make us a light from which people seek illumination. Give us the drink of your intimacy so that our thirst will be quenched and anyone who is thirsty will quench his thirst through us. Grant us gifts and satisfaction and inspire us with thankfulness in the state of being given favors and satisfaction in the state of having them withheld and having the doors closed. Confirm our truthfulness and obliterate our lies and falsehood. Amen.

⊛ O young man, retire from kingship if you wish for the permanent company of the King of kings. Kingship is a veil from the King, favor is a veil from the Benefactor, and tribulation is a veil from the One who causes it. Attachment to the creatures, who are made and fashioned, is shackles to the hearts, innermost beings, and essences. When Allah (mighty and glorified is He) wants to confer a lot of good on someone, He fetters him, makes him stand in His presence on the feet of his heart, and provides him with a pair of wings to fly in the air of His Knowledge and then seek refuge in the tower of His nearness. Despite that, He will impose on him fear, the renunciation of any interests, and the abandonment of any sense of conceit as a result of his state. He will fear that the hand of Divine jealousy might clip his wings and screen him off from knowing Him after he has known what is there. As long as the servant is in this world, he must have fear and give up any sense of vanity, regardless of the spiritual state that he attains. This is so because this world is the abode of change and replacement, whereas the hereafter is the abode of permanence wherein no change or replacement takes place.

⊛ O young man, pass through the market of the creatures. Enter from one door and leave from another. Move away from them with your heart and intention and be like a lone bird that does not offer intimacy or accept it. Make sure that you do not see others and do not show yourself to them. Be like this until the appointed time comes to pass and your heart draws near to the door of your Lord (mighty and glorified is He). You will see the hearts of the people of Allah there. They will receive you, say to you "congratulations on your safety," and kiss you on the forehead. The hand of subtle kindness will then come from inside, receive you, carry you, conduct you in a solemn procession, approach you, feed you, quench your thirst, and anoint you with perfume. It will then take you out and seat you at the door, watching and waiting for any questing seeker who will come. You will take him by the hand and hand him to the hand that received you when you arrived. When this has happened to you, come out to the creatures and be among them like the physician among the sick, like a man of reason among the insane, and like a compassionate father among his children. Before this happens, you remain unworthy of respect! You would be a hypocrite with the creatures, a servant for them, and a follower who works for their purposes. You think you are medicating them when in fact you are associating them with Allah. Your treatment of them turns into a form of punishment for you because it is based on ignorance and inexperience. This is why the Prophet (Allah's prayer and peace be on him) has said: "The person who worships Allah with ignorance causes more damage than good."

Solitude

✧ In the beginning there is discomfort and at the end there is tranquility. Our Prophet Muhammad (Allah's prayer and peace be on him) was made to love solitude. One day he heard someone saying: "O Muhammad, O Muhammad!" He ran away from that voice and did not know what it was. This kept happening to him for some time. He then knew what it was so he stood firm. The voice then disappeared, so he became depressed, wandered in the mountains, and was even about to throw himself off.

In the beginning he used to run away, whereas later he started seeking. In the first stage there is discomfort, whereas in the second there is tranquility. The seeker quests, whereas one who is sought after is quested. Moses (prayer and peace be on our Prophet and on him) was a seeker, whereas our Prophet (Allah's prayer and peace be on him) was sought after. Moses remained in the shadow of his own presence and his request to see Him on the mountain of Ṭūr in Sinai. Our Prophet (Allah's prayer and peace be on him) was one of the sought after, so he was granted the vision without requesting it and he was drawn near without endeavor or request. He was enriched without requesting affluence and he saw what is behind the veil without any quest.

Moses (prayer and peace be on our Prophet and on him) requested the vision, so he was denied it and was made to pay with a proportionate punishment for requesting what was not allotted to him in this world. Our Prophet (Allah's prayer and peace be on him) behaved with ultimate politeness, recognized his status, strived, behaved with humility, and never transgressed, so he was given what was not given to anyone else. This happened because of his neglect of anything other than the True One (mighty and glorified is He) and his compliance with Him.

Greed and over keenness are detested. Be content with whatever has been allotted to you by your Lord (mighty and glorified is He); be satisfied with it. The person who endures with patience will achieve attainment. When the person endures with patience, his heart will become rich and his poverty will be removed. You have to resort to solitude so that you can worship with sincerity, for loneliness is better than bad companions.

It is related that a righteous man had a dog about which he was asked: "Why do not you abandon this dog?" He replied: "It is better than a bad companion." How could not the righteous love solitude when their hearts are filled with intimacy with their Lord (mighty and glorified is He)? How could not they escape from fellow creatures when their hearts do not see their benefit and harm, as they see the True One (mighty and glorified is He) as the source of benefit and harm? The wine of nearness revives them, whereas soberness leaves them dead. The speech of yearning draws them near and the revelation of secrets to them is their Paradise. They are lunatic as far as fellow creatures are concerned, but sensible, wise, and knowledgeable in the sight of Allah (mighty and glorified is He). The person who wishes to be an ascetic must be like this. Otherwise, there is no point in making any effort.

O man of affectation, O man of artificiality, O you who is submerged in prattle! This business cannot be achieved by fasting by day, keeping vigil to worship by night, and practicing austerity in diet and dress, yet with the existence of the lower self, vagaries, natural inclination, wretchedness, ignorance, and interests in the creatures. This business cannot be done without His guidance. Woe to you! Act with sincerity and detach yourself, for there maybe some hidden things that you are not aware of. Be truthful and then you will attain and become near to Him. Lift up your aspiration and then you will rise high. Surrender and then you will be saved. Comply and then you will be granted success. Be satisfied and then you will be satisfied with. Hurry up and act and then the True One (mighty and glorified is He) will complete for you what you set out to do. O Allah, take charge of our affairs in this world and the hereafter, do not assign us to ourselves or to any of your creatures, and "give us good in this world and good in the hereafter and protect us from the torment of the Fire."

The Definition of the Sufi

⊛ Woe to you! You claim to be a Sufi, yet you are impure! The Sufi is one whose inward and outward have become pure by following the Book of Allah and the Sunna of the Messenger of Allah (Allah's prayer and peace be on him). As his purity increases, he further emerges from the sea of his existence and gives up his will, choice, and volition.

When someone's heart becomes pure, the Prophet (Allah's prayer and peace be on him) becomes an ambassador between him and his Lord (mighty and glorified is He), as Gabriel did. The foundation of good is to follow the Prophet (Allah's prayer and peace be on him) in both his words and works. When the heart of the servant becomes pure, he will see the Prophet (Allah's prayer and peace be on him), commanding him to do this and prohibiting him from doing that. He will become totally a heart. He will retire with full knowledge. He will become an innermost being with no publicity, purity with no impurity. Clear up everything from the heart. Pulling out the firm mountains requires mattocks of strife and enduring with patience the sufferings and the arrival of tribulations.

Extinction

⊛ If you continue to behave properly, you will come to see with the eye of certitude and become as the Commander of the Believers 'Alī bin abī Ṭālib (may Allah be satisfied with him and ennoble his face) has said: "Should the veil be removed, I would not have more certitude." He was also asked: "Have you seen your Lord?" He replied: "I would not worship a Lord that I have not seen." A certain righteous man was asked: "Have you seen your Lord?" He answered: "If I have not I would have died." If then someone would ask: "How can you see Him?" I would say that if the creatures left the servant's heart and nothing remained in it other than the True One (mighty and glorified is He), he will see Him and draw as near to Him as he likes. He will see Him inwardly as others see Him outwardly. He will see as the Prophet (Allah's prayer and peace be on him) saw in the night of the Heavenly Ascension, as he likes. His Lord will make such a servant see Him, draw near to Him, and talk to him in his sleep. He may also attract his heart to Him in wakefulness and close the eyes of his existence so the servant sees Him with His eye as He outwardly is. And He will give him another essence with which he sees Him. He will see His attributes, blessings, favors, and beneficence to him. He will see His bounty and protection.

The person whose servitude, servanthood, and knowingness have been realized will not say "show me" or "do not show me," "give me" or "do not give me." He will become extinct, fully absorbed. Therefore, a certain righteous person who attained to this spiritual station used to say: "Why would I care about myself?" How good this saying is! He meant: "I am His slave, and the slave has no choice or will in relation to the master."

A man once bought a slave who was of the people of religion and righteousness. He said: "O slave, what would you like to eat?" The slave replied: "Whatever you feed me." The master asked: "What kind of clothes would you like to wear?" The slave answered: "Whatever clothes you give me." The master then asked: "Where would you like to live in my house?" The slave replied: "Wherever you put me." The master asked: "What kind of work would you like to do?" The slave answered: "Whatever you order me to do." At this point, the master wept and said: "Blessed are you! If only I am with my Lord (mighty and glorified is He) as you are with me!" The slave then said: "O master, does the slave have any choice and will in the company of his master?" The master said: "You are a free man for the sake of Allah and I want you to stay with me so that I serve you with myself and my wealth." As for anyone who knows Allah, Allah will not leave for him will or choice, and he will come to say: "Why would I care about myself?" He will not challenge destiny about his affairs or others' affairs.

⊛ When the heart of the servant becomes connected to his Lord (mighty and glorified is He), He becomes his physician and intimate companion so that no one medicates him other than Him and no one becomes his intimate companion other than Him. David (prayer and peace be on our Prophet and on him) used to say: "O Allah, I have visited all the physicians of Your servants and all of them have referred me to You! O Guide of the bewildered ones, guide me to You!" When someone loves Allah (mighty and glorified is He), his heart becomes a total longing [for Him], total detachment [from anything apart from Him], and total extinction [in Him]. No doubt, all his concerns become one concern.

The reality of unveiling completes only after emerging from the veils. If you wish for attainment to Him, give up this world, the hereafter, and everything from beneath the Throne down to beneath the surface of the earth. Each one of the creatures is a veil except the Messenger (Allah's prayer and peace be on him), for he is the door: "And what the Messenger gives you, take; and what he forbids you, abstain from" (from 59.7). Following him is not a veil but rather the means of attainment.

Pardoning

⊛ O young man! Do all that you can to obey Allah, your Lord. Make strenuous efforts to give to the person who deprives you, maintain a connection with the person who cuts you off, and pardon the person who wrongs you. Make every effort to ensure that your body is with the servants but your heart is with the Lord of the servants. Do all that you can to speak the truth and never tell lies. Make strenuous efforts to work with sincerity and avoid hypocrisy. Luqmān the Wise used to say: "O my son, do not put on a show to impress people for you will not meet Allah (mighty and glorified is He) as long as your heart is infidel!"

The Light of the Believer

⊛ If the believer is endued with a light by which he sees, how could the same not be true of the truthful person who is drawn near? The believer has a light by which he sees, therefore the Messenger (Allah's prayer and peace be on him) has warned of his sight saying: "Beware of the insight of the believer for he sees by the light of Allah (high is He)". The knower who is drawn near is also given a light by which he sees his nearness to his Lord (mighty and glorified is He) and the nearness of his Lord (mighty and glorified is He) to his heart. He also sees the spirits of the angels, the souls of the prophets, the hearts and souls of the truthful, and their spiritual states and spiritual stations. All of this happens deep in his heart and in the purity of his innermost being. He is always in happiness with his Lord. He is a mediator, taking from Him and distributing to the creatures. Among them (the people of God) there are those who are knowledgeable with both tongue and heart and there are those whose hearts are knowledgeable but their tongues are inept.

⊛ The ambition of the worshipful ascetic is for miracles in this world and for gardens of Paradise in the hereafter, whereas the ambition of the knower is for his faith to remain intact in this world and for salvation from the Fire in the hereafter. His ambitions and desires will continue to be for these until his heart is told: "What is this? Calm down and be steadfast. Faith is firmly established in you and from you the believers can take a light for their faith. Tomorrow (on the Day of Resurrection) you will be asked to intercede and your word will be accepted. You will be a cause for the salvation from the Fire for many creatures. You will be in the presence of your Prophet (Allah's prayer and peace be on him) who is the master of intercessors. So, switch your concern to something else." This is a sealed assurance of the permanence of faith, knowingness, safety in the hereafter, and walking in the company of the prophets, messengers, and the truthful who are the elite among the creatures.

⊛ The truthful person sees by the light of Allah (mighty and glorified is He), not by the light of his eye or by the light of the sun and the moon. This is the general light from Allah and he is given a special light also. Allah has given him this light after mastering the second light of Knowledge. O Allah, grant us Your Law, Knowledge, and nearness and "give us good in this world and good in the hereafter and protect us from the torment of the Fire."

⊛ When someone acquires knowledge and puts it into practice with sincerity, both the flint and the fuel will come to be in his heart. A light from Allah (mighty and glorified is He) will come to be in his heart which he and others use for illumination. Turn away, O sons of babble, O sons of pages composed by lower selves and passions! Woe to you! You dispute what is written and predestined? You will lose and perish, whereas His writings will not change. How can the foreordination and foreknowledge be changed by your effort? Be believers, Muslims. Have you not heard His following words: "Those who believed in Our signs and were Muslims" (43.69)?

✸ O young man, you have not established Islam firmly, so how can you be a believer? You have not perfected faith, so how can you have certitude? You have not established certitude firmly, so how can you be a knower, saint, or spiritual substitute? You have not established knowingness, sainthood, and spiritual substitution firmly, so how can you be a lover and extinct to yourself and existing through Him only? How can you call yourself a Muslim when both the Book and the Sunna have delivered their laws concerning your affairs yet you have not applied these laws or followed them? The person who seeks Allah (mighty and glorified is He) will find Him and the person who strives for His sake will be guided by Him because He said in the manifest verses of His Book: "And those who strive in Our cause, We will certainly guide them to Our ways" (from 29.69). He is not a wrongdoer and He does not love wrongdoing. He (high is He) does not wrong the servants. He gives things in return for nothing, so how much more would He give in return for something? The Invincible One has said: "Is the reward of goodness anything but goodness?" (55.60). Whoever does good in this world, Allah will do him good in this world and in the hereafter.

✸ Worshipping is the closest thing to the believer. Performing prayer is the closest thing to himself. He sits in his house, while his heart waits for the muezzin,[22] who is the caller of the True One (mighty and glorified is He). When he hears the prayer call, happiness fills his heart and it flies to the mosques and places of prayer. He feels happy when a beggar comes to him, and if he has anything he gives it to him. He does so because he has heard the words of the Prophet (Allah's prayer and peace be on him): "A beggar at the door is a gift from Allah (mighty and glorified is He) to his servant." How could he fail to rejoice when His Lord (mighty and glorified is He) has come asking him for a loan through the hand of the poor man? The Prophet (Allah's prayer and peace be on him) is reported to have said: "Allah (mighty and glorified is He) will say to His faithful servants on the Day of Resurrection: 'You have preferred this world to the first world and you have preferred worshipping Me to your lustful desires. By My invincibility and exaltation, I have not created Paradise but for you'". This is what He will say

---

[22] The person who proclaims the times of prayer in the mosque.

to the former, whereas He will say to the lovers: "You have preferred Me to all My creatures, the first world, and this world, and you have evicted the creatures from your hearts and removed them from your innermost beings. Therefore, My face is for you, My nearness is for you, and My intimacy is for you. You are My true servants."

⊛ O young man, when someone does good works, they become a light in front of him and a riding animal beneath him. The deeds of his heart appear on his face and his face becomes like the full moon. He becomes like an angel who is drawn near. His heart feels happy because of what he sees of Allah's generosity to him. His deeds bring him the good tidings of what Allah (high is He) has prepared for him in Paradise. The good works assume a form and say to him: "I am your weeping, patience, piety, faith, certitude, prayer, fasting, striving, longing for your Lord (mighty and glorified is He), knowingness of Him, Knowledge of Him, good action, and good conduct and behavior in His (mighty and glorified is He) presence." Thus, his burden will be lifted from him, his fear will turn into security, and his hardship into prosperity. As for one who did no righteous works and waged war against his Lord (mighty and glorified is He) with the gravest of sins, he will carry the weight and burden of his acts of disobedience on his back, will have hunger and thirst inside, and fear and humiliation will show on him. The angels will drive him from behind while he crawls and drags himself until he attends the parades of the Resurrection. Then he will be subjected to interrogation and reckoning. He will receive a severe reckoning and then he will be cast into the Fire to be tormented. If he is one of the people who believe in the oneness of God, he will be punished in proportion to his evil deeds and then Allah (mighty and glorified is He) will save him from the Fire by His mercy. But if he is one of the people of disbelief, he will be left forever in the Fire with those of his kind.

⊛ The believer knows the creatures. He is able to recognize signs in them. His heart is sensitive. He can see by the light of Allah (mighty and glorified is He) who placed the light in his heart. The real light is the light of the hearts and the real cleanness is the cleanness of the hearts, innermost beings, and private lives. If your heart and private life are unclean, what would the cleanness of your outward benefit you? Even if you bathed yourself a thousand times each day, nothing of the dirt of your heart will disappear. The acts of disobedience have a nasty smell that is recognizable by those who see by the light of Allah, but they keep what they know about the creatures to themselves and do not expose them.

Woe to you! You are lazy. No doubt you will not achieve anything. Your neighbors, brothers, and relatives traveled and searched so they found treasures. They made a profit of ten or twenty silver coins and returned with their earnings, whereas you have been sitting in your place.

The little that you have will soon finish and you will start begging from people. Woe to you! Strive on the way of the True One (mighty and glorified is He) and do not rely on His destiny. Have you not heard His following saying: "And those who strive in Our cause, We will certainly guide them to Our ways" (from 29.69)?

Strive and then guidance will come to you. It will not come to you because of you, yet you have to be involved. It will not come about through you alone. Make a start and others will then come and complete your work for you. Everything is in the hand of Allah (mighty and glorified is He), so do not ask for anything from anyone else. Have you not heard Him say in His Book: "And there is not a thing but with Us are its storehouses; and we send it down only in a known measure" (15.21)? Is there anything else to be said after this verse? O seeker of the gold coin and the silver one, they are nothing! They are both in the hand of Allah (mighty and glorified is He) so do not try to obtain them from the creatures. Do not ask for them with the tongue of your attribution of partners to Allah and your reliance on means. O Allah, O Creator of the creatures, O Creator of all means, save us from the fetters of associating Your creatures and means with You and "give us good in this world and good in the hereafter and protect us from the torment of the Fire!"

❀ Each one of you will soon remember what he achieved in terms of believing in the oneness of God and attributing partners to Him, in terms of hypocrisy and sincerity. On that day, the Fire of hell will be made visible to those who are sighted. All those who are present at the Resurrection will see it and become terrified of it except a few individuals. When it sees a believer, it dies away and subsides so that he can pass safely through. This is why the Prophet (Allah's prayer and peace be on him) is reported to have said: "On the Day of Resurrection, the Fire will say: 'Pass through, O believer, for your light has put out my flames'"! It will call on him before he passes through it: "Hurry up, pass through, do not keep me back from doing my business, for my business is with others, not you." Passing through it is inevitable for the Muslim and the disbeliever, for the obedient one and the disobedient one. Once the foot of the believer has rested on the path that is stretched across it, the Fire will die away, subside, and say to him: "Pass through. Your light has put out my flames." Some of the believers will pass through it without even seeing it, so when they enter Paradise they will ask: "Has Allah (mighty and glorified is He) not said: 'And there is not one who will not come to it' (from 19.71)? We did not see it!" They will be told: "You passed through it while it was abating."

❀ The believer keeps on affirming his faith until he becomes a knower of Allah (mighty and glorified is He), knowledgeable of Him, and near to

Him. Once he has reached this stage, he will prefer Him over everything else and distribute his wealth on the entourage who are standing at the door, so entering the house of nearness will become his only concern. He will return the key to his castle in Paradise to its keeper. His innermost being will come to the doors of the gardens of Paradise and lock them up. He will shut the doors of the creatures and existence. He will throw himself at the door of the King, behave as if he was ill, and fall like a piece of motionless meat, waiting for the feet of subtle kindness to pass by and tread on him, waiting for a glimpse from the eye of mercy and for an extension of the hand of generosity and favor. While he is in this state, he will suddenly find himself in the chamber of nearness; on the lap of subtle kindness; in the hands of the Subtly Kind One, the Expert, who will medicate him, restore strength to him, entertain him, confer on him kingship, jewelry, and crowns, feed him from the food of favor, and offer him drinks of intimacy. Mercy will then have arrived at the house of nearness and happiness will have arrived at the balconies of attainment. All creatures will become beneath him, whereas he looks at them with the eye of mercy and graciousness. He will acquire the attributes of the True One (mighty and glorified is He), because the hearts of those who attain to Him become filled with mercy to the creatures. They look at both the Muslims and disbelievers, common people and the elite, with the eye of mercy. They have mercy for all of them, but at the same time they demand from them observing the limits of the Law. They demand outwardly but have mercy inwardly. O servants of Allah, when you meet anyone of these people, serve him and listen to what he has to say for he gives you good advice!

Denouncing this World

⊛ Woe to you! You are unceasingly busy accumulating one gold coin on top of another. These will be scorpions and snakes that will bite you. The gold coin is the house of fire and the silver coin is the house of cares. This world is an abode of engagements and the hereafter is an abode of terrors, and the servant is between them until he is finally made to settle, either in Paradise or in the Fire. O young man, do not consume that whose branch and root you do not know, for the consumption of prohibited things darkens the heart. How could the impatient person consume what is lawful? The person who consumes only lawful things is one who has patience to fight his lower self, passion, and devil. It is the patient warrior who consumes lawful things only. O Allah, grant us what is lawful and keep us away from the unlawful! Grant us from Your favor, good, and nearness, and grant our hearts, innermost beings, and limbs and senses from the same. Amen.

⊛ The wealth that you have is not yours but it is rather a deposit that has been entrusted to you. It is to be shared between yourselves and the poor. Do not appropriate the deposit, otherwise its Owner will take it from you. When one of you cooks a pot of food, he must not eat from it alone; he must feed from it his neighbor, the beggar who comes to his door, and the guest who asks for hospitality. Do not turn away the beggars when you are capable of giving them, for turning them away results in the removal of the favors. The Prophet (Allah's prayer and peace be on him) is reported to have said: "When someone turns a beggar away from his door without an acceptable excuse, the guardian angels will not come close to his door for forty mornings." You have made it common practice for your tongues to say the following when beggars come: "May Allah ease your hardship. May Allah help you!" You turn him away despite your ability to give him. What makes you certain that Allah would not enrich him and impoverish you? Woe to you! Were not you poor without a single atom then Allah enriched you, removed your poverty, and increased your benefits and sustenance beyond your expectations? Then, He sent to you a poor person, someone whom He referred to you, to console him with something of what He has given you, yet you turn him away in disappointment and do not accept His assignment. He will soon re-possess all that He has given you, return you to your poverty and beggary, cast hardness toward you in the hearts of the creatures, and at the same time leave you with little patience. O Allah, grant us wakefulness before death, repentance before death, guidance before death, knowingness before death, doing business with You before death, returning to Your door before death, and entering to the abode of Your nearness before death! Amen.

⚇ O slaves of this world, O slaves of the hereafter! You are ignorant of Allah (mighty and glorified is He); of this world, which is His; and of the hereafter, which is His! You are walls. As for you, this world is your idol; and as for you, the hereafter is your idol. In your case, lustful desires and pleasures are your idol; and in yours, praise, commendation, and people's acceptance of you are your idol. Everything other than Allah is an idol. The people of Allah wish for His face. Woe to you! The Resurrection is close to you. It is merely a nap followed by a wake-up. It is a retreat followed by an advance: "Is not the morning nigh?" (from 11.81).

The Day of Resurrection is the day of the pious, the day of the victory of the pious, the day of happiness of the pious. The pious are those who are so in both their private and public lives, in affliction and adversity, and in what they love and hate. They are the servants of Allah (mighty and glorified is He) and His brave men. They are the brave men and the heroes. They are the masters and the chiefs. They have the foundation of faith and its edifice. They avert attributing partners to Allah and hypocrisy, outwardly and inwardly. They renounce this world and the creatures. They do not satisfy the needs of their lower selves.

You will not attain nearness to Allah (mighty and glorified is He) until you leave everyone other than Him. How can you obtain what is in the presence of Allah when you love this world and work hard for it? When you donate some of your worldly possessions, you donate the worst of what you have! When fine food was brought to anyone of the righteous predecessors, he used to say to his servant: "Take this food to the house of the poor so-and-so." Do not you feel ashamed? When you have to pay obligatory alms, you produce the worst gold you have! You produce bad coins instead of good ones, silver instead of jewels. When you have something that is worth a gold coin, you evaluate it at half its real value in order to understate the obligatory alms that you must pay to the poor. And when you have in your possession some food, you donate what is unsavory and eat the tasty. You worship your lower self and you are unable to disagree with it. You are a follower of your passion, devil, and evil companions. The pious are free of any attachments to their families or relatives. They are one in a million. Do not exert any effort as Allah (mighty and glorified is He) will not accept from you other than what is pure. He will not give a seat at His table to someone unless he is clean. He does not allow on His table any meat other than what has been slaughtered by the hand of the person who will eat from that plate. He does not accept the meat of the dead. The seeker of the creatures and this world is a rotten, dead corpse. Attributing creatures and means to Allah is a filthy thing. Our Lord does not accept other than what is offered for the sake of His face. He does not take a share of anything that is not offered to Him exclusively. He relieves the partners attributed to Him from all obligations of this partnership.

⊛ You have made your only concern to work hard and secure your allotted shares in this world and protect them. You have forgotten death and what is after it. You have forgotten Allah and the fact that He can change things and left Him behind your backs. You have turned away from Him and accompanied this world, the creatures, and the means. Most of you worship the gold coin and the silver coin and neglect worshipping the Creator, the Provider. All these calamities are the product of your lower selves, so you have to imprison them in the jail of strife and you have to cut off their supplies and prevent them from acquiring what they like. Cut off their supplies so that all that they wish for will be a slice of dried bread and a drink of water. This will then come to be all that they long for. If you fatten them by satisfying all sorts of lustful desires, they will devour you. As one righteous person has said: "If you fatten your dog, it will devour you." What good is to be expected from them when Allah (high is He) has said about them: "surely the lower self commands committing evil, except such as my Lord bestows mercy on; my Lord is Forgiving, Merciful" (from 12.53)?

⊛ Woe to you! O servant of this world, O servant of the creatures, the cloak, the turban, the gold coin, the silver coin, praise, and dispraise! Woe to you! The whole of you is dedicated to this world, the whole of you is dedicated to things other than your Lord (mighty and glorified is He). Where is His share of you in your private and public lives? He has created you only to worship Him. Everyone who has reason, intelligence, and proper thinking worships his Lord (mighty and glorified is He) and consults Him in his affairs, whereas one who is reasonless does not do this, and his heart is metamorphosed because of his interest in the creatures and his love for this world.

Many people lay claim to Islam by their outward, yet they say as the disbelievers say: "There is nothing but our life in this world; we die and live, and nothing destroys us but time" (from 45.24). The disbelievers have said this and many of you say it but try to conceal it. They say it through the actions they commit, hence they are worthless in my eyes and they do not carry the weight of a gnat's wing; so what weight would they have the sight of the True One (mighty and glorified is He)? They have no reason and no faculty to distinguish between harm and benefit.

O servants of Allah, remember death and what is after it! Remember the True One (mighty and glorified is He) and His management of His creatures. Reflect on His Lordliness and greatness. Reflect on that when you have withdrawn from the company of your families and when the other eyes have gone to sleep. Once the heart has become suitable for

Allah (mighty and glorified is He), He will not allow it to remain involved
in buying and selling and relying on the means. He will distinguish it,
save it, raise it up from its fallen state, give it a seat at His door, and let it
sleep on the lap of His subtle kindness. O you who have turned away from
your Lord (mighty and glorified is He), you will see when the dust has
cleared! You will soon see the destruction of your house and the strike of
the True One (mighty and glorified is He) against you if you do not back
down from your wrongdoing, pay heed, and take notice.

Woe to you! The robe of your practice of Islam is shredded, the robe of
your faith is unclean. Your faith has no substance, your heart is not open
to Islam, your innermost being is impure, your breast is not expanded for
Islam, and your inward is in ruins although your outward is prospering.
The pages of your record are full, this world of yours which you love so
much is leaving, and the grave and the hereafter are approaching you. Pay
attention to your affairs and what you will be soon facing, for your death
may come today, or even this very hour, and you will be separated from
your hopes. The person who really knows what he is seeking sees
whatever he has to do as insignificant. The person who is truthful about
love does not sit with other than His Beloved. Someone may ask: "I have
heard about Paradise and the bliss it contains through His (mighty and
glorified is He) following words: 'And in it is all that the souls desire and the eyes
find sweet' (from 43.71), so what is its price?" We would answer: "Allah
(mighty and glorified is He) has said: 'Allah has bought from the believers their
lives and their wealth for the Paradise they are to have'" (from 9.111). Hand over the
soul and wealth and then Paradise will be yours.

⊛ O young man, there is no Paradise before this world and no getting
close to Paradise. The servant comes near this world and wishes to
possess it. Then once its shortcomings have become visible to him, he will
renounce it and come to be content from it with a single palm-date and
what is indispensable. He will take that from it with the hand of the Law,
piety, and pious restraint. He will take that with the hand of the heart not
the hand of the lower self, passion, and the Devil. When all this has
happened to him, Paradise will come to him, because renouncing this
world is the price that must be paid for Paradise and the key to it. So,
when his heart has entered it and his feet have settled there, he will be
able to walk, and its affairs will become easy for him. While he is in this
state he will see the men of the True One (mighty and glorified is He)
walking toward Him. He will ask them: "Where are you going?" They will
say: "To the door of the King." They will fill him with yearning for Him,
draw his attention to Him, urge him to renounce Paradise and what he
has, and say to him: "We are among those about whom Allah (mighty and
glorified is He) has said: 'They seek His face'" (from 6.52). The land of
Paradise will become too strait for him despite its spaciousness, and he
will seek to leave it, pleading to it: "Show me the door so that I can go out.

I have become like a bird in a cage. My heart is imprisoned in your jail, for the previous world is the prison of the believer, whereas you are the prison of the knower." He will then leave it running and catch up with the people who "seek His face." This is the way of the seekers. As for the way of those who are attracted, the lightening flash of nearness will snatch them at the first step not gradually and without means. O Allah, attract our hearts to You and "give us good in this world and good in the hereafter and protect us from the torment of the Fire."

⊛ No one can benefit from poverty other than the patient believer who practices pious restraint. How could he not be patient with it when this world is his prison? Have you ever seen a prisoner seek joy in his jail? The believer wishes to leave this world, wishes to escape from it. There is an enmity between himself and his lower self. He wishes for it enduring hunger, thirst, deprivation of clothing, and humiliation so that it can help him be obedient. Poverty is useful for him and he is able to endure it with patience. O traders of dates! Look after your dates and you will succeed!

Woe to you! You claim that you obey me, yet you travel away from me! You claim that you obey me; where are you going then? You are building walls. You work without sincerity, you start things but you never finish them, you are an outward with no inward, you are all about creatures with no Creator, you are full of this world with no hereafter, and you worship with no knowledge.

⊛ O young man, why do you care about this world? When it gives you things, it keeps you busy, and when it deprives you of things, it fills you with sighs of disappointment. If you have too little of this world you become weak, and if you have too much of it you feel too heavy. While any of you is in the midst of things that he loves, diseases, illnesses, grieves, and cares attack him. There is no benefit in it for anyone other than the person who spends it in obeying Allah (mighty and glorified is He).

⊛ O people, empty yourselves of the cares of this world as much as you can! Do not wish for something that will depart you soon. If the believer could renounce his food, drink, clothes, and wife, he would do. If he could rid himself of his lower self, natural inclination, and passion so that he would not seek anything other than his Lord (mighty and glorified is He), he would do. Prevent your tongues from talking about things that do not concern you. Increase your remembrance of your Lord (mighty and glorified is He). Stay at home and go out only when necessary and to attend the Friday prayer, collective prayers, and sessions of remembrance. If any of you can work from home, let him do so.

⊛ Every heart that is full of this world, lustful desires, and pleasures is a shell that is only suitable for the Fire. If you find in your heart anything from this world, you should know that you will be punished. Allah (high is He) has said: "I have not created the jinn and the human beings but to worship Me. I do not seek sustenance from them or ask them to feed Me. Allah is the Provider, the Powerful One, the Strong One" (51.56-58). Most of you are under an illusion — laying claim to Islam, yet possessing nothing of what Islam is about. Woe to you! The mere name of Islam will bring you no benefits. You rush to meet its requirements outwardly but not inwardly. Therefore, your work is worthless. Your outward is in the *miḥrāb*²³, but your inward is indulgent in dissimulation and hypocrisy. Your outward is the outward of a hermit, whereas your inward is full of unlawful things and you have a mistress at home! The Law will not call to your punishment outwardly because you have not shown any infringement. However, Knowledge will condemn you to hatred and castigation inwardly. Suppose that you escaped the punishment today, who would save you tomorrow [at the Resurrection]?

⊛ Respond to the Messenger, the Messenger of Allah (Allah's prayer and peace be on him), when he calls you to what revives you. What can a dead heart hear? How can it see? As for the heart that is dead because of its love for this world, love for the creatures, and pinning hopes on them, how can it hear or see?

Know this world and then you will renounce it. Know the lower self and then you will disobey it. Know the creatures and then you will renounce them. O you who are dead at heart because of seeking this world, wishing for it, and loving it! As for you, O ascetics, your quest for Paradise has constrained you from attaining to your Lord (mighty and glorified is He)! Woe to you! You have missed the way. Get the neighbor before the house, and the companion before the way.

⊛ If you glorify this world's tyrants, Pharaohs, kings, and rich yet forget Allah (mighty and glorified is He) and do not glorify Him, the verdict on you will be as the verdict on the idol worshipper. Those whom you glorify will become your idols. Worship the Creator of the idols and then the idols will humble themselves to you. Draw near to Allah (mighty and glorified is He) and then the creatures will come near to you. As much as you glorify Allah (mighty and glorified is He), His creatures glorify you. As much as you love the Creator, the creatures love you. As much as you fear Him, His creatures fear you. As much as you honor His commandments and prohibitions, His creatures honor you.

⊛ O seekers of this world, O lovers of this world, is it other than a

---

²³ A niche in a mosque showing the direction of Mecca.

temporary maidservant in comparison with Paradise? Paradise is the resident female slave. Paradise is the lady. Aḥmad bin Ḥanbal (may Allah, high is He, show mercy to him) used to say: "I feel sorry for hearts that have been corrupted by the love of this world although they have memorized the Qur'an."

⊛ You earn instead of religion worldly status and you amass rents, gold coins, clothes, houses, maidservants, horses, and servants. All these things will soon be separated from you. Return to your Lord. Reverse your actions in order to succeed. Give up falsehood, confusion, and madness. What is the point in collecting something that you will have to leave for others to inherit while you will alone face the reckoning and interrogation about it? You will not benefit even a single atom from what you accumulate. Nothing of it will fall into your hand, yet it is you who will have to face the reckoning, punishment, loss, and regret. You have no reason. Buy reason from me. Sit in front of me and listen to the good advice that I offer you. I know what you do not know and I see of the hereafter what you cannot see. Woe to you! It is righteous works that protect you from the torment when you are in your graves. The Prophet (Allah's prayer and peace be on him) is reported to have said: "When the believer is taken down into his grave, the charitable alms [that he gave] will sit at his head, his prayer to his right, his fasting to his left, and patience at his feet. The torment will then approach him near his head, so the charitable alms will say: 'There is no way for you from my side.' Then it will approach him from the right, so prayer will say: 'There is no way for you from my side.' It will then approach him from the left, so fasting will say: 'There is no way for you from my side.' Then patience will say [to the charitable alms, prayer, and fasting]: 'I am at the ready, if you need me I will help you'".

⊛ Be in this world with renouncing hearts. Do not settle in it as if it is the homeland, for it is not the homeland or the abode of permanent residence. There is another homeland. This abode is the prison of the believer in comparison with the abode of the hereafter. Therefore, the Prophet (Allah's prayer and peace be on him) has said: "This world is the believer's prison and the disbeliever's Paradise." It remains his prison even if he lives a thousand years in it, enjoying its bliss, whereas the hereafter is his salvation, happiness, Paradise, bliss, reward, empire, authority, and wealth. As for the practicing, truthful knower, his reward will be available in this world before the hereafter, which is nearness to his Lord (mighty and glorified is He). He wishes that Paradise will never be created. He sees the Resurrection and paradise too crowded. He can see that the Resurrection will result in the disclosure of his secret because on that Day the innermost beings will show on the faces. He can see that he will be raised from his grave covered with jewels and dressed up in fine clothes and will be received by processions and youths of Paradise, yet his heart is ever renouncing all that. He hates crowdedness for he feels completely satisfied with his Lord (mighty and glorified is He). He loves the Benefactor not the benefits. He loves to enter into the presence of the King from the door of the innermost being not in processions. He dislikes crossing Paradise because he has given up everything other than Him. He wishes not to see Paradise so that he will not become attached to it, he will not be changed by it, his footsteps will not end before reaching his Lord (mighty and glorified is He), and he will not be occupied with anything other than Him. What a loser is one who does not come to know Allah (mighty and glorified is He) in this world before the hereafter, smell the breeze of His nearness, eat from His food and His grace, and quench his thirst by the drink of His intimacy.

⊛ The Prophet (Allah's prayer and peace be on him) is reported to have said: "Woe to the person who leaves his dependents behind him with good things but come to meet his Lord with bad things!" I find that this is what the majority of you do. They amass silver and gold coins with a hand that is not the hand of pious restraint and leave them to their families and children to inherit. The reckoning will be for them to face, whereas it will be for others to enjoy the wealth they left. Sorrow will be for them to suffer, whereas joy will be for others. O you who will leave this world to others to inherit, listen to the words of your Prophet (Allah's prayer and peace be on him)! Do not leave for them what is unlawful and come to meet Allah (mighty and glorified is He) in the company of evil and torment. The hypocrite entrusts his children to the wealth that he leaves for them to inherit, whereas the believer entrusts his children to his Lord (mighty and glorified is He). Even if he were to leave for them this entire world with all that it has, he would not entrust them to it. He is experienced and well aware that many people placed their children in the care of the wealth they left for them, yet their children were humiliated and impoverished and begged from people. The blessing was taken away from the wealth they left for them. The blessing disappeared from it because it was not collected by the hand of pious restraint and because they relied on it, placed their children in its care, and forgot their Lord (mighty and glorified is He).

The hypocrites are slaves of the creatures, the silver and gold coins, authority, power, and earnings, and they are slaves of the wealthy, kings, and sultans, while they are enemies of the person who calls them to their Lord (mighty and glorified is He), guides them to Him, and shows them the ugliness of what they are involved in. The believers are always with their Lord (mighty and glorified is He), in affliction and in adversity, in hardship and in prosperity, at times of being given and at times of having things withheld from him, in good health and in sickness, in poverty and in affluence, when people gather around them and when people keep away from them, and under all circumstances. Their hearts do not leave Him, not even for a single moment. They are Muslims, submissive, obedient, satisfied, and compliant. They have given up disputation. They are unconscious and nothing awakens them other than the commandments and prohibitions.

⊛ The hour of courage is an hour of patience. Repent all of you this moment, with all of your hearts. Remember death and what is after it. The Prophet (Allah's prayer and peace be on him) used to say: "Remember frequently the destroyer of pleasures, for whenever it is remembered, when there is little of something, it increases it, and when there is excess of something, it decreases it." Remembering death is a remedy for the disease of the lower selves and food and benefits for the hearts. Forgetting death hardens the heart and makes it too lazy to exercise obedience, whereas being concerned with the creatures and seeing them as the source of harm and benefit drive it into disbelief, darken it, and screen it off from its Lord (mighty and glorified is He). Reliance on the means decreases faith, puts out the light of certitude, screens off the heart from its Lord (mighty and glorified is He), invokes His hatred, causes it to fall from His grace, and locks up the door of His nearness.

Alas for you, how can you be prepared to die when you are in the state you are in now, with your hearts being empty of faith, certitude, belief in the oneness of God, sincerity, and knowingness of your Lord (mighty and glorified is He)? How great your objection to your Lord (mighty and glorified is He) is! Woe to you! Who do you think you are? How impertinent you are! You have made objecting to your Lord (mighty and glorified is He) by the night and day your only business. The person who objects to His Lord will not find the breeze of nearness — not even a single atom of it. Give up objecting to your Lord (mighty and glorified is He), O you whose hearts are impoverished, O you who have turned your backs to faith! O Allah, gather us together with those whom You love, separate us from those whom You hate, and "give us good in this world and good in the hereafter and protect us from the torment of the Fire."

⊛ O seekers of this world, as long as you are seeking her, you will remain in tiredness! She seeks anyone who runs away from her. She tests the person who escapes from her by running after him. If he looks back at her, she takes this as an indication that he is a liar. She will catch him, put him at her service, and then kill him. But if he does not look back at her, she will conclude that he is truthful and put herself at his service. The person can benefit from her only after renouncing her and running away from her. Run away from her, for she is a murderer, cheat, and witch. Leave her with your hearts before she leaves you. Renounce her before she renounces you. Do not marry her, but if you marry her do not let your religion be her dowry. She marries then gets divorced. How fast she marries and gets divorced! If you seek her by means of your religion then your religion will be her dowry, for the religion of the hypocrite is the dowry of this world, the blood of the martyred believer is the dowry of the hereafter, and the blood of the lover is the dowry of the nearness to the Master.

Woe to you! As long as you serve this world, she will harm you and will not do you any good. But if she comes to serve you, she will be beneficial to you and will not harm you. Evict her from your heart and then you will see her good, service, and humility. She appears to the believer's heart in the best form, wearing all kinds of ornaments. He asks her: "Who are you?" She answers: "I am this world." Then he turns away from her, and immediately her flaws become visible and its beauty turns into ugliness. Woe to you! You lay claim to renunciation of this world, yet you love the gold and silver coins, run after them, and humiliate yourself to the kings and wealthy people for their sake. You have lied in your claim to renunciation! One of the righteous people (may Allah show mercy to him) is reported to have said: "Once I saw in a dream a beautiful, attractive woman, so I asked her: 'who are you?' She replied: 'I am this world.' I said to her: 'I seek refuge in Allah from you and your evil.' She replied: 'Dislike the gold and silver coins and then you will be protected from my evil'".

O liars, one of the essential attributes of the person who is truthful in obeying the will of his Lord (mighty and glorified is He) is that he hates anything other than Him in both the inward and outward realms! The outward realm is represented by this world, its lustful desires, its sons and their possessions, the praise and commendation of creatures, and their welcoming attitude and acceptance. The inward realm is represented by Paradise and its bliss. Anyone who meets these requirements will be truly obeying the will of Allah. His heart will draw near to his Lord (mighty and glorified is He) and he will sit near to Him and be His guest. At this point, this world and its plate and the hereafter and its plate will both come. The former will come with its ornaments and the latter will come with its modesty. They will both become maidservants for him. Their plates will be for the lower self not for the heart. The food of this world and the hereafter is for the lower self, whereas the food of nearness is for the heart. What I am calling to is what Allah (mighty and glorified is He) wants His creatures to do, not what you call to.

O hypocrites, the sensible person is one who reflects on the ultimate consequences and is not deceived by how things appear at first. The sensible person is one who carefully reviews this world and the hereafter, both of which are maidservants for the people of Allah — serve them and obey their orders. He listens to this world describing itself, and the hereafter speaks to him, so he buys from it what is useful to him. He renounces this world because it is ephemeral and turns away from the hereafter because it is not eternal but a created thing and because it screens off from its Lord (mighty and glorified is He) anyone who binds himself to it and wishes for it instead of Him. This world will say to him: "Do not seek me and do not marry me for I keep moving from one house to another, from one king to another. Whenever I get married to someone, I kill him and seize his wealth. Beware of me for I change husbands continuously and I am murderous and perfidious. I do not keep my word with the person that I make a covenant with." The hereafter will say to him: "I am marked for buying and selling, as my Lord (mighty and glorified is He) has said: 'Allah has bought from the believers their lives and their wealth for the Paradise they are to have' (from 9.111). I can see on your face the mark of nearness, so do not buy me, for Allah (mighty and glorified is He) will not let you stay with me." So if he achieves this, abandons them, and distances himself from them seeking his Lord (mighty and glorified is He), He will send this world back to him so he will get his allotted shares thereof, without him doing that out of necessity, and He will return the hereafter to him to be his housekeeper.

O seekers of this and that, listen to me! O you who are ill with this and that! What I have explained to you is a medicine, so use it. When the person renounces something, that thing starts to seek him. Renounce the creatures so that the Creator will love you. The likeness of the beloved who is in the presence of Allah (high is He) is as the likeness of a patient on the lap of a gracious physician who personally attends to him.

O people, listen to my words and renounce this world for your desire for and love of it screen you off from the hereafter and from the nearness to your Lord (mighty and glorified is He) and blind the eyes of your hearts. Your stay with this world screens you off from the hereafter and your stay with the lower self screens you off from the True One (mighty and glorified is He). O ignorant ones, do not seek this world at the expense of your quest for the hereafter so you lose in the end! The hereafter is a mistress, whereas this world is her female slave; the slave follows the owner. This world is inferior and the hereafter is superior; the inferior one follows the superior. Do not eat the food of this world before taking the antidote which is the renunciation of this world and the departure from it with your heart, from the sea of wisdom to the sea of divine providence, from the medicine to the physician who teaches you how to differentiate between its poison and meat. Have you not heard and seen that the snake-charmer seizes the snake, slaughters it, cooks it, extracts its poison, and then eats its meat? The True One (mighty and glorified is He) assigns the poison of this world to the disbelievers, those who are arrogant to Him, and those who forget Him. He assigns its meat from which poison has been removed to those who believe in Him, who are humble to Him, who remember Him, and who forget everyone else. How would not He prepare pure meat for them when they are His guests?

He treats them as the lover treats the beloved. He extracts for them the sweet from the midst of the bitter and purity from the midst of impurity. As for those who are sought after, food, drink, clothes and all that they need are purified for them.

The would-be ascetic is someone who tries his best to make the right judgment about things — so sometimes he purifies things and sometimes he does not, sometimes he stands and sometimes he sits. As for the ascetic, most things have become clear. His right decisions are more than the wrong ones. For the knower, however, everything has become totally clear. He recognizes the difference between the pure and the contaminated. What is pure calls on him, revealing itself, and what is impure does likewise.

The people of Allah have had all their directions united, so that only one direction is left for them. The directions of the creatures have become too narrow for them, whereas the direction of the True One (mighty and glorified is He) has become wide-open for them. They have blocked the directions of the creatures by the hands of their truthfulness and opened the directions of the Creator by the hands of their hearts. No wonder, their hearts have expanded, grown, and become great, and protection has stood at the doors of their hearts preventing anyone from entering into them except their Owner and Creator. Every one of these people is like the sun and the moon in this world. They are its two sources of light. Their faces are turned toward the True One (mighty and glorified is He), whereas their backs face the creatures. If their faces would turn to this world, everything that grows on it would burn.

You are dead walking on the face of the earth. Be sensible. You have no reason. You are not one of the men of Allah. The men of Allah know the men of Allah. The men of Allah are not interested in knowing the chiefs and heads of the creatures.

Your words reveal what is in your heart. The tongue is the speaker of the heart. If you find that you love one person and hate another, do not love the former and hate the latter because of your lower self and your natural inclination, but scrutinize them both by the Book and the Sunna. If they approve of the one whom you love, continue to love him, and if they disapprove of him, discontinue your love. And if they approve of the one whom you hate, abandon your hatred to him, and if they disapprove of him, continue to hate him. Woe to you! You hate me because I speak the truth and take you to task. No one hates me and is ignorant of me other than one who is ignorant of Allah (mighty and glorified is He), given to much talk but little work. No one loves me but one who is knowledgeable of Allah (mighty and glorified is He), given to much work but little talk. Nearness to the True One has left me in no need of anything. There is plenty of water all around me and I am like a frog, so I cannot speak of what I know. I wait for the water to seep away and then I speak. Then, you hear the news about you and about others.

The Fruit of Knowledge

⊛ O knowledgeable scholar! If you were in possession of the fruit and blessing of knowledge you would not go to the doors of sultans seeking shares for your lower selves and lustful desires. The knowledgeable scholar has no legs with which he goes to the doors of the sultans and the creatures, and the ascetic has no hands with which he takes people's property.

⊛ O young man, do not behave like a grown-up cock when you are still a young chick inside an egg. You have no right to speak until your body has fully developed, your egg has cracked and released you, and you have become a young chicken beneath the wing of your mother, beneath the wing of the Law of your Prophet (prayer and peace be on him and on his family), until he feeds you so that your faith becomes strong and complete. When righteousness has flowed into you, you will start to pick your sustenance from the grains of the favor of your Lord (mighty and glorified is He). At this stage, you will become a rooster for the hens. You will comfort them, love them, become a guardian for them, deal with the tribulations, and sacrifice yourself for them. Once the servant has become sound, he will carry the burdens of the earth and the creatures and become a spiritual pivot for them. The Prophet is reported to have said: "The person who acquires knowledge, puts it into practice, and teaches others will be called 'great' in the kingdom of heaven."

I say about you what the Commander of the Believers 'Ali bin abi Talib (may Allah be satisfied with him and ennoble his face) has said: "I have within me so much Knowledge. If I could find those who can carry it and who are its real people, I would not have locked up the door of secrets and would have opened its gates and manufactured its keys, but [I say] 'O my innermost being keep the secrets hidden until its people come'"! Keep what you have as a secret, but if you are asked for it, disclose it. I cannot reveal all that I have, because some spiritual states should be kept secret.

Ibn Sam'un (may Allah, high is He, show mercy to him) used to say: "Believing what I say merits the degree of sainthood. If the person is already a saint, he will further rise in ranking." Such words are accepted, believed, and put into practice only by someone who serves the Law, acts in accordance with it, and sincerely complies with it. It is the guidance of the Book and the Sunna. He has succeeded, by Allah, the person who is brought up according to their teachings, who grows up while complying with them, and who never exceeds their limits; he has succeeded indeed. I am afraid that your practice of Islam and your faith are mere façade. Perfect your practice of Islam and your faith. This way your fear, fasting, prayer, and night vigil will increase. The people of Allah went wandering, joined the wild animals, and competed with them for the herbs of the earth and the water of the springs, with the sun becoming their sunshade and the moon and the stars their lamp. Exert strenuous efforts in performing works of obedience and acts that draw you near before you arrive in His presence. Do not wrong yourselves by disobeying Him and being impudent to Him. O Allah, grant us success in obeying You, keep us away from the acts of disobeying You, and "give us good in this world and good in the hereafter and protect us from the torment of the Fire."

⊛ By Allah, you are a liar under all circumstances. You do not know the way to the door of Allah (mighty and glorified is He). How can you point to it when you are blind? How can you guide others when you are blinded by your passion, natural inclination, and pursuit of your lower self, love for this world, superiority, and lustful desires? Woe to you! You love to stay in this world, therefore you will achieve nothing. When will you find the door of your Lord (mighty and glorified is He)? When will you put prayers before the business of your shop and your profits? When will you put the hereafter before your worldly interests? When will you put the Creator before the creatures? When will you put the beggar before yourself? When will you put obeying the commandments of Allah (mighty and glorified is He), observing His prohibitions, and enduring with patience the tribulations that come from Him before your passion and habitual practice? When will you put answering Him before answering His creatures?

O young man, be sensible! You are in sheer illusion. You are a falsehood with no truth, an outward with no inward, and a show of publicity with no substance. Come to me since the acts of disobedience are still on your outward, before they reach your heart and you become persistent and then persistence develops into disbelief. Do something before it is too late. Use the little that you have to get the great amount that you lack. Do something since the rope is still in your hand. The Prophet (prayer and peace be on him and on his family) has said: "The repentant sinner is like one who has never committed any sin, even if he kept sinning seventy times a day." If you listen to the Prophet (Allah's prayer and peace be on him), act in accordance with his words, and behave well in his company by following his companions, he will introduce your heart to your Lord (mighty and glorified is He) and let you hear His words. When someone's obedience to Allah and his servitude to Him have become confirmed, he will become capable of hearing His words.

⊛ If you borrow another person's words and utter them, pretending that they are yours, the hearts of the righteous people will hate you. If you do not have works that match those words, you do not have the right to speak. On the face of it, the matter looks to be wholly about work. Allah (high is He) has said: "Enter Paradise a reward for what you have done" (from 16.32). The believer does not make the angels weary with much babble and talk about things that do not concern him. Rather, his heart fears the True One (mighty and glorified is He), so no doubt his limbs and senses are also afraid of Him. The tongue of his heart keeps silent, so his mouth's tongue also does not speak. His heart calms down because of His majesty so his limbs and senses follow suit, leaving the angels restful and at ease.

⊛ Among the speakers there are some who speak from their hearts and others who speak from their lower selves, passions, and devils.

⊛ O people, seek to be steadfast in worshipping your Lord (mighty and glorified is He) for He has praised those who are obedient in His presence. The Prophet (Allah's prayer and peace be on him and on his family) is reported to have said: "When the servant has stood praying for a long time in His (mighty and glorified is He) presence, his sins will scatter away as the dry leaves fall down from the trees on a windy day." As the servant behaves truthfully in his obedience to his Lord (mighty and glorified is He), his sins scatter away from his outward, inward, and the whole of him; his heart will become enlightened and his innermost being will become pure.

Denouncing Hypocrisy

⊛ Woe to you! Do not be double-faced, double-tongued, and with two different kinds of work like so-and-so. I have been given the authority to confront every liar, hypocrite, and impostor. I have been given the authority to confront everyone who is disobedient to Allah (mighty and glorified is He), the greatest of whom is Iblīs and the smallest is the sinful person. I have been given the authority to fight everyone who has gone astray, leads others astray, and calls them to falsehood. In doing so, I seek the help of [the following words of remembrance]: "There is no might or strength but by Allah, the High, the Great (*lā ḥawla wa lā quwwata illā billāhi al-'Alīyi al-'Adhīm*)". O Allah, guide us to what makes You satisfied with us, and "give us good in this world and good in the hereafter and protect us from the torment of the Fire."

⊛ Woe to you! Hypocrisy has become firmly stuck to your heart, so you need Islam, repentance, and cutting the waistband [which Christians wear]. Be sensible! You will see when the dust has cleared whether you are riding a horse or donkey: "And you will know its tidings after a while" (38.88). The person who listens to my words, puts them into practice, and acts with sincerity will be one of those who are drawn near because these are words from the kernel with no shell.

⊛ As for the hypocrite, he has a clever tongue but a clumsy heart. All his knowledge is in his tongue. This is why the Prophet (prayer and peace be on him and on his family) has said: "The most that I fear for my nation is a hypocrite with a clever tongue."

⊛ O hypocrite, you will not succeed in this business through your hypocrisy and pretence! You can see your cunningness, you can see your acceptance by the hearts of people, but you cannot see what lies in front of you! You are a source of misfortune to yourself in this world and in the hereafter, and to those whom you teach and order to follow you. You are a dissimulator, impostor, and swindler in relation to people's property. No doubt, you will not have a prayer answered or a place in the hearts of the truthful. You have gone astray from Allah's (mighty and glorified is He) way with His knowledge. You will see when the dust has cleared whether you are riding a horse or donkey. When the dust has cleared, you will see the men of the True One (mighty and glorified is He) riding horses and thoroughbreds, whereas you are on a broken donkey behind them and the demons and devils will grasp you. The people of Allah attain to a state in which they have no prayer of supplication and make no requests. They do not ask for benefits to be brought or harms to be repelled. Their supplication will come to be at the command of their hearts, sometimes for themselves and sometimes for the creatures, so they utter the prayer of supplication while being unaware of what they are doing. O Allah, grant us ultimate politeness with You under all circumstances and "give us good in this world and good in the hereafter and protect us from the torment of the Fire."

❀ It is the habit of the believer to reflect first and then speak, whereas the hypocrite speaks first and then reflects. The tongue of the believer is behind his mind and heart, whereas the tongue of the hypocrite is in front of his mind and heart. O Allah, include us among the believers, do not include us with the hypocrites, and "give us good in this world and good in the hereafter and protect us from the torment of the Fire."

❀ May Allah confer no blessing on you, O hypocrites! How many you are! Your efforts are totally dedicated to cultivating your relationships with the creatures and undermining your relationships with the Creator. If you treat me as your enemy, this means that you are treating Allah (mighty and glorified is He) and His Messenger (Allah's prayer and peace be on him and on his family) as your enemies because I support them. Do not overstep the mark for "Allah has full control over His affair" (from 12.21).

Joseph's (prayer and peace be on our Prophet and on him) brothers tried hard to kill him but without success. How could they have succeeded when he is a king in the sight of Allah (mighty and glorified is He), one of His prophets, and one of the truthful elite, and when He had preordained that benefits would flow to the creatures through his hands? Similarly, the Jews tried to kill Jesus, the son of Mary (prayer and peace be on our Prophet and on them), because they became envious of him as a result of the marvelous signs and miracles that he performed, so Allah Almighty revealed to him that he must leave their country for Egypt. He left it, and this happened when he was thirteen years old. It was one of his relatives who took him and helped him to escape. Then his influence increased and he became well-known throughout that country, so a group of people decided to kill him but they failed for "Allah has full control over His affair." You are doing the same, O hypocrites of this age! You wish to kill me. You are unworthy of respect! You will be kept well short of that.

Force yourselves to perform works of obedience and refrain from acts of disobedience and reprehensible deeds and then this forcing will turn into a natural inclination. Try to understand the words of your Lord, put them into practice, and act sincerely in accordance with them. Our Lord (mighty and glorified is He) speaks a speech that can be heard and understood. In this world, Moses (prayer and peace be on our Prophet and on him) and Muhammad (Allah's prayer and peace be on him) heard His words. In the hereafter, the believers among His creatures will hear His speech. Our Lord can be seen. We shall see Him on the Day of

Resurrection as we now see the sun and moon. We have no doubt about this today and we shall have no doubt about it tomorrow [at the Resurrection]. Allah (mighty and glorified is He) has servants who are willing to sell Paradise and its contents for a glance [of Him]. Once He has established the truthfulness of their intentions and that they are irrevocably ready to trade Paradise for a single glimpse, He will make glimpses available to them indefinitely. He will make their nearness permanent. He will compensate them for the pleasures of Paradise with His nearness.

O you who are ignorant of Allah (mighty and glorified is He), His Messenger (Allah's prayer and peace be on him), and His men! Woe to you! Advance one step with the feet of your hearts to the food of the favor of Allah (mighty and glorified is He). Can you not see how I am putting it in front of you? Anyone of you who accuses me of telling lies will himself be called a liar by his clothes, his house, and the angels who surround him. I do not care about the accusation of telling lies that you level at me, O hypocrite, O impostor!

⊛ I can see that the majority of you make public any bad thing they come across and conceal any good thing that they see. Do not do that. You are not in charge of people. Leave people under Allah's (mighty and glorified is He) veil. Release people from your hands for their reckoning is a matter for their Lord. If you have known Allah (mighty and glorified is He), you will have shown mercy to His creatures and left their shortcomings undisclosed. If you have known Him, you will have ignored anyone other than Him and you will have known the others through Him. If you deal with Him, you will resent dealing with others. If you have known His door, your hearts will have turned away from the doors of others. If you have seen the favors to have come from Him, you will have thanked Him and forgotten thanking others. Ask Him to provide for your needs and do not ask others. Believe in His oneness and then you will be unified. The person who believes in His oneness will be unified. The person who seeks [Him] will find [Him]. The person who surrenders and submits [to Him] will be saved. The person who complies with His will will be granted success. The person who disputes with destiny will be destroyed.

⊛ O hypocrite, it is natural that you do not understand what I have to say because you disbelieve my words. If you want to comprehend and understand what I say, repent from your hypocrisy, act with sincerity, and renounce your worldly interests and anything other than your Master. The first stage of this business is declaring that "there is no God save Allah (lā ilāha illā Allah) (from 47.19), Muhammad is the Messenger of Allah (Muhammadun rasūlu Allah)" (from 48.29), and its last stage is seeing stones and clay as equal. I mean by "stone" the gold which is the beloved of the creatures and the thing they seek.

⊛ Suppose that you have succeeded in concealing your reality from the people of the Law, how can you hide yourself from the people of Knowledge who can see by the light of Allah (mighty and glorified is He) and are able to know the creatures by their marks? In the sight of the common people, you are one who performs the prayer, keeps the fast, is obedient, pays the obligatory alms, makes the pilgrimage, practices pious restraint, is pious, and is an ascetic. In the eyes of the people of Knowledge, however, you are a hypocrite, impostor, and inhabitant of hell. When you come into their presence, they see the ruins of your house and of the house of your religion. They see the traces of hypocrisy on your face. They know you from your marks but they do not utter a word. The nearness to the True One (mighty and glorified is He) has sealed their mouths, His covering has held their tongues, and the tongue of His generosity and patience has prevented them from speaking. Otherwise, their secrets would have become public.

O hypocrites, fulfill the requirements of Islam so that you acquire faith, certitude, knowingness, private conversation, direct speech, and discourse. Be sensible, do not be satisfied with the appearances and neglect the substance. Work and act with sincerity and then you will be saved. Serve the practicing knowledgeable scholars. The person who serves will himself be served. The person who acts with humility will be elevated. Give service and then you will become a master. Have you not heard this saying: "The master of the people is their servant"? You serve very well yourself, your wife, and your son but you hide your money away from the poor and spend it in satisfying your passions and purposes. Your wealth will soon vanish.

You are afraid of the watchman on your street and the ruler of your town more than you fear your Lord (mighty and glorified is He). You treat them with veneration and present them with gifts because they know that your home is in ruins and are aware of your scandals. Woe to you! Soon, your wealth will disappear and your friends, who are evil companions, will abandon you and become your enemies. The watchman on your street and the ruler of your town will spread the word about your disgrace because you do not pay them anymore. How would Allah (mighty and glorified is He) bless you when you are spending His favors on acts of disobedience to Him? Soon, you will start to beg but no one will give you a handout and the garbage dumps and sewage places will be your abode. It is also possible that the Angel of Death will come to you while you are in this situation and thus you will move from one misery to another. Be sensible and feel ashamed in the presence of Allah (mighty and glorified is He). This world will not last forever but the hereafter will. The lustful desires of this world do not last but the pleasures of the hereafter do. The believer sells this world for the hereafter and the creatures for the Creator.

⊛ O hypocrite, your time is being spent on nothing. O backslider, your time is being wasted and your capital is melting away, so no doubt you will make no profit. Your capital is your religion, and since you are using your capital to consume worldly things, you are in effect consuming your religion, so it is diminishing and vanishing. It vanishes through your work for the sake of the creatures and your quest for fame, the gold coin, the silver coin, social prestige, and acceptance [by the creatures]. You are the enemy of Allah (mighty and glorified is He). You are hated by Him, by the hearts of the truthful among His servants, and by His angels. The angels curse you, the earth under you curses you, the sky above you curses you, and your clothes curse you. So you are cursed by the Creator and by the creatures. Have you not known that the hypocrite is "in the lowest depths of the Fire" (from 4.145)? Surrender (become a Muslim) and then repent. Do something before death surprises you, before you are suddenly overtaken and end up in regret when regret is useless. I know you but I cannot point at you. We are commanded in the Law to leave you and others unexposed. But I speak out, however, without mentioning names. I refer to you indirectly, without pointing to you explicitly. As the saying goes: "My words are aimed at you, so listen to what I am going to say to my neighbor." The slave may need to be beaten with a stick but a nod should be enough for a freeman.

The True One (high is He) looks at the private and public lives of the creatures and also at their hearts. He does not accept from them other than what they offer to Him and do for the sake of His face. Do not put on a show, do not cheat, and do not try to conceal your faults for "He knows the secret and what is yet more hidden" (from 20.7), and "He knows the treachery of the eyes and what the breasts conceal" (40.19).

⊛ How much I call on you but you do not hear me, and when you hear you pretend to be deaf and do not answer! How far you are! You are being called from a distant place. Your voice comes from the depths of the earth not from the castle of nearness and the shore of the sea of favor. Your whole concern is with your bellies, genitals, bodies, and amassing worldly goods. This is poison. Hunger is the food with which Allah (mighty and glorified is He) satisfies the stomachs of the truthful on earth. O you who are afraid of poverty, the real poverty is the fear of poverty, and the real affluence is being satisfied with Allah (mighty and glorified is He) not with the silver and gold coins! O young man, make yourself live the experience of the Resurrection [before it has come]! Enter with the feet of your reasoning to the Fire and Paradise and look at what is there with the eyes of your faith and certitude. The believer continues to work until both of his reasoning and sight come to be sound. After achieving this, he puts himself through the experience of the Resurrection. He stands in the presence of His Lord (mighty and glorified is He) and reads the scrolls of his works. He sees in them his good and bad deeds. He can see that his bad works have outnumbered his good ones and that because of his bad works he will fall into the Fire. He wishes to cross over the ṣirāṭ,[24] so he will step on it, poised between fear and hope, between falling to his death and crossing safely. While he is in this situation, Allah (mighty and glorified is He) will reach out to him with His mercy, giving the order for him to be brought back, widening the ṣirāṭ beneath his feet, and extinguishing with the water of His mercy the flames of the fire so that the fire will say to him: "Pass through, O believer, for your light has put out my flames!" The believer reflects on all of this, imagines it graphically, and believes in it as a fact. He keeps his belief in it until it becomes a matter of certainty for him.

⊛ One of the righteous is reported to have said: "The hypocrite remains in one and the same state for forty years, whereas the truthful person changes forty times every day." The hypocrite is involved with his lower self, passion, natural inclination, devil, and worldly interests. He never leaves their service. He never expresses an opinion that is different from theirs. He never says anything that contradicts what they say. His whole concern is with eating, drinking, dressing up, having sex, and amassing wealth. He does not care in what way he gets all that. He ensures the prosperity of his body and worldly affairs but ruins his heart and religion. He pleases the creatures but dissatisfies the Creator. The longer his hypocrisy lasts, the harder and darker his heart becomes, so he becomes more unmoved and undisturbed by any admonition, unable to learn a lesson from any advice, and incapable of remembering when he is given a reminder. No doubt, therefore, he remains in one and the same state for forty years. The truthful person, on the other hand, does not remain in one state because he is involved with the Transformer of hearts, submerged in the sea of His power, with one wave raising him up and another sending him down. With respect to the True One's (mighty and glorified is He) management of affairs, he is like a feather in the desert, like a stalk in the farmer's field, like the corpse in the hands of the washer of the dead, like the child on the lap of the nursing mother, and like the ball in front of the polo player's mallet. He has surrendered his outward and inward to Him and he is satisfied with His management of his affairs and His looking after him. He is not concerned with his eating, sleep, and lustful desires, but the whole of his concern is with the service of his Lord (mighty and glorified is He) and His satisfaction with him.

---

[24] A narrow bridge that every person will have to cross on the Day of Resurrection.

This is why a righteous man has said: "As for the people of Allah, their eating is like that of the sick, their sleep is like that of the drowned, and their speech is only uttered out of necessity." How could not they be like this when they have seen with their hearts what no one else has ever seen? They have forgotten everything other than their Lord (mighty and glorified is He). They have become unconscious as far as this world, the hereafter, and anything other than Him are concerned. They have camped at His door. They used compliance as their pillow at His doorstep, and content and satisfaction as their quilt, while the divine decree and destiny serve them, kiss them on the forehead, and carry them on their heads.

The Benefits of the Month of Ramadan

❀ O young man, the word Ramadan[25] consists of five letters: *rā'*, *mīm*, *dhād*, *alif*, and *nūn*. The *rā'* is derived from *raḥma* (mercy) and *ra'fa* (graciousness); the *mīm* from *mujāzāt* (recompense), *maḥabba* (love), and *minna* (favor); the *dhād* from *dhamān lilthawāb* (assurance of reward); the *alif* from *ulfa* (affinity) and *qurb* (nearness); and the *nūn* from *nūr* (light) and *nawāl* (earning of grace). If you give this month its due and act properly during it, these things will come to you from the True One (mighty and glorified is He). They will come to you in this world in the form of strength and enlightenment to your hearts, and as favors and earning of grace, outwardly and inwardly. In the hereafter there will come to you what no eye has ever seen, no ear has ever heard, and has never occurred to any human being.

Most of you are out of touch with Ramadan. Respect for any command comes in proportion to the respect shown to the commander. As for anyone who is out of touch with Allah (mighty and glorified is He), His Messenger, His prophets, and the righteous among His servants (prayer and peace be on our Prophet and on all of them), how can he be in touch with this month? Most of you have seen their fathers, mothers, and neighbors fast, so they joined them as a matter of habit not worship. They think that fasting is merely about abstaining from food and drink, so they do not fulfill its conditions and requirements.

O people, give up habitual practice and keep to worship. Fast for the sake of Allah (mighty and glorified is He). Do not get bored of fasting and worshipping in this month. Do righteous works during it, and make sure that you act with sincerity. Make a regular practice of doing the prayer of *tarāwīḥ*.[26] Illuminate the mosques, for this will be a light for you on the Day of Resurrection. If you obey and honor Allah (mighty and glorified is He) in this month, it will be an intercessor for you in the presence of your Lord (mighty and glorified is He) on the Day of Resurrection. Give fasting its due so that it gives you yours. Give it so that it gives you, becomes a witness for you in the presence of your Lord (mighty and glorified is He), praises you, and asks for you a share of His favor, generosity, blessings, grace, graciousness, subtle kindness, safekeeping, substance, and protection.

Woe to you! What benefit would you derive from fasting if you break it on unlawful food and sleep during these noble nights having committed acts of disobedience? Woe to you! You fast out of dissimulation and

---

[25] As written in the Arabic script.
[26] Special prayers performed in the month of Ramadan.

hypocrisy as long as you are among the creatures, and once you are on your own you break your fast! Then you come out and say: "I am keeping the fast," whereas throughout the day you are involved in verbal abuse, leveling defamatory accusations, swearing false oaths, and taking people's money by fraud, trickery, and exaction. This kind of fast does not do you any good and does not count as a fast. The Prophet (Allah's prayer and peace be on him) has said: "There are so many people who fast yet get nothing from it other than hunger and thirst, and there are so many people who spend the night worshipping yet earn nothing from it other than fatigue and vigil."

There are among you those who are Muslims outwardly but like idol-worshippers inwardly. Woe to you! Renew your practice of Islam, your repentance, your apology, and your sincerity so that your Master (mighty and glorified is He) will accept you and pardon your past sins. O you who are fasting, thank your Lord (mighty and glorified is He) for preparing you for the fast and enabling you to keep it! When one of you fasts, let his ears, sight, hands, legs, limbs and senses, and heart all fast. Let all his outward and all his inward fast. When you fast, give up telling lies, giving false witness, backbiting, defaming people, and embezzling their property. In principle, you fast in order to purify yourselves of your sins and keep away from them, so what would you benefit from your fast if you commit these sins yet again? Have you not heard these words of the Prophet (Allah's prayer and peace be on him): "The fast is a suit of armor (*junna*)", for it protects and covers the person who wears it? This is why the shield is called *mijanna*, because it protects its owner and prevents the arrows from striking him, and the person who is out of his mind is called *majnūn*, as his mind has been screened off.[27] The fast is a suit of armor for anyone who fasts with pious restraint, piety, and sincerity, for in this case it prevents the tribulations of this world and the hereafter from striking him.

O you who are fasting, comfort the poor and the needy with a share of your food at the time of breaking your fast for it increases your reward and is a sign of acceptance of your fast at the time of breaking it! All this will disappear and nothing will remain other than what you do in preparation for yourselves in the hereafter. Therefore, do such preparations as long as you can. On the Day of Resurrection, you will be gathered hungry, thirsty, naked, afraid, ashamed, and terrified. The person who feeds the poor and the needy in this world will be fed on that Day. The person who gives drink in this world will be given drink on that Day. The person who provides clothing for the poor and the needy in this world will be supplied with clothes on that Day. The person who is afraid and feels ashamed before the True One (mighty and glorified is He) in this world will be made to feel safe on that Day. The person who is

---

[27] The Arabic words *mijanna* and *majnūn* both share with *junna* the same root.

merciful to others in this world will have Allah (mighty and glorified is He) show mercy to him on that Day.

In this month, there is a night that is the greatest night of the year, which is *Laylatu Al-Qadr* (night of power).[28] This night has signs which the righteous can recognize. Among the servants of Allah (mighty and glorified is He) there are those who have the veil removed from their eyes so they see the light of divinity that is held in the hands of the angels, the light of their faces, the light of the doors of heaven, and the light of the face of the True One (mighty and glorified is He), because on that Night He manifests Himself to the people of the earth.

O people, do not make obtaining your food your concern because it is a low concern. You have been put to test by the need to eat and drink, but you have been spared the trouble of securing sustenance, so do not have any concern about it. Glory be to the Self-Sustained One who never eats or drinks. He gives but is never given substances, He feeds but is never fed, He is the Self-Sustained One who has no belly. He never eats, drinks, or sleeps. Your greedy keenness has increased, whereas your pious restraint and faith have decreased. Woe to you! This world lasts for only one hour, so spend it in obedience.

---

[28] The night on which the first verses of the Holy Qur'an were revealed to Prophet Muhammad (prayer and peace be on him).

The Benefit of Mercy

⊛ The Prophet (Allah's prayer and peace be on him) is reported to have said: "Gabriel has said to me: 'Allah will not treat mercifully anyone who does not show mercy to people'". Allah treats with mercy His merciful servants. Treat with mercy those who are on earth so that those who are in heaven treat you mercifully. O you who wish for mercy from Allah (mighty and glorified is He), weigh up its price and you will then get it. Its price is nothing other than showing mercy to His creatures, being compassionate with them, and treating them with good intention. You would like to get something for nothing, so you will get nothing. Pay the price first and then take the priced thing. Woe to you! You lay claim to knowingness of Allah (mighty and glorified is He), yet you show no mercy to His creatures! You have made a false claim. The knower treats with mercy every creature from the point of view of Knowledge, and he shows mercy to some people and not others from the viewpoint of the Law. The Law differentiates, whereas Knowledge unites. Allah (high is He) has said: "And enter the houses by their doors" (from 2.189).

The truthful, sincere, practicing shaikhs are the doors to the True One (mighty and glorified is He) and His ways to His nearness. They are the heirs and deputies of the prophets and messengers (prayer and peace be on them). They are the individuals whom the True One (mighty and glorified is He) has singled out and the ones who call to Him. They are ambassadors between Him and the creatures. They are the physicians of religion and the teachers of the creatures. Accept from them and serve them. Surrender your ignorant lower selves to their commandments and prohibitions.

All forms of sustenance are in the hand of Allah (mighty and glorified is He): the sustenance of the bodies, the sustenance of the hearts, and the sustenance of the innermost beings. So request them from Him not from someone else. The sustenance of the bodies is food and drink, the sustenance of the hearts is the belief in the oneness of Allah, and the sustenance of the innermost beings is the private remembrance [of Allah].

Show mercy to your lower selves by striving against them, instructing them to observe the commandments and prohibitions, and training them. Be merciful to the creatures by commanding them to do what is right, forbidding them from committing what is wrong, offering them truthful advice, and taking them by the hand to the door of their Lord (mighty and glorified is He). Mercy is one of the attributes of the believers, whereas harshness is one of the attributes of the disbelievers.

Maintain a connection with the person who cuts you off, give to the person who deprives you, and pardon the person who wrongs you. If you do this, your rope will be connected to the rope of Allah (high is He) and what you have will be connected to what He has, because these morals are among the morals of Allah (mighty and glorified is He). Respond to the call of the muezzins who call you to the mosques, which are the home of hospitality, the home of private conversation. Answer their call for you will find salvation and satisfaction in them. If you respond to the call of His caller, He will admit you to His house, answer your prayers, draw you near, teach you knowingness and Knowledge, show you what He has, teach your limbs and senses the proper conduct, clean your hearts, purify your innermost beings, confer on you guiding inspiration, place you in His presence, lead your hearts to the abode of His nearness, and give them permission to enter into His presence. He is generous. If you respond to His call and do not underestimate it, He will answer your prayers, treat you kindly, and confer favors on you. The Invincible One has said: "Is the reward of goodness anything but goodness?" (55.60). If you act properly, He will give you good rewards. The Prophet (Allah's prayer and peace be on him) has said: "As you treat others, you will be treated. As your state of affairs is, those who have authority over you will be. It is either in your favor or against you."

⊛ The Prophet (Allah's prayer and peace be on him) has said: "Keep to good manners in your social relationships with people so that when you are dead they pray for Allah to show mercy to you and when you are alive they yearn for you." Heed to this good advice. Tie it to your hearts and do not forget it. It points out to you an easy work that carries much reward. How good fine manners are! They are a source of comfort to the person who has them and to others. How detestable are bad manners! They are a source of fatigue to the person who has them and a source of harm to others.

The Prohibition of Injustice

⊛ O servants of Allah, beware of injustice for it results in darkness on the Day of Resurrection. Injustice darkens the heart and the face. Beware of the prayer of supplication of the wronged person. Beware of the weeping of the wronged person and of the burning in his heart. The believer does not die before revenge has been exacted on the person who did him injustice and before he has witnessed his death, the black signs of death covering his door, his children become orphans, the seizure of his property, and the transfer of his authority to someone else. When the believer's behavior becomes controlled by his heart, judgment will often be delivered not against him but in his favor, he will not be humiliated but humiliation will be inflicted [on others] in his favor, he will not have his shares reduced but reduction of the shares [of others] will be made to his advantage, and he will not have the women of his family exposed to publicity, humiliated, or surrendered to the hands of wrongful people.

⊛ O people, refrain from engaging in idle gossip, amassing worldly goods, and quarreling over them. You will be punished [at the Resurrection] on account of the worldly goods that you have in your hands if you do not give the dues of the poor and the needy and spend the rest in obedience to Allah (high is He) and in worshipping Him. Woe to you! You are trustees of this property, so do not you feel a sense of shame that you have neighbors who are poor and starving to death while you have turned away from them? Have you not heard His following words: "And spend of what He made you inherit" (from 57.7)? He has informed you that you have been appointed trustees of the wealth but you have considered it your personal property and engaged in mutiny, rebelling against Him. He has not commanded you to spend all of it on charity but appointed for the poor a specified entitlement which is the obligatory alms, expiatory gifts, and votive offerings. Discharge your obligations to the poor then discharge your obligations to the family and relatives. Comforting with charitable alms, in addition to giving the obligatory alms, is part of the good manners of the believer. The person who does business with Allah (mighty and glorified is He) makes profit. The Most Truthful of Speakers has said in His truthful Book: "And what you spend He replaces it" (from 34.39).

⊛ O people, do not do injustice to yourselves and do not do injustice to others. Injustice ruins homes, cuts off lineages, darkens hearts and faces, and decreases sustenance. Do not commit injustice for we will have a resurrection. We will certainly be resurrected. It will come soon. We have a Creator who will certainly make us stand before Him, call us to account, interrogate us, and ask us about what we did, be it insignificant or major, including the things that are as tiny as an atom. I am offering you good advice and I do not ask for a fee in return.

Do not come close to usury for this amounts to waging war against your Lord and causes the blessing to disappear from your property. Lend a gold coin for one gold coin. If anyone of you is able to give a loan to a poor person and after sometime donate it to him for the sake of Allah, let him do it. He will thus make him happy twice: the first time when he gives him the loan and the second when he turns the loan into a donation. Do this as an act of relying on your Lord (mighty and glorified is He) and having confidence in Him. He compensates, rewards, and gives blessings. Make strenuous efforts not to turn away a beggar. Give him whatever you can. Giving little is better than deprivation. If you have nothing at all to give, do not chide him, but send him away using kind words and never break his heart.

This world is a passage that is crossed as night and day alternate. When someone dies, he experiences his own resurrection and comes to know what he has to his credit and what he has against him. Everything has an opposite counterpart: well-being and affliction, good and evil, affluence and poverty, life and death, and honor and humiliation. All of these things are opposites. When one of them arrives, its opposite departs, and in the end there is death.

✿ The Prophet (Allah's prayer and peace be on him) is reported to have said: "Each one of you is a shepherd and responsible for his flock." The father will be held responsible for his children and his wife, and the children and the wife will be held responsible for him. Every master will be held responsible for his slave. Every slave will be held responsible for his master. The teacher will be held responsible for the pupils. The chief will be held responsible for the people of his village. The king will be held responsible for the people of his kingdom. The Commander of the Believers, who is the shepherd of all people, will be held responsible for his flock. There is no one among you who will not be held individually responsible.

Make every effort that you do not do injustice. Make every effort to give the rights to those who are entitled to them. Give gifts to one another. Show mercy to one another. Do not backbite one another. Do not subjugate one another. Help each other, ignore any wronging between yourselves, and do not expose each other's faults. Tolerate your wrongdoing to each other. Leave people under the veil of Allah (mighty and glorified is He). Command what is right and forbid what is wrong, without prying or spying. Denounce any wrongdoing that is apparent but do not concern yourselves with what may be hidden. Do not expose others' faults so that Allah (mighty and glorified is He) will not expose yours. The Prophet (Allah's prayer and peace be on him) loved refraining from exposing people's faults and hated keeping an eye on the shortcomings. Therefore he (Allah's prayer and peace be on him) has said: "Suspend the application of the punishments prescribed by the Law whenever there are doubts." He also said to 'Alī bin Abī Ṭālib (may Allah be satisfied with him and ennoble his face): "O 'Alī! Give evidence only on something [that is clear] like this," and he pointed to the sun.

O young man, the practice of beneficence is to give all that you are required to give and accept only some of what you are entitled to. If you can, donate all that is due to you and add more on top of it. This depends upon the strength of your faith, certitude, and confidence in your Lord (mighty and glorified is He). When you weigh some goods, tip the balance in the customer's favor, for thus Allah will tilt the balance in your favor on the Day of Resurrection. O you who are in charge of weighing, tilt the balance in favor of the person for whom you weigh so that the balance will be titled in your favor [in the hereafter]! It has been reported that the Prophet (Allah's prayer and peace be on him) once borrowed a few silver coins, and when he came to settle the debt he said to the man who weighs: "Weigh and tilt the balance in favor of the creditor." When anyone of you borrows something from another person, he should pay him back something that is better than what he borrowed from him and add some extra, even though this was not stipulated originally.

O people, buy from Allah the nearness to Allah (mighty and glorified is He), buy from Allah Allah! As for your allotted worldly shares, they and their dates of arrival have already been determined. They will not increase or decrease whether you seek them or not, whether you worship your Lord or disobey Him, whether you behave properly or badly. Those that are assigned for later dates cannot be made to come earlier and those that are assigned for earlier dates cannot be delayed. Allah is the Provider, whereas everyone else is provided for. He is the Wealthy One, whereas everyone else is poor. He is the Capable One, whereas everyone else is powerless. He is the One who sets things in motion, the One who causes things to come to a halt, the One who grants authority to someone over another, and the One who puts things at the command of others. All creatures are instruments in His hands. He has assigned a means for everything. Forget the creatures then the means and this world as far as your hearts, private lives, essences, and innermost beings are concerned. Evict from your hearts everything other than Him. Beware of the situation where He would look into your hearts while they quest for other than Him and wish for someone else. Submit and surrender to Him. Believe in the oneness of God and be consistent in this. Be satisfied with the preordained decree and be extinct to the One who preordains. Listen to your Lord (mighty and glorified is He), but be deaf to His creatures. Be deaf and blind as far as the creatures are concerned.

Neglecting What is of No Concern

⊛ The Prophet is reported to have said: "One result of the excellence of the person's practice of Islam is neglecting what does not concern him." Every person who practices Islam and applies it is interested in what is really relevant to him and turns away from what is irrelevant to him. Being busy with what is of no concern to you is the business of those who are idle and in illusion. The person who is deprived of the pleasure of His Master is he who did not act on what he was commanded but instead occupied himself with irrelevant things. This is deprivation itself, resentment itself, and banishment itself. Woe to you! Obey the commandments, refrain from the prohibitions, show acceptance at times of affliction, and then surrender yourself to the hand of destiny without asking "why" or "how." Allah's (mighty and glorified is He) care for you combined with His knowledge of you are better than your care for yourself combined with your ignorance of your Lord. Be satisfied with what He gives and occupy yourself with offering thanks for it. Do not ask Him for more, for you do not know where your best interest lies.

⊛ Give up the involvement in much babble and idol gossip and squandering money. Do not spend much time in the company of relatives, neighbors, friends, and acquaintances without good reason, for that is an illusion. Most of the telling of lies takes place between two, and disobedience does not happen but between two. None of you should go out of his home except to pursue essential personal and family interests. Make every effort not to be the first to speak and that your speech is only in answer to a question. When a person asks you about something, answer him only when there are benefits for both of you in doing so, otherwise do not answer him. When you see a Muslim brother do not ask him "where are you going to?" or "where are you coming from?" He may be unwilling to tell you about his personal affairs and thus he would lie, so it would be you who forced him to lie.

Feel a sense of shame from the Honorable Recording Angels (*Al-Kiram Al-Katibin*).[29] Do not dictate to them what you should not be saying. Dictate to them what would make you happy on the Day of Resurrection, words of glorification of Allah, recitation of the Qur'an, and words that relate to your and other creatures' interests. Increase their ink with your tears and strengthen their pens with your belief in the oneness of God, then leave them sitting at the door and enter into the presence of your Lord (mighty and glorified is He).

---

[29] These are the angles who record the works of every person.

Curtail hopes. Keep death in front of your eyes. When anyone of you comes across his brother, he should greet him and bid him farewell as if he is about to depart from this world. Similarly, when he leaves his home, he should greet his family with his heart, for the Messenger of Death may summon him and thus prevent him from returning to them. His final moment may be on the road. Therefore, the Prophet (Allah's prayer and peace be on him) has said: "None of you should sleep the night unless his will is written and placed under his head." If one of you has a debt and is capable of paying it back, he should repay it and not postpone the repayment, for he does not know whether or not he will have the opportunity to repay later. The person who is capable of repaying the debt but does not do is thus involved in wronging himself, because the Prophet (Allah's prayer and peace be on him) has said: "The postponement [of repayment] by the affluent person is an act of wrongdoing."

⊛ O young man, do not occupy yourself with what is irrelevant to you so you miss what concerns you! Thinking of the states of another person and his faults is of no concern to you, whereas reflecting on your states is of concern to you. All of the speech of the person with a lower self, passion, and natural inclination will be against him rather than in his favor. He is like the person who collects firewood by night so he does not know what he is gathering. When the lower self has calmed down and the fire of passion and natural inclination has subsided so that it cannot reach the lower self, the faculty of reason will grow, faith will strengthen, tranquility will arrive, and the differentiation between the truth and falsehood will come, so the person will refrain from falsehood and speak the truth. The Law will then come to him and he will act according to it, so he will become a servant of the Law. He will obey the Messenger (Allah's prayer and peace be on him) with regard to his commandments and prohibitions because he has heard the True One (mighty and glorified is He) say: "And what the Messenger gives you, take; and what he forbids you, abstain from" (from 59.7). He has come to know that this verse applies to all the commandments and prohibitions brought by the Messenger (Allah's prayer and peace be on him). He will, thus, perform the works of obedience that he commanded and refrain from committing the sins he (Allah's prayer and peace be on him) prohibited. At this stage, he will become a pious Muslim. If he continues like this, he will become a knower of Allah (mighty and glorified is He) and knowledgeable of Him. He will have tranquility, silence, and ability to listen to what is spoken to him in his heart. He will be continuously spoken to and he will be in permanent happiness. O Allah, grant us the pleasure of Your nearness, the delight of Your private conversation, and feeling happy with You, and "give us good in this world and good in the hereafter and protect us from the torment of the Fire."

⊛ Be sensible and do not talk about things that do not concern you. Occupy yourselves with what you have been commanded to do and do not waste your time on irrelevant things. Be pious to your Lord (mighty and glorified is He) and repent to Him. When someone shows piety to Him, He protects him; and when He protects someone, He elevates him to the door of His nearness. He elevates him to everlasting life. He elevates from the stars to the Seventh Heaven. You will soon see the Resurrection. You will see how Allah (mighty and glorified is He) will gather those who are pious to Him in the shade of His Throne and seat them at tables on which there is white honey, whereas the other people are immersed in heat and sweat. While sitting at those tables, they will see the creatures and their states; some people will be taken to the gardens of Paradise and others will be carried away to the Fire. They will be sitting there and their houses in Paradise are in front of them. Their wives and their youths of Paradise will be visible to them. They will see the things that have been assigned to them before they reach them.

⊛ O you who are forgetful! Take little from what leaves you and take in abundance from what stays with you and does not leave you. Do many righteous works. Fast and be sincere in fasting. Perform prayer and be sincere in your prayer. Make the pilgrimage and be sincere in that. Pay the obligatory alms and be sincere in it. Remember your Lord (mighty and glorified is He) and be sincere in remembering Him. Serve the righteous, draw near to them, and be sincere in your service to them. Occupy yourself with your own faults and do not pay attention to the faults of others. Command the practice of what is right and prohibit what is wrong. Do not expose the private affairs of people and keep them secret. Disapprove any wrongdoing that is apparent but do not concern yourselves with what may be hidden. Focus on yourselves and do not pay attention to others. Do not speak a lot about things that are of no concern to you, for the Prophet (Allah's prayer and peace be on him) has said: "One result of the excellence of the person's practice of Islam is neglecting what does not concern him." Your faults are your business but the faults of others are of no concern to you.

⊛ O young man, talk about things that concern you and give up discussing matters that are irrelevant to you. When you know Allah (mighty and glorified is He), your fear of Him will increase and your speech in His presence will decrease. This is why the Prophet (Allah's prayer and peace be on him) has said: "When someone comes to know Allah, his tongue becomes exhausted," meaning that he becomes mute. The tongue of His lower self, passion, natural inclination, habit, telling of lies, slander, and falsehood will become dumb, whereas the tongue of his inward will speak, and the tongue of his heart, innermost being, essences, truthfulness and his purity will speak. The tongue of his falsehood will become dumb, but the tongue of his truth will speak. The tongue of his talking about things that are of no concern to him will become incapable of speech, whereas the tongue of his heart will speak about things that concern him. The tongue of his quest for his lower self will become dumb, whereas the tongue of his quest for the True One will speak. In the early stage of acquiring knowingness, speech will stop and the person's whole existence will melt away. He will become extinct to himself and to everyone else. Then, if the True One (mighty and glorified is He) wills, He will resurrect him. If He wants him to speak, He will create for him a tongue with which He enables him to speak. He will cause him to speak what He wants of words of wisdom and secrets. His speech will be a remedy within a remedy, a light within a light, a truth within a truth, a rightness within a rightness, and a purity within purity, for he will speak only at the command of Allah (mighty and glorified is He), by means of his heart. If he speaks without being commanded to do so, he will perish. He will not speak unless he is given a command, or as a result of an irresistible thing that overcomes him. If this was the case, the True One (mighty and glorified is He) is far too generous to call someone to task because of an irresistible motive that has no lower self, passion, natural inclination, devil, and willfulness, as He does not call the dead to task for making some utterance, or a dreamer for his wet dreams and for what he sees and does in his sleep. The words of those whose lower selves have died were heard only after the death of their lower selves. As for someone who speaks before reaching this stage, his silence is better than his speech. No one should advance to the first row save the brave. The person who advances to the first row without having bravery and expertise will perish.

Humility

⊛ Be humble and do not be arrogant. Humility raises people up, whereas arrogance brings them down. The Prophet (Allah's prayer and peace be on him) has said: "When someone behaves with humility with Allah, Allah (mighty and glorified is He) raises him up." Allah has some servants who do righteous works that are as great as the mountains, like the deeds of the predecessors, yet they humble themselves to Allah and say: "We have done nothing that can cause us to enter Paradise. If we would enter it, it would be by the mercy of Allah (mighty and glorified is He), and if He would deny us admission, it would be on account of His justice." They continue to stand in His company on the foot of bankruptcy.

⊛ Be humble, for the more you humble yourself the more you become prominent, get elevated, and gain a higher status. If you do not behave with humility, this will indicate your ignorance of Allah (mighty and glorified is He), His Messenger (Allah's prayer and peace be on him), His prophets, His saints, His Law, His Knowledge, His power, His status, this world of His, and the hereafter of His. How often you hear but do not understand, understand but do not work, and work but with no sincerity so that your presence and your absence are one and the same!

⊛ O hypocrite, why do you want to listen to these words? Get out of here. You are the enemy of Allah (mighty and glorified is He), the enemy of His Messenger (Allah's prayer and peace be on him), His prophets, and His saints (Allah's prayer and peace be on all of them). Were it not for my patience and sense of shame in the presence of Allah, I would come down, grab you by the scruff of your neck, and throw you out.

You are in illusion. O people, work and be sincere! Do not be conceited and do not claim doing a favor to Allah (mighty and glorified is He) for deeds that He Himself has enabled you to do! The vain person is ignorant. The person who claims to have done Allah a favor is ignorant. The person who behaves arrogantly with the creatures is ignorant. Humility is from Allah and arrogance is from Satan. The first one who behaved with arrogance was Iblīs, so he was cursed, hated, thrown out, and deprived. If self-abasement and humility did not represent such a high spiritual degree He would not have used them to describe those whom He loves and who love Him, as in His (high is He) following saying: "O you who believe! If anyone of you turns back from his religion, Allah will bring a people whom He loves and who love Him — [who are] humble to the believers, proud with the disbelievers" (from 5.54). The believers humble themselves to the believers, but are honorable in their attitude toward the disbelievers.

Their humbleness to the believers is an act of worship and their honorableness with the disbelievers is a work of worship. The believer never adopts an attitude of arrogance toward the creatures, but he rather abases himself and behaves with humbleness to them. He conceals his spiritual state by his self-abasement and humility. He is in fact close to the king and is in his house. When he goes out and about with him, he disguises himself as a servant so that no one would recognize his nearness to the king. If the vizier and the king went out, having disguised themselves, and then the vizier was recognized by one of his friends and started to talk to him, the vizier must not treat him with arrogance and respond by saying: "The king is with me." Instead, he must smile to him, do his business for him, and give him the impression that the person who is with him is his servant, thus concealing his true identity.

O young man, you have no knowledge of the spiritual states of the people of Allah and you do not believe in their words! It is your involvement with the creatures that has screened you off from them. Your pursuit of worldly status and your quest for leadership have screened you off from them. If you were truthful in seeking the people of Allah, you would have seen them and benefited from their words.

⊛ Be humble so that you will be given a high status. Take off the clothes of arrogance and put on the cloths of humility so that you will be raised. All that you are involved in is an illusion within an illusion. If you turn away from the notion of the lower self, the notion of passion, the notion of Satan, and the notion of this world, the notion of the hereafter will come to you, as well as the notion of the angel, and finally the notion of the True One (mighty and glorified is He), which is the ultimate goal. When the heart has become sound, it will stop the notion and ask it: "What kind of notion are you? Where are you from?" It will reply: "I am the notion of such-and-such." Woe to you! Most of you are in illusion within illusion. You are worshipping the creatures in your cells.

Denouncing Dissimulation

⊛ One who is ignorant of Allah behaves with dissimulation and hypocrisy, whereas one who is knowledgeable of Him does not do that. The fool disobeys Allah (mighty and glorified is He), whereas the sensible person obeys Him. One who is full of hatred disobeys Him, but the lover obeys Him. One who greedily accumulates worldly goods behaves with dissimulation and hypocrisy, whereas one who has curtailed hopes does not do that. One who is forgetful of death puts on a show, whereas one who remembers it does not behave hypocritically. One who forgets that Allah (mighty and glorified is He) looks at him behaves with dissimulation, whereas one who is aware that He watches him does not do that. One who is neglectful behaves dissemblingly, but one who is wakeful does not put on a show.

⊛ O young man, do not speak to any creature about what you are involved in of the affairs of this world and the hereafter. Keep what you are involved in out of sight, behind locked doors. Cover the face of your spiritual state and do not let anyone see anything of it except the eyes. If the cover is a veil that totally covers the face, it will be even better for you.

This is the end of the days of intermission. There are the market of hypocrisy and the market of dealing on the basis of hope of salvation and fear of punishment. You wish to obtain worldly things and fear their remoteness. You wish for nearness to the creatures and fear that they may keep away from you. The kings have become gods for many creatures. This world, affluence, well-being, might, and strength have all become gods. Woe to you! You have mistaken the branch for a root, the one who is provided for for a provider, the slave for a master, the poor person for a rich one, the powerless person for a powerful one, and the dead person for a living one. You are unworthy of respect! We do not follow you and do not adopt your creed. We would rather keep away from you. We stand on the hill of safety — on the Sunna, and on the relinquishment of heretical innovations. We stand on the hill of the belief in the oneness of God, of sincerity, of abandoning dissimulation and hypocrisy, and of seeing the creatures as powerless, weak, and overpowered. We accept the divine decree and give up dissatisfaction. We adhere to patience and give up complaining. We walk with the feet of our hearts to the door of our King (mighty and glorified is He). Putting someone at the command of another and giving authority to someone over another are both from Him. The ability to create and provide sustenance are also both from Him.

Envy

⊛ O young man, beware of envy for it is a bad companion. It was envy that wrecked the house of Iblīs, destroyed him, rendered him one of the people of the Fire, and made him cursed by Allah (mighty and glorified is He), His angels, His prophets (Allah's prayer and peace be on them), and His creatures. How can a sensible person be involved in envy when he has heard these words of Allah (high is He): "We have apportioned between them their livelihood in the life of this world" (from 43.32), and "or do they envy people for what Allah has given them?" (from 4.54); these words of the Prophet (Allah's prayer and peace be on him): "Envy consumes good deeds as the fire consumes firewood"; and these words of one of the learned scholars: "How good envy is! How just it is! It kills first the envier!" The envier is in fact objecting to Allah (mighty and glorified is He) and disputing with Him about His actions, creatures, and distribution of shares.

⊛ How long will it be before you give up envying your brothers and hoping to obtain what they have? Woe to you! You envy your Muslim brother for his wife, children, house, and worldly possessions, although all those are already created to be his and you have no share in them. You hope to have his wife, although she is created to be his in this world and in the hereafter. You wish for affluence, although it has already been decreed that straitened circumstances will be your lot. You will be punished and hated because you quest what has not been allotted to you. How enthusiastic you are in seeking this world despite the fact that you will not have of it other than what has been allotted to you! O Allah, awaken our hearts from their forgetfulness, awaken us so that we heed to You, put us at Your service, and "give us good in this world and good in the hereafter and protect us from the torment of the Fire."

The Curtailment of Hopes

⊛ O young man, curtail your hopes and decrease your greedy keenness on this world. Pray like someone who is about to depart this world. Come here into my presence as someone who is about to leave this world. If destiny would allow you to come on another day, that would be something you had not counted on. The believer should not sleep unless his will is written and placed under his head, so that if the True One (mighty and glorified is He) awakens him in good health that would be good fortunate, otherwise his family would act according to his will after his death and ask Allah to show him mercy. If you do that, your eating will become like that of someone who is about to leave this world, your presence among your family will become like that of someone who is about to depart from this world, your meeting with your brothers and friends will become like that of someone who is about to leave this world. How can it not be like this for someone whose affairs are in the hand of someone else? Only a few creatures will come to know what they will do, what will happen to them, and when they will die. All of this is stored in their hearts. They see that as clearly as you see the sun, yet their tongues do not reveal it. The first to view this is the innermost being. Then the innermost being informs the heart, the heart then informs the tranquil self (*an-nafsu al-muṭma'enna*) which keeps it secret. It gets informed of this after acquiring good manners and serving and accompanying the heart. It qualifies for this after a lot of strife and suffering. The person who attains to this spiritual station is the deputy and representative of the True One (mighty and glorified is He) on earth. He is the door of the innermost beings. He has the keys of the safes of the hearts, which are the safes of the True One (mighty and glorified is He). This is something beyond the comprehension of the creatures. All that appears of it is merely an atom from its mountain, a drop from its sea, and a lamp from its sun. O Allah, I apologize to you for speaking about these secrets, but You know that I am overwhelmed. A certain righteous person once said: "Beware of what merits an apology." But when I get up to sit on this chair [to preach], I become unaware of you [O people!] to the extent that no one is left in front of my heart to apologize to and restrict myself because of.

⊛ You have to curtail your hopes, for everyone who has succeeded has done so by the curtailment of hopes. Decrease your greedy keenness on this world for your allotted worldly shares will come to you even if you were not keen on getting them. You will not leave this world before receiving all that is yours. Woe to you! You are in illusion. Abandon the lower self and passion for you have no escape from the hand of death. Death cannot be escaped. Whichever direction you take and whatever you do, it will be in front of you and around you. Do not be concerned with the Day of Resurrection, for the day of your death is a private resurrection for you, whereas the Day of Resurrection is a universal resurrection for you and for others. The first resurrection will show you the second one. If you see the Angel of Death (prayer and peace be on our Prophet and on him) come to you with a laugh and relaxed face, and his assistants likewise, greet you, and take your soul gently, as he took the souls of the prophets, the martyrs, and the righteous (Allah's prayer and peace be on all of them), then expect good at the Resurrection. The first day will show you the second Day and its details. If you see good [on the first day], you will have good [on the second], and if what you see [on the first day] is bad, it will be bad [on the second]. The Angel of Death came to Moses (prayer and peace be on our Prophet and on them) holding an apple in his hand. He let him smell it and took his soul during that. Similarly, anyone who is close to Allah will have the Angel of Death take his soul in the easiest manner and in the most beautiful way.

Death

⊛ O you who are enjoying the bliss of this world, you will soon leave your bliss! How fine this piece of poetry is:

Listen, for you are able to hear
if you do not take the initiative it will be too late.
Eat as you like and live in ease,
the end of all of this will be death.

Soon, your wealth and life will vanish, your eyesight will deteriorate, your mind will lose its sanity, and your capacity for food and drink will decrease. You will see the pleasures but you will be unable to have anything of them. Your wife, children, and maidservant will hate you and wish for your death. Care and grief will be thrown on you. This world will abandon you and the hereafter will receive you. If you have done good for the hereafter, it will receive and embrace you, but if you have no such works, the grave will be your place and the Fire will be your final abode. It is illusion [that you are in]. The Prophet (Allah's prayer and peace be on him) used to say: "The real life is that of the hereafter" and repeat it to himself and to his companions (may Allah be satisfied with all of them).

⊛ Use your good health and your leisure time in obedience to Allah (mighty and glorified is He) before the approach of an illness that ruins your health and business and a matter that takes away your leisure time. Make full use of your affluence before you become poor, for affluence does not last forever. Be generous to the poor and share with them your wealth, for what you give them is credit that you have with your Lord and will be useful for you in the hereafter. Woe to you! Take full advantage of your life before your death. Learn a lesson from death, for the Prophet (Allah's prayer and peace be on him) used to say: "Death is sufficient a preacher." Death wears out every new thing, brings near every distant thing, and muddles every pure thing. There is no escape from death. It may come in this very hour and on this very day. This matter is under the control of someone else; it is not in your hands. Everything that you have is a loan: your youth, good health, leisure time, affluence, and life are all on loan to you. Therefore, make what really matters to you your concern.

⊛ Death is watching you while you are unaware. You have forgotten to wait for it despite the fact that it is standing in front of you. It will soon come your way — targeting your well-being and lives. The soul of one of you will go, while his body stays behind like the corpse of a sheep. Who will have mercy for you will bury you in the ground before the earth's wild beasts and insects eat you. Your family, friends, and enemies will stay with their food, drink, and pleasures, and they may or may not ask Allah to show mercy to you. Many kings were killed by their enemies who then threw them in the wilderness, deliberately without burial, to ensure that they are devoured by dogs and insects. How ugly the king who ends up like this is! How good this piece of poetry of one of them is:[30]

> One that death can remove is not a real kingdom
> The real kingdom is that of the One who does not die!

The sensible among you is one who remembers death and is satisfied with whatever destiny brings, thanking for what he likes and enduring with patience what he dislikes. Focus your reflection on matters related to your religion, instead of reflecting on lustful desires and pleasures, and reflect on death and what follows it.

⊛ O people, die before you die. Die as far as your lower selves and your wills are concerned. Remember death frequently and prepare for it before its arrival and then you will have died before you die. Death, then, will be easy for you and will not represent a burden or grief. The arrival of the day of death and the Day of Resurrection is inevitable, so wait for them. These two days have been decreed by Allah (mighty and glorified is He) and cannot be turned back.

⊛ Remembering death is a remedy for the diseases of the lower self. I have spent years remembering death frequently, by night and day. I have prospered by remembering it and I have overpowered my lower self through that remembrance. One night I remembered death and wept from the onset of night until the beginning of dawn. I kept on weeping and saying: "O Allah, I ask You that the Angel of Death does not take my soul away but that You do." At the beginning of dawn, my eyes dozed off and I saw a handsome old man with beautiful features coming in through the door. I said to him: "Who are you?" He replied: "I am the Angel of Death." I said to him: "I have asked Allah (mighty and glorified is He) that He not you would take away my soul." He asked: "But why did you ask Him for that? What is my guilt? I am just a servant following orders. I am commanded to be gentle to some people and rough to others." He then embraced me and wept, so I wept with him. I then woke up while I was still weeping.

⊛ O you who are in the company of their worldly goods and great expectations! The appointed times of death will soon come and separate

---

[30] The poet is the pious Umayyad caliph 'Umar bin 'Abd Al-'Azīz (682-720).

you from your hopes. Hurry up before the arrival of these appointed times. Look at sudden death. Death is not necessarily preceded by an illness. Iblīs is your enemy so do not heed to his advice. Do not trust him for he is not trustworthy. Beware of him. He wants you to die while you are standing on the foot of heedlessness, disobedience, and disbelief. Do not be forgetful of your enemy for his sword will not be prevented from hitting the truthful person or the disbeliever. Only a few individuals escape it. He removed your father Adam and your mother Eve (prayer and peace be on our Prophet and on them) from Paradise and he works diligently to prevent you from entering it. He urges you to commit disobedience, sins, disbelief, and noncompliance. All acts of disobedience are attributed to him, after Allah's decree and His destiny. All creatures are subject to affliction except Allah's sincere servants who have realized their servanthood to Him (mighty and glorified is He), so he has no authority over them. At times, he can cause them some harm, for when it is time for a decreed matter to take place, the eye becomes blind. His effect on them touches only the body, not the heart or the innermost being; only matters relating to this world, not matters pertaining to the hereafter; only matters relating to the creatures, not matters related to the Creator (mighty and glorified is He). He approaches the creatures mainly through the attachment to this world and the lower self. Seeking this world is a burning fire.

O young men, occupy yourselves with what concerns and is good for you. Preparing for what follows death is of concern to you, striving against your lower self is of concern to you, paying attention to your faults is of concern to you, but attending to the faults of other people is of no concern for you. Remember death and work in preparation for what is after it, for the Prophet (Allah's prayer and peace be on him) has said: "The intelligent person is one who calls himself to account and works in preparation for what follows death, whereas the incompetent person is one who lets his lower self follow its passion, yet still wishes for forgiveness from Allah."

Thinking Well of Others

⊛ O young man, attach your heart to your Lord, so when Iblīs comes to seduce you and make you change course, seek the help of Allah (mighty and glorified is He) to drive him away. Seek His help as did those before you. Do good works then think well of your Lord (mighty and glorified is He). Thinking well of Him and obeying Him will bring about marvelous results for you. There is so much good in thinking well of Allah (mighty and glorified is He), His prophets, His messengers, and the righteous among His servants (Allah's prayer and peace be on all of them).

⊛ O people, strive, work diligently, and do not despair for relief may come at any time. Have you not heard that Allah (mighty and glorified is He) has said: "Allah may bring after that something new to pass" (from 65.1)? Fear your Lord and pin your hopes on Him; have you not heard His following words: "And Allah warns you of Himself" (from 3.28)? As much as you have fearfulness and caution you will have safety. Put your trust in your Lord; have you not heard His following saying: "And whoever puts his trust in Allah, He will suffice him" (from 65.3)? O Allah, let us do without Your creatures! Let us do without those who amassed the wealth of Your creatures, placed it beneath their feet, and withheld it from Your creatures while being totally indulgent in their pompous pride. The poor beg and appeal to them for help but they turn a deaf ear to them. O Allah, include us among those who get what they need through You and appeal to You for help in their serious problems! Amen.

Sufyān Ath-Thawrī (may Allah, high is He, show mercy to him) was asked: "Who is the ignorant person?" He replied: "One who ignores Allah (mighty and glorified is He) until he asks Him (mighty and glorified is He) for help with his needs." His likeness is as the likeness of a man to whom the king assigned a job in his house, yet he left his work and went out to the door of a man in the same neighborhood and asked him for a piece of bread to eat. Should the king know about that, would not he hate him and prevent him from entering his house?

O you who are dead at heart, listen to these words! What losers you are that you die without knowing your Lord (mighty and glorified is He)! O Allah grant us knowingness of You, working sincerely for You, and ceasing to work for other than You! Grant us knowledge of Your outward Law and Knowledge of the inward. Grant us patience and satisfaction. Sweeten for us the bitterness of Your affliction which You foreknow will come our way. Cause the flesh of our hearts to die so that we do not feel the pain of the scissors of Your power, and thus Your companionship will last for us forever. Amen.

Having a Sense of Shame

⊛ The Prophet (Allah's prayer and peace be on him) is reported to have said: "The sense of shame stems from faith." O servants of Allah, how impudent and how daring you are to your Lord (mighty and glorified is He)! Showing modesty to the creatures but impudence to the True One is utter foolishness and madness. The reality of modesty is feeling a sense of shame with your Lord (mighty and glorified is He) in both your private and public lives so that modesty with the creatures comes to be a consequence not a cause. The believer feels a sense of shame with regard to the Creator, whereas the hypocrite feels a sense of shame with respect to the creatures.

Enduring Affliction

⊛ The people of Allah accustom themselves to afflictions and do not get annoyed like you. One of them used to be afflicted everyday with a tribulation so that on the day when no affliction came his way he used to say: "O Allah, what sins have I done today that You have not sent to me my daily affliction?" Afflictions are of various kinds; some target the body, while others target the heart. Some of them are suffered in relation to the creatures, whereas others in relation to the Creator. There is no good in someone who has not been subjected to suffering. Afflictions are the hooks of the True One (mighty and glorified is He).

⊛ A few individuals have on them remnants of sins of which they are cleaned by the tribulations and afflictions, so they earn degrees in the hereafter that they would not earn without them. You have to be satisfied with the divine decree, observe the Law, and perform good works under all circumstances: in hardship and prosperity, when it is something you love and when it is something you hate. The Prophet (Allah's prayer and peace be on him) is reported to have said: "If a person is not satisfied with the decree of Allah, there is no medicine for his foolishness." What He has decreed will come to pass, whether the servant is dissatisfied or satisfied. Woe to you! O you who protest against Allah (mighty and glorified is He), do not speak nonsense! No one can turn back or stop the divine decree. Submit and then you will find comfort. You cannot turn back the night and day. When the night comes, it sets in whether you agree or disagree, and the same is true of the day. Both come without you having a say in the matter. The same is true of the decree of Allah (mighty and glorified is He) and His destiny. They are either in your favor or against you. If the night of illness comes, submit and say good bye to the day of well-being. If the night of poverty comes, submit and bid farewell to the day of affluence. If the night of what you hate comes, submit and say goodbye to the day of what you love. Receive with a patient heart the night of diseases, illnesses, poverty, and the loss of worldly goods. Do not reject anything of the decree of Allah (mighty and glorified is He) and His destiny, otherwise you will perish, your faith will vanish, your heart will become impure, and your innermost being will die.

Allah (mighty and glorified is He) has said in one of His books: "I am Allah. There is no god other than Me. When someone submits to My decree, receives My affliction with patience, and offers thanks for My favors, I record him in My presence as a truthful person and I gather him on the Day of Resurrection in the company of the truthful. As for one who does not submit to My decree, does not endure with patience My afflictions, and does not give thanks for My favors, let Him seek a lord other than Me." If you do not submit to the divine decree, do not endure with patience the affliction, and do not give thanks for the favors, you do not have a lord. Seek a lord other than Him, but there is no lord other than Him. If you like, be satisfied with the divine decree and believe in destiny, whether good or bad, sweet or bitter, for what has come your way could not have been averted through precaution and what has passed you by could not have been made to come your way by exerting efforts and seeking it. When your faith has been confirmed, you will come to the door of sainthood. At this stage, you will become one of the men of Allah (mighty and glorified is He) who have fulfilled their servitude to Him. The distinctive sign of the saint is his compliance with his Lord (mighty and glorified is He) under all circumstances. He becomes total compliance without asking "why" and "how," while carrying out the commandments and observing the prohibitions. No doubt, then, his company [of Allah] will last. He becomes a front with no back, a state of nearness with no remoteness, purity with no impurity, and goodness with no evil.

⊕ Nothing turns you away from the obedience to Him and the belief in His oneness other than your sins, your ignorance, and the ruined state of your homes and sanctuaries. You will soon regret. Listen to the verses of the Qur'an with the ears of your hearts. Rush to Him from every door, bid farewell to every door, and cling to the door of your Lord (mighty and glorified is He). It is He who is the Remover of harm. It is He who "answers the cry of the distressed person when he calls on Him" (from 27.62). Be patient with Him and then you will experience goodness. Thank Him when He answers you and be patient when His answer is delayed. Courage is an hour of patience.

O Remover of harm and affliction, remove the harm and affliction from us, for You answer the needy person when he prays to You! O Doer of what He wishes, O You who are Capable of everything, O Knower of everything! It is You who has full knowledge of our needs, and it is You who is capable of providing for them. It is You who knows about our faults and sins, and it is You who is Capable of erasing and forgiving them. Do not refer us to someone other than You, do not assign us to someone else, do not send us to the door of someone other than You, and do not turn us to someone else.

⊕ O young man, go out with your heart, stripped naked of all of your possessions, and be secluded from the whole of you so that you will be compensated for all of that. Woe to you! The creatures cannot bring you any benefit or cause you any harm unless Allah (mighty and glorified is He) gives His permission first. Your hearts are in His hand and He moves them as He wishes, sometimes putting them at the service of others and sometimes giving them authority over others. Have you not heard that

Allah has said: "Whatever mercy Allah opens to people there is none to withhold" (from 35.2)?

O young man, when affliction comes your way, receive it with faith, patience, submission, and a smile! Be patient with it until its days are gone and its times are over. O seeker, do not escape from the door of your Sought After One because of the arrows of His afflictions! Stand firm and then you will find your Sought After One. When the seeker is afflicted, he needs a master who medicates him during his ordeal, heals him with drinks of patience and thankfulness, commands him to take one thing and keep away from another, and instructs him to turn away from his lower self and refuse to accept its advice. If the person is truthful in the company of his shaikh, Allah (mighty and glorified is He) will sooner or later bring benefits to him. O You who separate between the salty water and the sweet water, separate us from any anger at You and dispute with You against Your decree! Separate us from the acts of disobedience to You with an isthmus of Your mercy. Amen.

⊛ O young man, if Allah causes you any harm or affliction, no one else can remove it. Why, then, do you say to someone who is as powerless as yourself: "Save me from what has hurt me"? If sickness or harm from the creatures comes your way, causing you loss of worldly property and wealth, no one can remove it other than Him. If you suffer loss of property, hunger in your stomach, or abandonment by the brothers and neighbors to the extent that they refuse to give you a morsel or as little as an atom, and if this world seems too strait for you despite its spaciousness, be certain at heart that all of that is from Allah (mighty and glorified is He) and that there is no remover of all of that except Him. No one can remove it other than the One who caused it. It is He who threw it at you so it is He who can remove it. It is He who dressed you with these clothes and it is He who can take them off.

Be sensible and do not associate creatures and means with Allah. Believe in one Lord only not in many. It is He who puts things at the command of others, the One who gives authority to someone over another, the Ruler, the Judge, and the Doer. His destiny comes with sickness in its hand and knocks on the door of your good health. His destiny comes with hardship in its hand and knocks on the door of your prosperity. His destiny comes with grief and sadness in its hand and knocks on the door of your happiness. His destiny comes with fear in its hand and knocks on the door of your sense of security. All these come from Him, and no one can remove them other than Him.

This world is the prison of the believer. Having been put inside it, his feet will start to move and then he will attain the spiritual state of knowingness, at which point the walls of the prison will collapse and the doors will become wide open before him. His heart will acquire feathered wings, so it will fly to the heaven of the Knowledge of Allah (mighty and glorified is He) and join the spirits that are there. This is something beyond your comprehension. The hearts of the people of Allah and their souls eat from the plate of the favor of Allah (mighty and glorified is He) while they are still in this world, as the souls of martyrs eat in Paradise. It is here where becoming in no need to the creatures happens. It is here where the kingship of the heart takes place. They are kings in this world and kings in the hereafter. They are chieftains in this world and chieftains in the hereafter.

⊛ Obey and do not disobey. Believe in the oneness of God and do not attribute partners to Him. Your reliance on the creatures and means is a form of polytheism. Woe to you! You are mad! Dissatisfaction and protestation do not give you something or take away another. Your anger would not delay something or bring forward another. The strike of affliction and its removal are both in Allah's hand. It is He who has sent down the disease and the remedy. It is He who has created the disease and the remedy. He subjects you to afflictions to make you know Him through them, to show you His signs and His power in sending down the affliction and in removing it, and to show you His ability to remove and send down His plate [of grace]. Afflictions show the way to the door of Allah (mighty and glorified is He) and knock on it. They bring the heart and the True One (mighty and glorified is He) together. They promote one's status. Do not hate afflictions for you have benefits in what you hate. Set aside asking "why" and "how." If you endure the afflictions with patience, they will purify you of the outward and inward sins.

The Prophet (Allah's prayer and peace be on him) is reported to have said: "Affliction will continue to come the believer's way until he comes to walk on earth with no sin." His sins will be erased from his scrolls and the angels who recorded them will forget them. A certain righteous person used to say: "O Allah, people love You for Your favors and I love You for Your affliction!" One of the people of Allah used to say on the day when no affliction came his way: "O Allah, what sin have I committed today so that you have deprived me of affliction?"

Woe to you! If you are not satisfied with His decree, do not consume His sustenance and seek a lord other than Him. Allah (Exalted is His affair) has said in one of His utterances: "O son of Adam, if you are not satisfied with My decree and are impatient with My affliction, go and seek a lord other than Me!" Be patient with your Lord (mighty and glorified is He), for you have no lord other than Him. There is no second lord. There is no other creator. There is no other provider. Be patient with the will of this One Lord.

⊛ O young man, do not escape from affliction but endure it with patience. It is inevitable and enduring it with patience is also inevitable.

How could the nature of this world and the how it was created be changed for your sake? The prophets, who are the best of all creatures, had always to suffer afflictions. The same applies to the followers who emulate them, who walk on their path, and who follow in their footsteps. Our Prophet Muhammad (Allah's prayer and peace be on him) was the beloved of the True One (mighty and glorified is He) and the one for whose sake everything exists yet he was constantly afflicted with poverty, need, hunger, fighting, wars, and harm from the creatures up to the time when he left this world. Take, for instance, the case of Jesus (prayer and peace be on our Prophet and on him) who is the spirit of Allah and His word, who was created by Him without the involvement of a male, who used to heal the blind person and the albino and raise the dead, and whose prayers were always answered. Allah caused his people to insult him, defame his mother, and beat him. He finally escaped from them with his companions, but they tracked them down, arrested them, beat them, and tortured them. Then they intended to crucify Jesus (prayer and peace be on our Prophet and on him) but Allah (high is He) rescued him from them and caused the person who led them to him to be crucified instead.

Moses (prayer and peace be on our Prophet and on him) was also afflicted with the calamities that happened to him, and each one of the prophets (prayer and peace be on them) had his share of affliction. This is what He did to the prophets and messengers (prayer and peace be on them) who are His beloved ones, so who are you to wish to change Allah's foreknowledge about you and about this world?

Renounce your will and your choice. Renounce your conversation with your lower self, passion, and this world of yours. Renounce your conversation with the creatures and your intimacy with them. If you accomplish this, the conversation of your heart will come to be with your Lord (mighty and glorified is He) and your intimacy will be with Him. His remembrance will camp in your heart. You will be remembering Him and He will be remembering you. He will snatch your heart and your limbs and senses to Him and keep them. You will come to want what He wants, and anything else will be resented by you. When a person becomes one of the spiritual beings who have attained to Him, he will wander among the servants of Allah and various countries, and He will use him to protect the creatures from tribulations and afflictions. He will take what His lord (mighty and glorified is He) has given him. This is the real gift, while everything else is worthless.

⊛ The best interests are enclosed within the folds of disliked things. Be sensible and acquire politeness. Afflictions come to the hearts of the truthful persons, salute them, and intercede on their behalf. The person who has established a strong relationship with Allah embraces afflictions, kisses them on the forehead, and endures them with patience, compliance, and contentment. They stay with him for a while before being taken away and asked: "How did you find the place and the hospitality?" They will reply: "An excellent place and an excellent host. An excellent gift and an excellent receiver!" One of these righteous people (may Allah show mercy to him), who was afflicted with a tribulation, was asked: "How are you doing in this affliction?" He replied: "Ask the affliction about me!"

Be patient with your Lord (mighty and glorified is He) for He removes your affliction and promotes you spiritually in His eyes as a reward for your patience. Be with Him against your lower selves. Be with those who are truthful in His company — who work with Him, by Him, and for His sake. O Allah, put things at our command, provide for us, open up opportunities for us, and make things easy for us and on us! Amen.

Faith that is shaken by illness, poverty, hunger, and loss of worldly things is not real faith. The essence and the well-being of faith become visible and its light shines at the time of affliction. Its courage also becomes apparent when the army of affliction comes. Your Lord (mighty and glorified is He) is fully aware of what you do. O kings, O slaves, O elite people, O common people, O rich, O poor, O people of private cells, O people of public places, no one has a veil that can hide him from Him! He (high is He) is with you wherever you may be. O Allah, protect, forgive, pardon in the form of subtle kindness, patience, tolerance, care, sufficiency, good health, and well-being! Amen.

With regard to everything that you are involved in of good and evil, truthfulness and lies, sincerity and polytheism, obedience and disobedience, He (high is He) is Knowledgeable, an Expert, Watchful, Present, and a Witness. Feel a sense of shame as He has His eyes on you. Look with the eye of faith and then you will see His glances coming from your six directions. Is this preaching not sufficient for you? Only if you heed and hear with the ears of your hearts! All that you need is fear of your Lord (mighty and glorified is He) in both your private and public lives. Be vigilant with Him (high is He) and be aware of His glances at you and of the Honorable Recording Angels who are with you. Be afraid of Him, not of the punishments prescribed by His Law and which may be applied to you by your sultan and your prince. If you will be afraid of Him, your ruler will not tire with you.

O you who are poor, O you who are hungry, O you who are naked, O you who are in need! You appeal to other than Him for help? Your silence is better and more beneficial to you. His knowledge of your situation should be sufficient for you not to put in a request. He has afflicted you in order for you to come back to Him. So, return with your heart to Him and stand firm and then you will experience good. Do not insist on a quick response from Him, do not accuse Him of stinginess, and do not harbor doubts about Him. He has caused you to experience hunger, nakedness, and poverty in order to look and see, in terms of differentiation not in terms of knowledge, whether you will cling to His door or to someone else's door, whether you will be satisfied or dissatisfied with Him, whether you will complain to Him or complain from Him, and whether you will shout at Him or beseech Him gently. He afflicts you with tribulations to see how you behave.

O ignorant ones, you have left the door of the Wealthy One (high is He) and clung to the door of someone who is poor! You have left the door of the Generous One and clung to the door of someone who is stingy. You have left the door of the Merciful One and clung to the door of one who is merciless. You have left the door of the Capable One and clung to the door of one who is powerless. O ignorant ones, He will soon gather you together and make you stand in His presence! This will happen on the Day of Assembly. He will gather you, you of all races, O all of you creatures! The Invincible One has said: "This is the Day of Separation. We have assembled you together with those of the ancient times. So if you have a scheme, try it against Me" (77.38-39).

On the Day of Resurrection, Allah will assemble all creatures on an earth other than this; an earth on which no blood of an innocent creature had ever been shed and on which no sin had ever been committed. There is no doubt or uncertainty about that. Allah (mighty and glorified is He) has said: "And because the Hour is coming, there is no doubt about it; and because Allah will raise up those who are in the tombs" (22.7). The Day of Resurrection is "the Day of Loss and Gain" (from 64.9), "the Day of the Sigh [of Remorse]" (from 19.39), the Day of Remorse, the Day of Reminding, the Day of Compliance, the Day of Testimony, the Day of Retribution, the Day of Happiness, the Day of Sorrowfulness, the Day of Fear, the Day of Security, the Day of Bliss, the Day of Torment, the Day of Rest, the Day of Toil, the Day of Thirst, the Day of Giving Drinks, the Day of Clothing, the Day of Nakedness, the Day of Wining, the Day of Losing, the Day on which "the believers will rejoice in the victory from Allah" (from 30.4-5). O Allah, we seek refuge in You from the evil of that Day, beg You to grant us its good, and [pray to you that You] "give us good in this world and good in the hereafter and protect us from the torment of the Fire."

⊛ Evict from your hearts all opponents, peers, and partners, for the True One (mighty and glorified is He) does not accept any partner — in particular in the heart, which is His abode. One day, when they were still little boys, Al-Ḥasan and Al-Ḥussein[31] (peace be on them) were playing in the presence of the Messenger of Allah (Allah's prayer and peace be on him), and he was happy with them and totally busy with them. So Gabriel (peace be on him) came and said to him: "This one will be poisoned and that one will be killed." He told him this in order to remove them from his heart and to convert his happiness with them to grief about them. The

---

[31] The grandsons of the Prophet Muhammad (prayer and peace be on him).

Messenger of Allah (Allah's prayer and peace be on him) loved [his wife] 'Āisha (may Allah be satisfied with her), so she came to be involved in that notorious story. She was, thus, removed from his heart despite his certainty of her innocence, because he (Allah's prayer and peace be on him) recognized the aim of the True One (mighty and glorified is He) behind that event. And as Jacob (prayer and peace be on our Prophet and on him) loved Joseph (prayer and peace be on our Prophet and on him), he came to experience what he experienced and He separated him from Joseph. Similar things frequently happened to the prophets and saints (Allah's prayer and peace be on all of them), who are the beloved of the True One (mighty and glorified is He). Because He is jealous, He evicts from their hearts anyone other than Him.

⊛ Afflictions and tribulations realize faith, knowingness, and Knowledge. They differentiate between the kernel and the shell. The person who remains compliant throughout is a kernel, whereas one who disputes about them is a shell. When the person is compliant with His Lord (mighty and glorified is He), the shell of creatures is peeled from his heart so he becomes a kernel with no shell. When the person's belief in the oneness of God and his trust in Him have gathered strength and he has come to see Him with the eye of certitude, he will never turn back and leave the way of the True One (mighty and glorified is He), will never run away from His door, and will adhere to truthfulness and integrity.

⊛ How much you fear hunger and poverty! If you had certitude you would not have thought of these. Comply with your Lord's (mighty and glorified is He) will. If He subjects you to hunger, endure it with patience, with a good feeling in your hearts. If He satisfies your hunger, offer thanks to Him. He knows your best interests better than you do. He is not stingy or gives little. It is related that seventy prophets (prayer and peace be on our Prophet and on them), who are buried between Al-Multazam[32] and Al-Muqām,[33] were killed by hunger and lice. Did not he have something in His kingdom to satisfy their hunger? But He chose and accepted that for them. He did that to them in order to promote them; not because they were insignificant in His eyes, but because this world is insignificant in His sight. When He wants one of His servants exclusively for Himself, He deprives him of his will and places a screen between him and other things so that his lower self melts down, the fire of his natural inclination subsides, and his soul finds living in this world a heavy burden and longs for the hereafter where His Lord (mighty and glorified is He) is. He will therefore wish for and enjoys the taste of death in order

---

[32] The spot between the Black stone and the door of the Ka'ba.
[33] The station of prophet Abraham next to the Ka'ba.

to be alone with His Lord (mighty and glorified is He). This is what happens in most such cases.

⊛ The Prophet (Allah's prayer and peace be on him) has said: "We prophets are subjected to afflictions more than other people, next are those who are closer to us, and so on." When the believer is afflicted, he endures his affliction with patience. He conceals his affliction from other creatures and does not complain to them. This is why the Prophet (Allah's prayer and peace be on him) has said: "The cheerfulness of the believer is on his face, whereas his sorrow is in his heart." He greets people cheerfully to conceal what is in his heart. The believers hide the treasures of their inwards. They place a cover over the true nature of their hearts. Sorrow is the true nature of the hearts, whereas fear is the true nature of the souls. Sadness is a cloud that showers on the hearts various kinds of wisdom and secrets.

Why do not you endure with patience sadness and heartbreaking when Allah has said in one of His utterances: "I am with those whose hearts are broken on My account"? Whenever the hearts are broken because of remoteness, the setter of nearness sets them. Whenever they become estranged from the creatures, intimacy with Allah (mighty and glorified is He) comes to them. Whenever they become alienated from the creatures, they seek the intimacy of the nearness to Allah (mighty and glorified is He). The longer their sorrow in this world lasts, the longer will their happiness be in the hereafter. The Prophet (Allah's prayer and peace be on him) was in continuous sorrow and in permanent reflection as if he was listening to a speaker who speaks to him or to someone who was calling on him. Those whom he ordered the people to follow — his representatives, deputies, and heirs — are likewise in relation to the lengthiness of their sadness and the permanence of their reflection. How could they fail to emulate his works when they are in his station, being fed his food, having their thirst quenched by his drink, and being put on the backs of his horses, and fight with his swords and spears?

page 84

Epilogue

⊛ O young man, your speech is from your tongue not from your heart, from your appearance not from your essence. The sound heart runs away from the speech that comes from the tongue. Upon hearing it, it becomes like a bird in a cage and like a hypocrite in the mosque. When a truthful person meets a hypocrite scholar in a session, leaving that session becomes his only wish. The people of Allah are able to recognize marks on the faces of the dissimulators, hypocrites, impostors, pretenders, enemies of Allah (mighty and glorified is He), and enemies of His Messenger (Allah's prayer and peace be on him). Their signs are on their faces and in their words. They flee from the truthful as they flee from lions, for they are afraid of being burnt by the fire of their hearts. The angels move them away from the truthful and the righteous. Each one of them is great in the sight of the common people but is worthless in the eyes of the truthful; a human being in the sight of the common people, but a cat that carries no weight in the eyes of the truthful.

O young men, you have to find a physician of the Law, for he can treat your illnesses. Follow his instructions and take the medicine that he prescribes and then your good health will be restored. Follow the young servant and he will take you to the master. The Law is a young servant, whereas Knowledge is a master. Follow it, see where it enters, and enter after it. Seek the door of your Lord (mighty and glorified is He) and behave well in the company of the Law, which is the young servant that stands at the door. If you do not follow the Law you will not reach Knowledge. Have you not heard these words of your Lord (mighty and glorified is He): "And what the Messenger gives you, take; and what he forbids you, abstain from" (from 59.7). If you become well-mannered in the company of the Law at the door of your Lord (mighty and glorified is He) and cultivate good behavior with Him, He will love you, open to you the door of nearness, and seat you at the table of His favor and generosity. You will become His guests. He will speak to your hearts, entertain your innermost beings, and teach them the Knowledge that He teaches to the elite among His creatures. So, His Law will be between Him and the creatures, whereas His Knowledge will be between Him and you, because the Law is common, whereas Knowledge is special. The Law is faith, whereas Knowledge is direct seeing.

⊛ O Allah, make us work and be sincere in our works, grant us acquaintance with Your Knowledge, steadfastness in our acquaintance and "give us good in this world and good in the hereafter and protect us from the torment of the Fire." Praise be to Allah Lord of the worlds. "O Our Lord, perfect our light for us, and forgive us. You are Capable of everything" (from 66.8). "O My Lord, enable me to be thankful for Your favor that You have conferred on me and on my parents, and to do righteousness that is pleasing to You, and do good to me in my offspring. I repent to You and I am one of the Muslims" (from 46.15). "Glory be to your Lord, the Lord of invincibility, above what they describe. And peace be on the messengers. And praise be to Allah, the Lord of the Worlds" (37.180-182). Praise be to Allah with whose favor all good works are completed.

Glossary

This is a list of Arabic words and our chosen translations.

'abd	servant/slave
'ārif	knower
'Arsh	the Throne
'Ilm	Knowledge
'uzla	seclusion
abdāl	spiritual substitutes
ādāb	refined behavior
al-Ḥaqq	the True One
al-aqsām al-maqsūma	allotted worldly shares
al-ḥukm (Sharī'a)	the Law
asbāb	means
badaliyya	spiritual substitution
bāṭin	inward
bid'a	false innovation
dhāhir	outward
dunya	this world
fanā'	extinction
farīdha	obligatory duty
ḥāl (ḥālāt)	spiritual state(s)
hawā	passion
himma	aspiration
ḥirṣ	greedy keenness
imān	faith
ishrāk	association of someone with Allah or attribution of partners to Allah
īqān	certainty [of belief]
jalwa	public life
jawāriḥ	limbs and senses
jihād	strife or striving
kadr	impurity
khalwa	private life or solitude
laththāt	pleasures

lutf	subtle kindness
ma'nā	essence
ma'rifa	knowingness
maqām	spiritual station
mi'rāj	Heavenly Ascension
mu'min	believer
mujāhada	striving
munājāt	private conversation
mutazahhid	would-be ascetic
muttaqī	pious to Allah
nafs	lower self
qadar	destiny
qadhā'	divine decree
qutb	spiritual pivot
sādiq	truthful person
safā'	purity
shahawāt	lustful desires
sirr	innermost being
tab'	natural inclination
taqwa	piety
tawakkul	trust
tawhīd	belief in the oneness of God
walī	saint
wara'	pious restraint
wāsita	mediator
wilāya	sainthood
yaqīn	certitude
zāhid	ascetic
zakāt	obligatory alms
zuhd	renunciation

Also by Louay Fatoohi:

The Mystery of the Historical Jesus
The Messiah in the Qur'an, the Bible,
and Historical Sources

Publication Date: September 2007
ISBN: 978-1-906342-01-2
Available from Amazon and other bookstores

- Jesus in the Qur'an, Christian writings, and historical sources

- The scriptural Jesus in the light of history

- The life and teachings of the historical Jesus

- The time and places in which Jesus lived

- Jesus and the Jews and the Romans

- The historical Jesus versus the theological one

About the book

Jesus remains one of the most studied characters in history. In the two millennia since his birth, countless writers have published numerous books and articles on every aspect of his life, personality, teachings, and environment. Depending on the backgrounds, goals, and trainings of their respective authors, these works relied on the New Testament, other Christian sources, Jewish writings, or other historical sources, or on combinations of these writings. The Qur'an is rarely mentioned, let alone seriously considered, by the mainly Christian authors of these studies. This explicit or implicit neglect reflects a presumed historical worthlessness of the Qur'an.

Muslim scholars have also written extensively about Jesus. Contrary to their Western counterparts, they have studied in detail what the Qur'an and other Islamic sources say about Jesus. The Christian image of Jesus is often cited to be dismissed, usually on the basis of what Islamic sources say, but at times also because of its incoherence and inconsistency. Like Western scholars who have ignored the Qur'an, Muslim writers have shown no interest in independent historical sources.

This book fills a gap in the literature on the historical Jesus by taking the unique approach of considering together the Qur'an, the Gospels, and other religious and historical sources. This genuinely new contribution to the scholarship on the historical Jesus shows that, unlike the New Testament accounts, the Qur'anic image of Jesus is both internally consistent and reconcilable with known history. While showing that our understanding of how the New Testament was formed and our growing knowledge of history confirm that the Christian Jesus is unhistorical, this study makes a strong case for the historicity of the Jesus of the Qur'an.

About the reader
Its friendly style makes this comprehensive book suitable for the general reader as well as the specialist. Readers with interest in the historical Jesus, the Messiah in the various scriptures, modern Qur'anic exegesis, or comparative religion will find this compelling study highly informative and thought-provoking. No specialist knowledge of any scripture or history is required for reading the book.

Also by Louay Fatoohi:

The Prophet Joseph in the Qur'an, the Bible, and History
A new, detailed commentary on the Qur'anic Chapter of Joseph

Publication Date: August 2007
ISBN: 978-1-906342-00-5
Available from Amazon and other bookstores

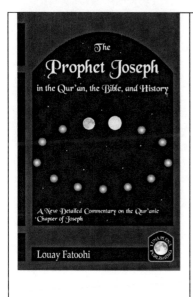

- Modern and comprehensive interpretation of the sūra of Joseph

- Verse by verse analysis and commentary

- Comparative references to classical interpretations

- Comparison between the story in the Qur'an and its Biblical counterpart

- Examination of the historical time and place where Joseph lived

- Explanation of the Qur'an's style in relating history

About the book

The Qur'anic sūra (chapter) of Joseph deals almost entirely with the story of this noble Prophet, his brothers, and their father Prophet Jacob. Since the revelation of the Qur'an fourteen centuries ago, there have been numerous attempts to interpret this sūra. The present study is a genuinely new look at the sūra — including careful examination of the historical background of its story and detailed comparison with the corresponding Biblical narrative. While referring to interpretations from classical exegetical works, this book offers new insights into the meanings and magnificence of this Qur'anic text.

The author is not only concerned with analysing the individual verses;

he is equally focused on showing how various verses are interrelated, explicitly and subtly, to form a unique textual unit. He shows particular interest in unveiling subtle references and meanings that are often overlooked or missed by exegetes. Through this comprehensive study, the author elucidates why the Qur'an has always been firmly believed to be a unique book that could have only been inspired by Allah.

About the reader

Thorough and scholarly but easy to read, this book is intended for both the general reader and the specialist. Whether you are a scholar of Qur'anic exegesis (*tafsir*), have general interest in Qur'anic studies and the Qur'anic story of Prophet Joseph, or interested in comparative religion, you will find this in-depth and detailed study of the sūra of Joseph informative, enlightening, and thought-provoking. No knowledge of Arabic or the Qur'an is required for reading the book.

Printed in the United Kingdom
by Lightning Source UK Ltd.
128711UK00001B/241-285/P